GLOBAL IMPERIALISM AND THE GREAT CRISIS

Global Imperialism

—————— and the ——————

Great Crisis

The Uncertain Future of Capitalism

by ERNESTO SCREPANTI

MONTHLY REVIEW PRESS
New York

Library of Congress Cataloging-in-Publication Data
Screpanti, Ernesto, 1948–
  [Imperialismo globale e la grande crisi. English]
  Global imperialism and the great crisis : the uncertain future of
capitalism / by Ernesto Screpanti.
    pages cm
  ISBN 978-1-58367-447-5 (paperback) — ISBN 978-1-58367-448-2 (cloth)
  1. Capitalism—Political aspects. 2. Imperialism. I. Title.
  HB501.S47613 2014
  337—dc23
                        2014011018

Monthly Review Press
146 West 29th Street, Suite 6W
New York, New York 10001

www.monthlyreview.org

5 4 3 2 1

Contents

Acknowledgments

Some parts of a previous version of this book have been read by Ash Amin, Gianni Betti, Sam Bowles, Emiliano Brancaccio, Alex Callinicos, Sergio Cesaratto, Geoff Hodgson, Jerry Levy, Massimo Livi Bacci, Mario Morroni, Edward Nell, Ugo Pagano, Anna Soci, Andrew Tylecote, Michael Yates, and Maurizio Zenezini. I warmly thank them all for their valuable comments and suggestions, and of course assume responsibility for any errors or oversights. Special thanks go to Emma Thorley, who helped me not only to translate the book into English, but also helped in the more challenging task of writing it in a language accessible to the lay reader, that retains analytical rigor.

THE BOURGEOISIE HAS THROUGH its exploitation of the world market given a cosmopolitan character to production and consumption in every country. To the great chagrin of Reactionists, it has drawn from under the feet of industry the national ground on which it stood. All old-established national industries have been destroyed or are daily being destroyed. They are dislodged by new industries, whose introduction becomes a life and death question for all civilised nations, by industries that no longer work up indigenous raw material, but raw material drawn from the remotest zones; industries whose products are consumed, not only at home, but in every quarter of the globe. . . . In place of the old local and national seclusion and self-sufficiency, we have intercourse in every direction, universal inter-dependence of nations. . . . The bourgeoisie, by the rapid improvement of all instruments of production, by the immensely facilitated means of communication, draws all, even the most barbarian, nations into civilisation. The cheap prices of its commodities are the heavy artillery with which it batters down all Chinese walls, with which it forces the barbarians' intensely obstinate hatred of foreigners to capitulate. It compels all nations, on pain of extinction, to adopt the bourgeois mode of production; it compels them to introduce what it calls civilisation into their midst, i.e., to become bourgeois themselves. In one word, it creates a world after its own image.

—MARX AND ENGELS, 1848

Introduction

The main thesis of this book is that contemporary globalization is bringing about a type of imperialism that differs fundamentally from those of the nineteenth and twentieth centuries.

The most significant difference is that the great capitalist firms, by becoming multinationals, have broken out of the confines within which they operated and that they exploited in the era of colonial empires. Nowadays capital accumulates in a global market. One of its dominant interests is therefore to dismantle all the barriers, obstacles, and political pressures that states can place in its way. Whereas in the past every nation's monopoly capital took advantage of its state's drive to imperialist expansion, because it could use this as a way to enlarge the domestic market, today the boundaries of national empires are seen as obstacles to commercial expansion and accumulation. And whereas monopoly capital previously had an interest in raising trade barriers and implementing mercantilist policies, which it saw as defenses against the competition of foreign firms, nowadays multinational capital votes for free trade and financial globalization. I call this new form of capitalist domination of the world *global imperialism.*

A second difference involves the relationship between state and capital. Their long-established symbiotic bond, based on the convergence of the state's interest in building political power and the interest of capital in creating a protected imperial market, is weakening. Big capital now places itself above the nation-state, toward which it tends to take an instrumental and conflicting attitude—"instrumental" because it seeks to bend the state to its own interests, both through the direct action of lobbies and the indirect action of "markets"; "conflicting" because the shift of its interests into a global space generates difficulties in national economies, especially advanced ones, which threaten the function of "national collective capitalist" previously played by states.

In the imperial regimes of the nineteenth and twentieth centuries, this function was *necessary* to provide national support for the interests of capital. And it was made *possible* by the inflow of surplus value from the colonies. States sought to distribute part of the surplus value among the various social classes in order to create a social block capable of drawing the collective interests around those of the capitalists. Colonial imperialism thus generated significant labor aristocracies in the metropolises, since the money inflows from the colonies allowed some strata of the working class, especially skilled workers in manufacturing, to think they had a real stake in the maintenance of capitalism in the rich countries. This facilitated the formation of reformist parties, which sought to serve the interests of the proletariat by reconciling them with those of the "nation."

This function has now been lost, as the free movement of capital and goods places the workers in the South in competition with those in the North. Contemporary globalization has brought about a redistribution of income from wages to profits, which generates growing inequality throughout the world. Consequently, all countries are failing to achieve domestic social harmony, while the conditions for an exacerbation of class conflict increase. The state only maintains the role of "social gendarme": it must guarantee the legislative, judicial, and policing conditions to control labor and make it prepared for increasing exploitation. The demise of labor aristocracies and the consequent reorientation of labor policies toward repression is the third novelty of today's globalization. True, there was a great deal of labor repression in the United States and European countries even in the 1970s and 1980s, but the market liberalization begun in the 1990s exacerbated the process.

A fourth novelty involves the way in which the world is governed. In global imperialism the use of military force by the capitalist Center to put down and control the Periphery has certainly not ceased, but it is becoming of secondary importance compared to the regulatory mechanisms that work via the "natural" laws of the market. The global empire needs no emperor; nonetheless its *imperium* is becoming ever more effective, and this effectiveness is guaranteed by objective mechanisms against which populations seem defenseless. Even if they are in competition with each other, the innumerable heads that manage multinational firms univocally contribute to reinforcing these mechanisms because they are all pursuing the same objective: capital accumulation.

The global imperialism of multinationals, buttressed by neoliberal ideology, tends to establish in the world the utopia of *stateless global governance*. This is the ideal of a world order that is not ruled by a state, but only by market laws. It was theorized by such neoliberal economists and political philosophers as Friederich von Hayek, Robert Nozick, and Milton Friedman against the traditional neoclassical liberalism of economists such as John M. Keynes, Arthur C. Pigou, Paul A. Samuelson, and Franco Modigliani. In the late 1980s it was actualized in the policy recipes of the Washington Consensus, and now is being more fully realized. The role of national states is under reconsideration. In a perfect world they should become "minimal states," mainly dedicated to their role of domestic "social gendarmes," reflecting the fact that workers worldwide often refuse to behave as simple sellers of a good. The markets would deal with all the rest, that is, with the "social balance" on a global scale.

However, three functions of central governance are necessary for the working of the global empire, and these demand the action of some great state or states on the international scene. The first of these functions is that of *global sheriff*: a role that needs to be filled by a military power capable of disciplining the countries that resist globalization and the opening of their markets to multinational capital. The second role is that of *global banker*: some governance mechanism must serve to produce the currency used as the main instrument of payment and international reserve. The third role is that of *driver of growth*: since capital accumulation in emerging and developing countries is led by exports, there must be at least one large advanced economy that grows by sizably increasing its imports. We shall see that the great powers have not always agreed on the fulfilment of these three roles over the last twenty years, giving us our fifth novelty.

To perform these three functions, the political actions of the traditional great powers need to be bent to serve the collective interests of
multinational capital, rather than the interests of national bourgeoisies
or the mass of a country's citizens. Thus, to be precise, one should talk
of *sovereignless* (rather than *stateless*) *global governance*. To the extent
that states are the expression of the citizens' will, they are forced by
markets to empty democracy of any substance and transform deliberative institutions into simple apparatuses for the formation of consent
and repression of dissent. Global imperialism tends to kill democracy
and it does so through the markets. To borrow the compelling metaphor of a leading multinational capitalist, "The market is sovereign."
This is the sixth novelty.

A seventh novelty pertains to the role played by economic crises in
disrupting and restructuring international political equilibriums and
domestic social relations. On the one hand, the crises of globalization appear as explosions of capitalist contradictions, especially in the
state–capital relationship. On the other, they accelerate the disciplinary
processes to which the "markets" subject states, populations, and subordinate classes.

I seek to deconstruct a pervasive ideology that has managed to con-
found a large part of critical thought: that globalization is a panacea for
all the economic ills of the world, a process that will boost development
and increase well-being, reducing poverty and inequality in all countries that open up to international trade. The first chapter is dedicated
to unmasking this myth.

The reality behind the mask is imperialism, today taking on a new
form, one for which the analytical tools of twentieth-century imperialism theory are only partially useful. The second chapter develops the
idea that contemporary globalization is establishing an entirely new
form of domination, global imperialism, the projection of big capital
onto what Marx called the "world market."

The third chapter explores this issue in greater depth, studying the
disciplinary mechanisms that globalized capital sets in motion, both
directly and indirectly, in the markets for goods, finance, and ideologies, as well as by waging war and terror. These mechanisms take an

"organic" form. They do not derive from the intentional actions of a sovereign authority. Instead, they consist of certain feedback processes that emerge as the unintentional effects of the actions of many heterogeneous players.

The fourth chapter presents the principal actors on the global stage: multinational firms and nation–states. A section is dedicated to three major international organizations: the International Monetary Fund (IMF), the World Bank (WB), and the World Trade Organization (WTO). I argue that multinational firms are the primary and states the secondary actors. The former, by operating in a regime of oligopolistic competition, transform markets into instruments for the coercion of political and social powers. As a consequence, the policy autonomy of nation–states turns out to be rather limited. Finally, it appears that despite being constituted as creations of the states the international bodies in reality play at the service of the multinational firms.

The fifth chapter describes the great crisis of 2007–2013, highlighting above all how its eruption was brought about by the policies of financial market deregulation in the United States and monetary union in the European Union (EU). The crisis has turned out to be W-shaped (dip-recovery-dip-recovery). At present we are perhaps at the beginning of the second recovery, but it seems that the governments of the major countries have not yet succeeded in finding a way out of the basic difficulties that brought about the crisis, so much so that some observers fear a third dip.

The crisis, which is an intrinsic phenomenon of capitalist accumulation, is also one of its most effective disciplinary mechanisms. In the sixth chapter, I explain the present crisis as a process that restores the domination of capital and its markets over politics. The real causes of the great crisis are to be sought in the effects of globalization on the distribution of income in advanced countries. The prolonged declining trend in the wage share has depressed their economies. The governments of some great countries—those with archaic imperial ambitions, especially the United States and Germany—have adopted economic policy schemes aimed at countering or politically exploiting these effects. For a while they were successful. In the United States, a politically engineered speculative bubble boosted GDP growth. In Germany, the single currency created a German mercantilist empire in Europe that is striving to compete with the dollar on global markets. Yet, in the end, the "markets" have thwarted those schemes, triggering the crisis.

Finally, chapter 7 focuses on interstate rivalries, arguing that they can no longer be explained as irreconcilable inter-imperialist contradictions. Instead, they are produced by the geopolitical ambitions of the great powers' ruling classes. Those ambitions have been only partially conducive to the working of contemporary capitalism. Mostly, they produce disorder and instability. In this chapter I interpret the crisis as the climax of a period of transition from old forms of imperialism to global imperialism. Like the economic turmoil between the First and Second World Wars, the present depression is marked by a striking disarray in international relations. And like the crisis that started in 1929, the one ignited in 2007 has revealed the need to reform the system. Therefore, I conclude by portraying a scenario of the resolution of the crisis in terms of a possible reshuffling of the relationships among the great powers and a reordering of the international payment system.

The theory I develop in this book describes a system of global domination by capital that is still far from full realization, although the economic trends of the last twenty years show it is rapidly taking hold. The present great crisis may accelerate this process and bring to light what will emerge as the fundamental contradictions of global imperialism. It is not a question of inter-imperial rivalries, which will certainly continue to exist as consequences of the former great powers' nationalist policies, but a question of class opposition between workers and capital, and between the Center and Periphery of the empire. With globalization these two contradictions tend to blend into one and take on the form of an increasingly harsh and widespread class antagonism between multinational capital and the proletarians of the whole world.

—JANUARY 2014

1. Mythologies in the New Millennium

There is no such thing as national welfare.
—KRUGMAN, OBSTFELD, AND MELITZ, 2012

The ideology of globalization is based on a series of clichés responsible for many grand narratives of contemporary capitalism. At the most abstract core of this ideology is a pure theory of international trade that seeks to demonstrate the positive effects of free trade on global welfare. In the present chapter, I criticize this doctrine[1] using a deconstructive method that has proven particularly effective in the field of pure economic theory. I will show that according to neoclassical economics, upon whose methodology the theory of comparative advantages is founded, the most conventional propositions on the beneficial effects of free trade are flawed.

Another common belief is that financial globalization is the principal cause of the wave of global economic growth experienced over the last twenty years. This opinion will be criticized simply by presenting the empirical evidence that disproves it.

Lastly, I will deconstruct the neoliberal rhetoric about the successes of the global fight against poverty. In recent studies many doubts have been raised regarding the complex problems involved in defining and measuring poverty. Besides recalling these, I present a selection of statistics on relative poverty, income inequality, and the wage share in national income, all of which unequivocally demonstrate the negative effects of globalization on the living conditions of the lower classes.

Two terminological clarifications are necessary before getting to the heart of the matter. One deals with the notion of the "multinational firm."

I use the adjective "multinational" rather than "transnational," because the second, apart from giving the nouns it is associated with, "capital" or "firm," the sense of a holistic agent, tends not to convey the meaning of a group of dominant subjects with its head in the Center of the empire.

The second clarification has to do with the North-South dichotomy, which I will use as a synonym of "Center-Periphery of the empire," even though the geographic borders do not exactly coincide with the economic and political ones. The categories of *Core* and *Periphery*, as well as that of *Semi-periphery*, were developed by Immanuel Wallerstein (three volumes, 1974–89) and various advocates of "dependence theory." In contemporary imperialism it is difficult to define the boundaries of the Center. Based on the notion of an "advanced economy," the Center could include the OECD countries. In a more restrictive definition, referring to the nations in which the parent companies of the greatest number of multinationals are based, the Center would be composed of the United States, the major European countries, and Japan. Developing and least-developed countries would belong to the Periphery. It is more difficult to define the Semi-periphery, which could include various emerging countries and those "in transition." However, many of these are almost ready to join the OECD, and some, given their spasmodic development, will soon join the Center. This is another reason why I will avoid using the notion of Semi-periphery, which in any case is not relevant to the argument I want to make. Clearly, with the passing of time, any overlapping of the North–South and Center–Periphery dichotomies will become blurred. Therefore I avoid using it in the last chapter and the conclusions, in which I look at the future developments of global imperialism, and argue about the transformation of some major emerging countries into first-rate imperial centers.

GLOBALIZATION AND ITS IDEOLOGY

The last act in the GATT saga, the Uruguay Round (1986–94), led to the birth of the WTO, officially on January 1, 1995. The original member states were 123, becoming 156 in 2012. The WTO soon drew up a series of important multilateral agreements that helped smooth the way for multinational firms. Trade barriers rapidly fell by 40 percent and international trade boomed, coinciding with the start of a new wave of global accumulation and production. The old classification of countries into first, second, and third world became obsolete and a new one was substituted: advanced, emerging, and developing countries, with the addition of underdeveloped countries.[2] The long wave was driven by emerging countries, which had outstanding GDP growth rates of between 5 and 12 percent. The advanced countries, in contrast, had growth rates fluctuating between 0.5 and 3 percent.

Neoliberal thought celebrates the WTO's triumphs, taking every opportunity to attribute the miracle of global development to the adoption of free trade policies. In reality, as we shall see, the miracle took place thanks entirely to the emerging countries, and mainly as a consequence of the violation of certain free trade rules. The process of global accumulation was primarily the work of multinational firms, rather than an effect of neoliberal economic policies. Indeed, such policies, in the form of the advanced countries' fiscal, monetary, and trade programs, have produced more crisis than development.

Nonetheless, the ideology rapidly established itself and was accompanied by the rise of conservative and anti-worker ruling classes in all the main centers of power around the world, the administrations of advanced countries, the governing bodies of central banks, the WTO, the WB, and the IMF. In economic theory the Washington Consensus[3] was established, on the strength of which the IMF sought to impose its deflationary and pro-privatization policies on the whole world.

A systematic reconstruction of neoliberal ideology is not necessary here. Instead, I will focus and comment on the essential features of some of the most common arguments.

However, I first need to clear the field of two widespread myths that proliferated in the early 1990s. The revolution in information and communication technologies brought about a time-space compression of the world, enabling fast and extensive information and financial connections between production units and different decision-making centers that would have been unthinkable only thirty years previously. This process is supposed to have favored the birth of *transnational* corporations, which propelled themselves into global markets in order to counter the slowdown in demand and production caused by the entrance of many goods into the maturity phase of the product life cycle.

The big firms were supposed to lose their national roots and spread globally, adopting network-based rather than hierarchical organizational structures. This is the hypothesis on the *globalization of production*. They were also supposed to perform technological research activities in all their global production centers, no longer concentrating this research in their headquarters. Thus the process of innovation was supposed to be transformed into a polycentric international phenomenon. And this is the hypothesis of *technological globalization*.

The two beliefs were already discredited by empirical research in the 1990s. Ruigrok and van Tulder (1995), for example, set out to test the hypothesis of the *globalization of production* by studying the 100 biggest firms in the world, discovering that "with very few exceptions, executive boards and management styles remain solidly national in their outlook" (159). In other words, the great multinational companies have decentralized production but centralized control.

As to the second proposition, Patel and Pavitt (1991; 1994) found, in the vast majority of the 686 biggest manufacturing multinationals, that technological research was concentrated in the parent company and firmly based in the advanced countries in the North of the world. Similar results were obtained by Archibugi and Michie (1995), while Ruigrok and van Tulder's (1995) investigation showed that in the 100 biggest firms research continued to be carried out nationally. It is true that various emerging countries, headed by China, have made huge investments in R&D and now produce a growing number of patents. However, most of their innovations boil down to the improvement, adaptation, and creative imitation of imported technologies.

What counts, in any case, is not so much in which country the management and *advanced* technological research of the big multinationals are concentrated, but the fact that they remain located in the developed North. Innovations, then, are transferred, through direct investments, into various emerging and developing countries, where they produce a derivative form of technological research. As a consequence, the process of expansion of foreign direct investments involves a constant flow of profits from the South to the North, that is, from the Periphery to the Center of the imperial power of multinational capital.

The ideological propositions dealt with in the next three sections refer to *trade* globalization, *financial* globalization, and their effects on poverty and inequality. *Trade globalization* consists of lowering trade barriers and the consequent increase in the volume of international trade. This is a real trend but nothing substantially new. The drive to expand global trade began centuries ago and is intrinsic to capitalist development. Particularly strong in the second half of the nineteenth century, up to the First World War, it was put on hold in the inter-war period following the breakdown of the Gold Standard, the international payment system based on gold as the main reserve instrument and the role of the Bank of England as global banker. Nevertheless, by the 1950s trade globalization had already recommenced, and the current trend cannot be interpreted as a structural change or a qualitative jump. *Financial globalization* is also a long-term trend whose origins can be traced back to the nineteenth century. However, the acceleration that has taken place over the last thirty years has become a phenomenon of gargantuan proportions and constitutes a significant leap compared to previous centuries.

The effects of the two processes are clearly visible to anyone. Trade globalization has allowed many countries, especially emerging ones, to engage in export-led growth. On the other hand, financial globalization, through the abolition of controls on capital movements and the consequent rise in foreign investment, has helped to export the capitalist mode of production together with capital.

Therefore the facts are indisputable. What can be questioned are the neoliberal theories used to interpret them, especially the following three propositions:

1. Free trade makes it possible to exploit the comparative advantages of all economies and increase welfare in all countries that accept it.

2. The free movement of capital allows savings to go where they are needed to finance investments and thus fosters high growth rates while reducing growth volatility in all countries that open up to international financial flows.
3. The combined effects of the two types of globalization reduce inequality and poverty all over the world.

COMPARATIVE ADVANTAGES AND DISADVANTAGES

The theory of comparative advantages claims that each country should specialize in whatever production makes intensive use of its most abundant and least costly production factor. This factor cost need not be lower in absolute terms compared to other countries. It is sufficient for the *relative* cost to be lower, for example, the cost of labor in relation to that of capital. Specialization enables a country to efficiently produce the goods it is better equipped for, increase its exports, and consequently buy abroad the goods it is not well equipped to produce. All this would raise the quantity of goods produced, cut prices, and improve global welfare. The political and ideological implication is powerful: protectionism lowers total output and reduces welfare.

The contemporary theory, in the canonical version of Heckscher-Ohlin-Samuelson (HOS), is formulated using the general equilibrium model, and can be criticized for the marked lack of realism of its basic hypotheses.[4] But there is no need to gloat about this. Let's take the model as a parable telling us something about reality, and check whether it tells the story well. As we shall see, the most edifying stories are inconsistent on the ground of its very methodology.

One of the first hurdles concerns the *distributive effects* of free trade policies. The theory is sometimes presented taking trade between individuals as a metaphor for that between nations. However, nations are composed of many individuals, and the effects of free trade can be felt in different ways by different subjects, enriching some and impoverishing others: "In the real world trade has substantial effects on the income distribution within each trading nation, so that in practice the benefits of trade are often distributed very unevenly." In fact, to put it clearly, trade "often hurts significant groups within the country in the short run, and potentially, but to a lesser extent, in the long run" (Krugman, Obstfeld, and Melitz, 2012, 80). Nowadays even many advocates of free trade recognize this limit, that "opening up to free trade makes some-body poor or poorer is possible, even probable, due to the reallocation of resources associated with it" (Bonaglia and Goldstein, 2008, 34).

What happens to workers manufacturing cars in Italy when the country starts to import "Italian" cars produced in Poland and Serbia? Many lose their jobs and many others will have to accept pay cuts. There is no guarantee that all the unemployed will find jobs in the Italian high-fashion clothing sector which, let us assume, will increase production and exports. There may be an aggregate increase in income, for example, because of a marked profit rise in the high-fashion firms. The fact remains that some groups of individuals will suffer a loss of welfare. The theory maintains that free trade is beneficial in any case, as the increase in welfare of some will be greater than the decrease in welfare of the others. A compensation scheme for the worse-off individuals can then be designed, to return them to a welfare level no lower than the one they enjoyed prior to opening up to free trade. This is the most simplistic and misleading way of putting the question: the individuals who benefit from trade could compensate those who lose out, and still maintain some advantages, in which case international trade would *potentially* constitute a source of greater welfare for everyone.

Yet, is the existence of a simple *possibility* of compensation suf-ficient to be able to speak of an improvement in collective welfare? Certainly not. If some suffer losses due to the change, this will not result in a Pareto improvement.[5] At any rate, in such a case it would be difficult to convince the metalworkers who have lost their jobs due to the introduction of free trade that their troubles have grown but are in the national interest, especially if this coincides with the interests of the profits earners. Therefore Samuelson (1962) is right in claiming that the simple existence of a *potential* aggregate advantage does not allow us to draw any conclusions about the collective benefits of free trade in terms of welfare. Indeed, *effective* compensation needs to be provided before we can speak of a real advantage for everyone (Hahn, 1998, 13). Unfortunately, all compensation schemes generate changes in prices, incomes, and endowments that alter equilibrium conditions in an unpredictable manner, so there is no guarantee that the potential welfare improvement will be achieved after compensation. To all this we should add that compensation entails administrative costs, which may reduce welfare in an unpredictable way (Driskill, 2007, 10; Rodrik, 2011, 63–66). In conclusion, we can say that, bearing in mind its distributive effects, the simple proposition that "the introduction of free trade in a country improves collective welfare" is deceptive: either the aggregate advantage is purely potential, in which case it needs to be explained why more importance is given to the greater profits of some than to the losses of others; or the losses have to be effectively compensated, in which case it is impossible to say that an improvement in collective welfare takes place.

Moreover, free trade can generate redistributive effects not only within a single nation, but also between different nations. Let's take the case of a developing country, A, selling a forest of premium wood to a multinational based in an advanced country, B. The living conditions of the indigenous communities that inhabited the forest and lived on its products will deteriorate. Some, but not all, of them will be employed by the multinational as woodcutters. The firm will make an enormous amount of profits exporting the premium wood. If the multinational's profits are higher than the net disadvantages of all the other economic actors in country A, an increase in aggregate income will take place. However, a global redistributive effect could also occur. If the multinational exports its profits, the developing country could witness a real decline in its level of welfare. The comparative advantage theorist could maintain that there has been an overall increase in potential welfare, as the winner's profit increase outweighs the losers' losses. However, if this reduction is not adequately compensated with a transfer from country B to country A, it is difficult to maintain that the latter obtains a real advantage from free trade. On the other hand, if the transfer does take place, it is difficult to maintain that global welfare has really improved, considering that the transfer itself and its administrative costs will have unpredictable effects on the general equilibrium conditions. In conclusion, the proposition "free trade generates an increase in global welfare" is also deceptive.

Real life is often worse than theory predicts. It would be easy to present a host of examples of developing countries that, though increasing their exports through multinationals, find themselves with deteriorating balances of payments due to capital outflows or reduced export prices, as well as countries that obtain "compensation" loans at high interest rates that increase their foreign debt and therefore decrease their level of welfare in the long run.

There are other problems. The traditional theory of comparative advantages is based on a flex-price model, that is, on the hypothesis that prices respond promptly and completely to demand and supply changes. In this theory it is assumed that prices are fixed by an abstract auctioneer and all economic agents take them as parameters. But what happens when the prices of some goods are fixed by firms? This is not a purely hypothetical case. In reality the big multinational companies enjoy oligopolistic power and are capable of fixing the prices of their own goods. On the other hand, the prices of commodities, which are mainly produced in developing countries, are quite flexible and beyond the control of their producers. In such cases the theory of comparative advantage can no longer even claim that free trade produces a potential increase in welfare by reducing prices. Indeed, the opposite can occur. For example, country A raises its production of commodities and the volume of exports, but its trade balance does not improve because export prices fall due to the increase in supply. If the prices of the industrial goods it imports do not fall, country A could see its collective welfare deteriorate. If, as a result of this, its demand for industrial goods drops, country B, which exports them, could see its welfare increase less than required to compensate for the deterioration. Note that here I am not considering global redistributive effects. I am merely pointing out another theoretical flaw in the doctrine. In the presence of fixed prices, the neoliberal economist could not even maintain that free trade increases *potential* welfare.

The workings of the "labor market" are a case in point. General equilibrium theory assumes full employment and flexible wages. But what happens when the job markets don't work in this way? As an example, consider two advanced countries, G and F. Labor productivity and the full-employment wage are higher in G than in F. At a certain point the government of G adopts a restrictive fiscal policy that creates unemployment. Moreover, with the threat of further reducing employment and the enticement of placing workers' representatives on firms' boards of administration, it induces the unions to accept pay cuts. On the contrary, the unions of country F do not collaborate and do not accept pay cuts because wages are already very low. Having reduced labor costs, G will expand its exports toward F and, as aggregate demand has fallen, its imports will decrease. Thus G exports unemployment to F. Many comparative advantage theorists may continue to use the general equilibrium model and maintain that, as the wage changes were accepted voluntarily by the workers (via the unions), both of the economies enjoy full employment. They will therefore continue to claim that international specialization always reflects differences in production costs. But will they be able to claim that free trade has brought about an increase in collective welfare, albeit potential? After all, the wage bill will have dropped in both countries (while firms' profits have probably grown in G). I will come back to this not particularly imaginative example in the fifth chapter, to explain the current problems of the European economies.

Now consider another macroscopic drawback of general equilibrium theory: the no externalities assumption. It is maintained that there are no social effects that are not quantified by the markets, that is, cases in which private costs and advantages do not coincide with social costs and advantages. Let's go back to the example of the forest of premium wood acquired by a multinational. The private profits will be enormous and will mainly be collected by the multinational itself. However, the markets will not be capable of valuing the environmental damage; its social cost will not have a price and the multinational will not be obliged to pay for it. The community will bear a welfare loss. There is no guarantee that, if this disadvantage is calculated against the net private advantage produced by free trade (if indeed there is any), the change in potential welfare will still be positive. The neoliberal economist comes unstuck when faced with externalities.

Technological change exemplifies a particular case of externalities that is also overlooked by comparative advantage theory. This theory usually assumes that technology is given, known, and accessible to everyone. There are no economies of scale, age, scope, no learning by doing, no endogenous improvements in human capital, and no endogenous technical progress. On these assumptions, it seems easy to demonstrate that Portugal would benefit from specializing in wine production, while England specializes in cloth production. However, if the production of cloth prompts increasing returns to scale, investments in scientific and technological research, and human capital growth, it is difficult to argue that Portugal will benefit from opening up to free trade. In a long-run view, adopting protectionist policies to favor the development of an industrial sector may be more profitable. In the short run Portugal may produce cloth at higher prices than England, but in doing so it could foster the growth of human capital and the technological know-how that would subsequently allow it to manufacture many products at lower costs than those imported from England. Neoliberal economists have serious difficulties countering such assertions. For example, they cannot deny the existence of an optimum tariff capable of coping with an internal market failure better than free trade.

FINANCIAL GLOBALIZATION AND DEVELOPMENT

Given the lack of realism of comparative advantage theory, and given the long series of caveats that need to be raised when proposing it, few neoliberal economists promote it to the general public and the political classes. It is nevertheless taught in all universities, presumably for its moral principles and character-building properties.

In constructing an ideological hegemony, the free movement of capital is a more frequently used and apparently less controversial propaganda tool, as it evokes the miraculous effects of *financial* globalization. Instead of focusing on the international trade of goods, which, according to the theory, depends on differences in endowment and production costs, the focus shifts to capital flows, which depend on arbitrage operations on asset returns. And instead of speaking of welfare, which is difficult to measure, it deals with the "easily" quantifiable concepts of gross domestic product and poverty.

The theory maintains that developing countries offer great investment opportunities but, given their low levels of per-capita income, suffer from a chronic lack of savings. If these countries liberalize capital movements by allowing multinationals to invest in them under the same conditions as national firms and then export profits without any obstacles, the savings required to fund growth will come from the advanced countries. Moreover, foreign direct investment will bring with it technology transfer, which will pump up total factor productivity. GDP growth would consequently rise. The global liberalization of capital markets would also allow savers to diversify their risks, leading to the convergence of interest rates, which is a sign of improvement in the efficiency of resource allocation. A closed economy with great investment opportunities and few savings would have high interest rates; financial liberalization would increase the availability of capital and lower interest rates, with significant advantages for development. Lastly, the free movement of capital has been claimed to have beneficial effects on currency markets, preventing the misalignment of exchange rates. In this case, liberalization means abandoning fixed exchange rate systems. Governments that renounce control over exchange rates would gain a degree of freedom in their implementation of economic policies. By exploiting currency depreciation, for example, they could loosen external constraints and adopt autonomous monetary policies to support growth (Rodrik, 2011, 116). For all these reasons the free movement of capital on a global scale would favor development.

Alas, the myth of a positive correlation between financial globalization and growth has been resoundingly falsified by empirical research. Rodrik and Subramanian (2009) showed that between 1970 and 2004 the correlation did not exist in a sample of 105 countries. Obstfeld (2009) came to a similar conclusion.

This is not entirely surprising. In a study commissioned by the IMF, Kose, Prasad, Rogoff, and Wei (2006) reviewed forty-three studies published between 1994 and 2006, reaching the conclusion that "the majority of empirical studies are unable to find robust evidence in support of the growth benefits of capital account liberalization" (4).[6]

How can this be true? Wasn't the world in the peak of a long upswing in 2006? And weren't GDP and global production booming? What about the resounding successes of emerging countries? And wasn't this all coinciding with a strong tendency to lower trade barriers and remove controls on capital movements?

All these rhetorical questions would imply a positive answer, which demands clarification. There is no doubt that lowering trade barriers at a global level stimulates international trade and enables many countries to benefit from export-led growth. But this phenomenon is the result of free trade, not financial liberalization. It is brought about by the effects that a growing global demand for imports has on the effective demand of exporting countries and the consequent activation of increasing returns to scale at industry and firm level.[7] Moreover, this kind of growth only occurs in some countries, not all those that open up to international trade.

In many developing countries the abolition of trade barriers can slow growth, and the abolition of controls on capital movements can exacerbate the situation. This mainly occurs in countries that have not launched adequate processes of industrialization. In these economies the direct investments of multinationals result in the hyper-specialization of production. Once they have agreed to participate in the international division of labor as producers of commodities, such countries tend toward monocultures and manage to intensify their exports by focusing on the supply of a few natural resources or agricultural products. Yet their balance of payments does not always improve and often experiences long phases of deterioration both because the prices of commodities are determined by markets in which the producers do not enjoy oligopolistic positions (unlike the producers of manufacturing goods), and because the profits made by multinationals in their countries are systematically exported. All this causes long cycles of foreign debt, leading to profound crises and growth slowdowns.

In most emerging countries, on the other hand, opening up to international trade was preceded by a long period of transformation in which their governments guided modernization and industrialization. They achieved this through investment-oriented industrial policies, protectionist policies targeted at favoring import substitution, and the development of a strong industrial sector, social policies aimed at training human capital, and supporting scientific and technological research, and so on. A classic example is China, which joined the WTO only in 2001, following half a century of forced and planned industrialization.[8]

Once open up to foreign trade many emerging countries continue to politically guide development in defiance of free trade theories. This has been done, for example, by adopting strategic trade policies to control and channel trade flows and foreign direct investments with the aim of favoring the formation and expansion of national firms in technologically advanced sectors.[9] Moreover, exchange rate policies have been aimed at artificially increasing international competitiveness.

A consistent group of emerging countries propped up the growth in global production before the 2007–13 crisis. Without them, the world would have been in the midst of a deep depression rather than a long wave of development in the decade preceding the crisis, given the tendency to stagnation of advanced countries and the growth volatility of developing and least-developed countries. It is clearly wrong to attribute the benefits of this type of development to financial globalization. On the contrary, such growth is explained by some violation, and even opportunistic exploitation, of the free trade rules by most emerging countries: certainly not by comparative advantages, and least of all by financial liberalization. Comparative advantages cannot take the credit; emerging countries manage to benefit from the expansion of international trade only because, by refusing to specialize their production, they adopt similar industrial structures to those of advanced countries. Nor can the merit be of financial liberalization, as the flows of both direct and portfolio investments in such countries are shrewdly controlled by political authorities.

In some cases, though, there does seem to be a positive correlation between financial globalization and growth. Even so, it has been observed that in such cases "it is perfectly possible (indeed likely) that the causation goes the other way, from faster growth to [financial] integration" (Wolf, 2005, 283).

Another "strong point" of contemporary free trade ideology lies in the argument that financial globalization contributes to reducing growth volatility, lessening the frequency and intensity of crises. The explanation goes as follows: as the flow of savings that serves to finance investments in any single country no longer depends on local economic conditions alone but is fed by global wealth, growth will be less exposed to national shocks (famines, uprisings, political errors, etc.). International finance would perform a risk-sharing function, could hedge against the idiosyncratic risks of every single country, and mitigate the destabilizing effects of crises.

It is amusing to witness the joy of Kose, Prasad, Rogoff and Wei (2006) when they reveal that empirical research has brought to light a decrease in growth volatility during the globalization era. Even more so if we look at the date of publication of their survey: the eve of the crisis that began in 2007. Would empirical research still show such impressive results if it were conducted after one of the greatest crises in the history of capitalism? In answering this question, we should reflect on the fact that financialization played a key role in the explosion and international spread of the crisis. What free trade theory seems to ignore is that though financial globalization may help to provide some hedging against idiosyncratic risks, increasing international financial integration still exposes many countries to systemic global risks and makes them vulnerable to the endogenous shocks of the global economy (speculative bubbles, financial crashes, chain bankruptcies, etc.).

In any case, the empirical evidence of lower volatility prior to the great crisis does not appear to be particularly solid. Leaven and Valencia (2008) brought to light the following historical facts: 124 banking crises, 208 currency crises, and 63 sovereign debt crises occurred between 1970 and 2008. Eichengreen and Bordo (2002) demonstrated that crises were twice as frequent in contemporary globalization as in the period of globalization prior to 1914. Reinhart and Rogoff (2009) assessed the existence of a clear overlap between the historical series of banking crises (from 1800) and the series of increases in capital mobility, deducing that the second phenomenon caused the first. Bush, Farrant, and Wright (2011) discovered that though 0.1 banking crises per year, 1.7 currency crises, and 0.7 external defaults occurred in the Bretton Woods era (1948–72), in the years 1990–2000 there occurred 2.2, 5.4, and 1.8, respectively.

All this explains why the existence of a positive correlation between financial globalization and growth cannot be proven: because it does not exist. The reason may be that the liberalization of capital movements, by increasing financial instability, dampens growth in the long run. Even if the inflow of foreign capital can feed a country's prosperity during boom phases by raising direct investments, credit availability, and optimistic expectations, when the crisis blows up, the flight of capital has the opposite effect and exacerbates production slumps. It has been estimated that a currency crisis reduces GDP by an average of 8 percent, and that a currency crisis coupled with a banking crisis can reduce it by 18 percent. The causal nexus is easily identifiable, as it has been "proved that banking crises are more probable and frequent when countries open up to international capital movements" and that the former phenomenon is preceded by the latter (Bonaglia and Goldstein, 2008, 63–64). To conclude, it could be said the main reason why financial globalization does not foster growth is that it feeds international speculation. In a speculative climate portfolio investments are destabilizing, being *markedly* pro-cyclical, and therefore have little effect in boosting growth *trends* (Calvo and Reinhart, 1999, 2001; Wolf, 2005, 283).

POVERTY AND INEQUALITY

Over the last fifteen years, intense debate and an important field of research have developed on the issue of globalization's effects on income distribution.[10]

One of the most exciting assertions made by neoliberal ideology is that globalization has made a decisive contribution to reducing the number of people living in poverty. The theory is simple. States that liberalize trade and capital movements obtain access to global markets.

They can attract private investments, as well as international aid and funding from the IMF and WB, and can export to rich advanced countries. Thus they foster economic growth. Even if the investments, aid, and funding do not go directly into the pockets of the poor, the growth in income and wealth rapidly spreads to the whole of society, according to the "trickle-down" fable, as the increased production creates new jobs, and technologies imported with the FDI boost productivity.

The statistics seem unequivocal.[11] In about thirty years the number of poor people (with an income lower than $2 per day) has fallen slightly: from 2.585 billion in 1981 to 2.471 billion in 2008. The percentage of poor people out of the total global population has fallen more noticeably: from 69.9 percent to 43 percent. The number of extremely poor people (with an income lower than $1 per day) has decreased even more, both in absolute terms, having passed from 1,545.3 million to 805.9 million, and as a percentage, from 41.6 percent to 14 percent (Chen and Ravaillon, 2012, 4–6).

World Bank studies seek to measure *absolute* poverty, understood as "an *inability* to attain a *minimal standard* of living" (World Bank, 1990). People who are incapable of satisfying their primary needs, from housing to food, from clothing to health, are considered poor. Herein lies a first problem. This definition should prompt the adoption of multidimensional measures of poverty,[12] and the use of a *direct method* of measurement that takes into account the basket of goods needed to satisfy basic needs. However, this would make it difficult to measure and survey poverty, and use it to support a superficial ideology. Therefore many prefer to simplify the problem by defining a *poverty line* in terms of income. They also propose adopting an *indirect method*, known as the *budget standard approach*: using market values, the basic consumption basket is transformed into the level of income necessary to buy it. The many dimensions of poverty are thus reduced to a number, a quantity of dollars.

Nevertheless, the poverty threshold cannot disregard the general living conditions of a society, its wealth, mean income, models of consumption, technology, social institutions, welfare systems—in short, the commonly accepted norms and practices of social decency (Borghesi and Vercelli, 2005, 205). So the same poverty line cannot be adopted for all societies and all periods, as the composition of a basket capable of fulfilling basic needs varies in place and time (Townsend, 1979). The income of a poor person today could have given him a middle-class lifestyle fifty years ago. The income of a poor North American today would allow him or her to live a more than decent life in Burkina Faso. Someone living in the Amazon rainforest will be able to satisfy his housing, clothing, and food needs with a much lower monetary income than an inhabitant of New York. Thus if poverty has to be measured by a synthetic index, it would be better to define it in relative terms, that is, in terms of distance from the mean or median income of any given society.

In other words, there are two options: either *absolute* poverty is measured in terms of ability to fulfil basic needs, in which case a multi-dimensional definition needs to be adopted and a spatial and temporal context provided (Sen, 1983, 155), or a synthetic index of income is used and the notion of *relative* poverty has to be adopted.

Anyone who does not accept this methodological choice can justifiably be suspected of bias. Economic growth in itself (without a reduction in inequality) does not contribute to reducing relative poverty (Ravallion, 2004, 47). This does not thrill those who maintain that globalization leads to a drop in the number of poor: hence their preference for the notion of absolute poverty. On the other hand, if the latter is contextualized in space and time, it may transpire that there are poor people in rich countries too. To detect them, a high-income threshold would need to be set. But the higher the threshold, the lower the rate of decline in poverty: an increasing trend could even emerge. The thresholds recently used by WB researchers to define poverty and extreme poverty ($2.5 and $1.25), although higher than those used a few years ago ($2 and $1), are still so low that there would appear to be no poor people in the whole of Europe and North America. Certainly, global poverty measured in this way is much lower and decreases more rapidly than real poverty.

To justify the setting of a decontextualized threshold, it is sometimes claimed that contextualization would lead to different thresholds being set for different countries, rendering international comparisons impossible. The World Bank began collecting data based on national poverty lines, but subsequently turned its attention to global poverty, using a universal income threshold. Its purported aim was to permit international comparison and aggregation. However, many comparisons can be made in terms of mean income, inequality indexes, or the like. Why should it be necessary to perform comparisons in terms of absolute poverty? Wouldn't it be better to stick to different statistics for different countries in order to see how the number of poor people evolves in each of them?[13]

On the other hand, if, as they claim, the threshold should be the same for the whole world, it would have to be low enough to detect poor people in the poorest countries in such a way that not (almost) all the inhabitants of those countries are considered poor. But why should people with incomes near the mean in poor countries be considered not poor, if they earn less than poor people in a rich country? Obviously it is because the assessment of poverty is contextualized. In other words, a very low and non-contextualized threshold is set in order to measure absolute poverty in the poorest countries (to reduce the level of poverty detected), yet an implicit contextualization is applied in order to justify that low threshold.

The theoretical problem of the very notion of "absolute poverty" is accompanied by other conundrums of a methodological nature. Many of these emerged from the extensive debate prompted by the periodic publication of World Bank data, and by some triumphalist declarations of its directors. There is no need to enter into the technical details here, but some information is necessary, if only to make it clear that the official records have been anything but acknowledged by the scientific community.[14]

The most important problem concerns the arbitrariness of the poverty threshold, as the World Bank made no effort to define the basket of goods necessary to fulfill basic needs. Critics have pointed out that the budget standard approach, that is, the definition of the basket of subsistence goods required to calculate minimum income, was not used to identify the threshold. Instead a money-metric methodology was adopted, thus making the index of absolute poverty absolutely arbitrary.

This first drawback leads to another—one that impinges on the methods used to homogenize monetary incomes at an international level. It is clearly not sufficient to use nominal exchange rates to measure all incomes in terms of a single currency, the dollar, as the price level, and therefore the real value of a dollar, varies from one country to another. This is why an exchange rate adjusted for purchasing power parity (PPP) is used. PPP requires the use of price indices calculated on the basis of different baskets of goods in different countries. Clearly, a U.S. basket will differ from a Tanzanian basket. This means that the calculation of minimum income in many countries in terms of PPP dollars is influenced by irrelevant information, by the prices of goods and services that the poor never consume. More than that, the use of PPP dollars provides information that is not only redundant, but distorting. In fact, some goods and services have higher prices in the United States than, for example, in Tanzania. Therefore conversion with PPP taking into account all goods will artificially boost the purchasing power of Tanzanians, and the number of poor will be underestimated. More generally, it has been pointed out that the World Bank's efforts to adjust the methods of detection in response to criticism have instead contributed to increasing the arbitrariness of the datasets produced.[15]

Besides the methodological problems, others of an interpretative nature emerge as soon as an indiscreet question is asked. The neoliberal ideologists maintain that poverty diminishes thanks to the economic growth fostered by countries opening up to free trade. Now, let's concede that extreme poverty in poor countries has decreased over the last thirty years. But are we sure that this miracle was produced by globalization?

One particular phenomenon that should give us pause for thought is exhibited by the poverty time series when the Chinese data are removed: the decreasing trend becomes much less evident. These datasets were produced by the World Bank in response to critics pointing out the significant contribution of certain big emerging countries, like China, in which poverty decreased more than in other nations. The critics suggest that it is deceptive to attribute the decrease in global poverty to globalization, as China is not particularly liberal in its industrial, trade, and currency policies, and systematically uses state capitalism and *dirigisme* to govern growth and counter the negative effects of free trade on its economy. If anything, China shows that resistance to neo-liberal globalization is more effective than globalization itself in the fight against poverty. The filtered datasets displayed by the World Bank would seem to defy the critics as they show that global poverty diminishes even when the Chinese poor are excluded, albeit less rapidly. But this is a rather weak defense. For China is not the only country that seeks to politically control the markets: various other emerging countries do so too. To clarify this issue, World Bank researchers would need to classify the countries into two groups, pro- and anti-free trade, and then collect data on poverty separately for the two groups. It might emerge that most of the successes in the fight against poverty could be attributed to resistance to global liberalization.[16]

The concept of absolute poverty is intrinsically ideological. It conveys the idea that poverty is simply caused by the inability of underdeveloped economies to counter a lack of resources with technical progress and capitalist accumulation. The backward economies are those that have proven incapable of launching the development process by opening up to modernization. In other words, poverty is presented as a product of the resistance of many traditional cultures to capitalist penetration. In breaking down that resistance, globalization would help the underdeveloped countries to begin the process of modernization by opening up their markets, and would therefore force them to reduce poverty.

What the concept of absolute poverty tends to obscure is the social dimension of the phenomenon: the fact that great masses of people can become poor *because* the privileged social classes get richer, and that the capitalist extraction of profit on a global scale can cause growing relative impoverishment in both advanced and developing countries. It is revealing that the minimum income thresholds used to quantify the phenomenon have been set so low that poverty in advanced countries cannot even be detected. Yet studies on *relative* poverty show it is increasing in many rich countries. For example, between 2005 and 2011 the percentage of the population "at risk of poverty"[17] in seventeen EU countries increased from 15.2 to 16.2 percent; in Germany from 12.2 to 15.8; in Spain from 19.7 to 21.8; and in France from 13 to 14 (Eurostat, 2012). In the United States, the percentage of the population with an income below the threshold of relative poverty grew from 11.1 percent in 1973 to 15 percent in 2011 (NPR, 2012).

The notion of "inequality" is less ideological, as it defines a phenomenon that is essentially relational, even though it does not measure class relations. Then again, debate on the measures and trends of inequality at a global level has been no less fierce than that on absolute poverty. In this case, however, the prevailing opinions of the scientific community are not quite as triumphant, as serious empirical research has brought to light results that neoliberal ideologists find it hard to accept: globalization appears to have increased rather than reduced inequality.

A convincing and decisive result has recently been published by Milanovic (2012): between 1988 and 2005 the Gini coefficient of inequality rose from 0.68 to 0.71 and the Theil index from 0.87 to 0.98; the share of income of the top decile also rose, from 51.4 percent to 55.5 percent. Milanovic's result is convincing because it deals with the methodological difficulties in a satisfactory manner, and decisive because it confirms the findings of many other studies.[18] These indices refer to *global* inequality, to inequality between the incomes of all the citizens in the world.

Other researchers have instead focused on *international* inequality, that is, between the mean incomes of nations, which, in some studies, seems to show a decreasing trend in the era of globalization. Now, there is no use in being ironical about a concept of inequality that assumes all the citizens in every nation to have the same income. After all, this measure could serve to see whether globalization has contributed to increasing or decreasing the gap in per-capita income between advanced and developing countries. In any case, even here an interesting result comes to light. The Gini coefficient shows a trend of increasing inequality if the incomes of the various countries are not weighted with the ratio of their populations to the global population. If, instead, they are weighted, the trend becomes decreasing. Does this mean that globalization works in reducing the income gap between rich and poor countries? Alas, the result is less sensational when China and India are excluded from the global data. The trend of the weighted international inequality index without China and India shows the same increasing trend as the non-weighted overall index, which could be interpreted very simply. If China and India have higher mean incomes than most developing and least developed countries, the weighted international index tends to decrease because the population or mean income of those two countries grow more than in the others. This rekindles a suspicion: perhaps some of the successes in the fight against inequality, like those in the fight against absolute poverty, are due to the resistance of the governments of certain large countries to the negative effects of globalization, rather than to globalization itself.

One advantage of the concept of inequality, compared to that of absolute poverty, is that it does not depend on the definition of an arbitrary level of minimum income and can therefore also be applied to advanced countries. Interestingly, it appears that inequality has increased in the era of globalization in these countries too. An OECD (2011, 24) investigation showed that between 1985 and 2008 the Gini coefficient increased in seventeen out of twenty-two advanced countries, remained more or less constant in three and decreased in only two: Greece and Turkey.

It should also be pointed out that the Gini coefficient is an imperfect measure of inequality, as it does not take into account asymmetry in the distribution of income. It does not enable us to detect the most extreme forms of inequality. Interdecile and interquintile ratios may not be as elegant as the Gini coefficient and similar indices, but they are more intuitive and, above all, come closer to grasping the class nature of the phenomenon.[19] In the United States, the ratio of the mean income of the wealthiest quintile to that of the poorest grew from 10.19 in 1968 to 14.74 in 2004, while the income share of the wealthiest 1 percent grew from 8.3 percent in 1981 to 16.08 percent in 2004 (Fiorentini and Montani, 2012, 87–8).

We get closer to an understanding of the class nature of inequality if we focus on labor. A recent International Labor Organization study (ILO, 2008) reviewed seventy-three countries for which reliable data are available, bringing some impressive phenomena to light. For instance, the ratio of the top manager-to-worker's mean income in the fifteen biggest companies in the United States rose from 360 in 2003 to 500 in 2007.

The trend of the wage share in national income is also highly significant. This is an indicator of worker exploitation: the lower the share the greater the exploitation. Revealingly, in fifty-one of the seventy-three countries the share has fallen in the last two decades. In Latin America and the Caribbean it fell by thirteen points between 1993 and 2002, in Asia and the Pacific by ten points between 1985 and 2002, and in advanced countries it fell by nine points between 1980 and 2005. A decreasing trend was registered in the majority of countries,[20] and the fall was particularly rapid between the early 1980s and the start of the new millennium (ILO, 2008, 1–6).

I must conclude by saying that after about fifteen years of research and debate the arguments of the neoliberal ideologists have been largely discredited by empirical evidence. The data on absolute poverty, despite being flawed by measurement methods and by the setting of arbitrary thresholds, show that the decrease in poverty in the era of globalization has been rather slight, and is mainly the outgrowth of countries that have adopted non-liberal policies. The data measuring *social* distribution show that the gap between the income of the privileged classes and that of the lower classes has grown, the wage share has fallen, and inequality and relative poverty have increased. And this has occurred almost all over the world, including in the advanced countries.

2. A New Form of Imperialism

Imperialism is not a stage—not even the highest—of capitalism.
It is immanent to its expansion since the beginning.
—SAMIR AMIN, 2002

If the neoliberal ideology of globalization is unable to account for the transformation of present-day capitalism, we must look elsewhere. The theories of imperialism, with their critical incisiveness, would seem to be the best analytical alternative, except for the fact that the core of these theories was developed in the early twentieth century and reflects a reality that has, in many ways, been superseded by contemporary globalization. Current imperialism theorists are forced to perform speculative contortions in their attempts to explain today's capitalism while remaining faithful to conventional doctrine. This frequently leads to misrepresentations that hamper rather than improve understanding of the subject. We are then led to ask whether Marxist-Leninist orthodoxy may be a more incisive analytical tool than neoclassical theory.

In any case, I believe that anyone wishing to understand capitalist globalization should read Lenin's *Imperialism*, but use it as a benchmark, and only after reading Marx's speech *On the Question of Free Trade* and *The Modern Theory of Colonization*. Observing the similarities and differences between the current situation and Lenin's scheme can clarify what contemporary globalization is not. The scheme of interpretation provided by Marx's texts, on the other hand, helps to distinguish the essential from the incidental and clarify what globalization really is.[21]

In the final chapter of volume 1 of *Capital* (1867, 932), Marx captures the essence of capitalist imperialism:

> Just as the system of protection originally had the objective of manufacturing capitalists artificially in the mother country, so [the] theory of colonization, which England tried for a time to enforce by Act of Parliament, aims at manufacturing wage-labourers in the colonies.

In advanced countries primitive accumulation was imposed partly by employing protectionism—"a means of manufacturing manufacturers" (921)—and by using the *"power of the state,* the concentrated and organized force of society, to hasten, as in a hothouse, the process of transformation of the feudal mode of production into the capitalist mode" (915–16). Hence imperial capital expanded in the colonies by creating wage workers, rather than by manufacturing manufacturers. There it used the power of the state not to support the primitive accumulation of local capital, but to destroy the precapitalist systems of production, reduce independent producers, artisans, and farmers to poverty, and thus create a class of workers ready to be exploited. And that is

> the secret discovered in the New World by the political economy of the Old World and loudly proclaimed by it: that the capitalist mode of production and accumulation, and therefore capitalist private property as well, have for their fundamental condition the annihilation of that private property which rests on the labour of the individual himself; in other words, the expropriation of workers. (940)

This is the essence of globalization. In the nations of the imperial Center, trade barriers have been used to support the formation of big capital. In the Periphery, protectionism is not necessary. What is needed is free trade to expose those countries to accumulation, and the power of multinational capital to export the capitalist mode of production there.

Historical Forms of Capitalist Imperialism

Before dealing with theoretical issues, it will be helpful to provide a brief overview of the history of imperialism and identify the forms it has taken in previous centuries. The story began in the twelfth century. Since that time, imperialism has assumed five different forms or, in other words, brought about five different systems of international economic relations.

The first form can be defined as *financial imperialism*. This imperial regime lasted from the twelfth to the fifteenth century and gravitated around three geographic centers: Central-Northern Italy, Northern Germany, and Flanders. The Crusades had opened the Middle East and Mediterranean markets to the Italian maritime republics. Thus, from the twelfth century onward, Venice, Genoa, Pisa, and other cities began their commercial and military expansion, leading to the creation of great maritime empires. Spices, silks, wool, brocades, damasks, ivory, dyes, perfumes, drugs, precious stones, and slaves were all goods exported via their trade routes to Europe, with large profit margins. In other cities, such as Florence, Milan, Siena, and Lucca, manufacturing industries were set up. Among these, the textile sector became particularly efficient and innovative, and exported its products to the rest of Europe. Meanwhile, a similar process took place in the German coastal cities, giving rise to the Hanseatic League, whose principal centers were Lübeck and Hamburg. This league controlled the trade routes of the Baltic and North Seas and linked up the Russian, German, Scandinavian, and English markets. It traded wood, salt-fish, wheat, copper, furs, wool, and cloth. Lastly, a flourishing textile industry developed in Flanders. Its principal centers, especially Bruges and Antwerp, provided a connection between the markets of the North and South of Europe.

Although large manufacturing and trading companies had formed in the most advanced cities, the big capital established its predominance through multinational financial companies. These were initially subordinate to trade concerns, but soon prevailed over both mercantile and industrial capital. The most powerful banking companies became capable of influencing the policies of the great monarchies, the Holy Roman Empire, and the Church. The gold coins minted in Florence, Venice, and Genoa circulated as the principal means of international payment.

The predominant form of state was that of *liberi Comuni* in Italy and *Reichsstädte* in Germany. The states were constituted as "people's" republics, but governed by the upper middle class. Capital had direct, and sometimes even constitutional, control over the state, either through the system of grand councils (to which only members of the high bourgeoisie had access), or through the system of major guilds (controlled by bankers, merchants, and industrialists). The city-states' financial and trade policies were therefore patently subordinated to the interests of capital.

There were two main types of conflict. On the one hand, commercial and financial competition gave rise to bitter inter-imperial rivalries. The Italian republics, for example, found themselves in a permanent state of war with each other. In the fourteenth century alone, Florence was involved in approximately 170 wars. On the other hand, the creation of a class of wage workers led to the explosion of vast social conflicts in the most advanced cities of Northern Europe and Central Italy. In the same century violent popular uprisings broke out in many cities, such as Siena, Florence, Perugia, Lübeck, Bruges, Ghent, and Liège.

This imperial regime entered a period of decline between the end of the fifteenth and the early sixteenth centuries, for two main reasons. First, the discovery of the Americas led to the development of Atlantic trade routes and the marginalization of Mediterranean and Baltic ones. Second, the formation of the great European nation–states and the irreconcilable inter-imperial rivalries of the city-states led to the political subjugation of the latter and then to their loss of economic power.

Hence, a second form of imperialism emerged in the sixteenth to eighteenth centuries, which can be defined as *mercantile imperialism*. It was characterized by the extraction of natural resources and colonial agricultural products, by the pillaging of American precious metal deposits, by the emigration of European settlers, by the triangular trade of African slaves, and by the extermination of Native American populations. International trade was now dominated by big commercial companies, which operated as monopolies and maximized profits "upon alienation."

In this imperial regime the states pursued power politics and strategies of geographic expansion, but their primary motivation was not profit. The absolute monarchies sought to exploit the interests of capital to achieve their own geopolitical objectives, if nothing else because the accumulation of gold reserves was necessary to boost military power. Meanwhile, the increased circulation of money facilitated the expansion of domestic transactions, the lowering of interest rates, and the development of manufacturing production. In order to favor money inflows, economic policies constantly aimed to create trade surpluses through exchange rate "depreciation" (such as clipping—reducing the metallic content of coins), protectionism, and export subsidies. In some cases, such as in France under Colbert, a good number of exporting companies were state-owned.

The third form was that of *colonial imperialism*. This began in the first half of the nineteenth century and peaked in the second half. It finally expired with the Thirty Years' War (1914–45), when the inter-imperial rivalries exploded with the utmost virulence. In this system of international relations, capitalist interests again prevailed over state power politics, which they subordinated to the impulse to accumulate. The states became republics or constitutional monarchies, in which restricted suffrage was used to turn governments into the "business committees" of the capitalist class. Firms tended to organize into large financial and industrial groups, giving life to cartels and conglomerates that sought to gain monopolistic power over national markets. The urgency of accumulation implied the need to enlarge markets and therefore expand empires. These spread toward Africa, the Middle East, and the Indian subcontinent in the form of colonial occupation, and toward the Americas and the far East in the form of influence zones.

The fourth type of imperialism was born after the Second World War and lasted until the end of the 1980s. This can be termed *postcolonial imperialism*. It was dominated by the United States and the Soviet

Union, which replaced the old European powers by building a new kind of empire. The two big states ideologized themselves and became champions of the anticolonial movement, or "missionary powers motivated by ideals" (Kaplan, 2010). Yet the liberal and socialist ideologies they vaunted actually served to mask two different types of capitalism: one based on private property, the other on state property. The two hegemonic powers bulged toward the South of the world, seeking to substitute colonial rule with informal relations of dependence, influence, and alliance. The nuclear threat prevented the explosion of a direct military conflict between the two empires, but they nonetheless clashed continuously in friction zones, triggering many local wars in Asia and Africa.

In the era of postcolonial imperialism, various Third World countries tried to achieve economic autonomy from the former colonial powers. Some, through national liberation wars and revolutions led by modernizing political classes of socialist or liberal leanings, began processes of primitive accumulation under the guidance of the state and with the help of one of the two imperial superpowers. The successful nations managed to build the infrastructures and create the cultural and social preconditions of capitalist development, and are now classified as emerging countries.

The inter-imperial conflict between the two superpowers ended with the victory of market capitalism and the collapse of the Soviet Union. But the defeat of its rival empire did not lead to the triumph of an American super-imperialism. In fact, the United States entered a crisis of economic and political hegemony. The upswing in the process of neoliberal globalization in the 1990s then paved the way for a fifth form of imperial rule, which I am now going to illustrate.

ULTRA-IMPERIALISM AND "IMPERIALISM"

The classic text of twentieth–century theories of imperialism is John A. Hobson's *Imperialism: A Study* (1902a).[22] In the chapter dedicated to the "economic roots of imperialism" there is the original sin of almost all such theories: the conviction that imperialism has its economic roots in some shortcoming of capitalism.

The particular root suggested by Hobson is a tendency toward under-consumption caused by a distribution of income that penalizes wages in favor of profits. The formation of monopolistic markets, by prevent-ing technological progress from depressing the prices of goods, causes profits to soar and is responsible for unequal income distribution. The resulting weakness in domestic demand generates overproduction, excess capacity, and oversaving. This induces firms to target foreign markets and then push the nation-states to expand their empires.

Rosa Luxemburg embraced Hobson's thesis and formulated a theory in which the contradiction at the heart of imperialism is a lack of effec-tive demand due to low wages. Imperial expansion into foreign markets, Luxemburg maintained, occurred because the accumulation of capital could only proceed if outlets were found abroad.

Various Marxist scholars subsequently felt the need to identify the roots of imperialism in one or another of capitalism's economic short-comings: the tendency of the rate of profit to fall, over-accumulation, increasing surplus, etc. All these drawbacks imply that the domestic market does not offer profitable investment opportunities, so that international expansion is the only option left to prop up accumulation.

Still, today some explain globalization as a consequence of the fall-ing rate of profit in advanced countries and the consequent tendency toward depression, trends that are supposed to have led to an increase in exports and foreign direct investments. Whoever reasons in this way commits an error of perspective. In fact, from the point of view of mul-tinational capital, investment opportunities span the global economy, and worldwide GDP growth around the turn of the millennium is cer-tainly not stagnant. Instead, as I will explain in the last three chapters, the slowdown of growth and domestic investments in advanced countries should be seen as a consequence rather than a cause of globalization.

My conviction is that Marx (1857–58, 408) was right: "The ten-dency to create the *world market* is directly given in the concept of capital itself." Imperial expansion is not born of a defect of capitalism, but is an intrinsic property of enlarged reproduction.[23] The only real root of imperialism is "accumulate, accumulate!" Moreover, this explanation is universally applicable: it fits all eras and all countries, and is not dependent upon a particular hypothesis about the trend of income distribution or technological progress. Imperialism has been inherent to capital accumulation from the start (Amin, 2002, 71).

Lenin, especially thanks to the influence of Hilferding (2010), does not suffer from Hobson's original sin. He only accorded a few cursory observations to under-consumption, focusing instead on the theory of monopoly. This "superficiality"[24] rendered his theory far more general that those of his predecessors. Nonetheless, it did not make it general enough to fully account for the transformations brought about by contemporary globalization.

According to Lenin (1917, chap. 7), imperialism can be defined by five main characteristics:

- The development of monopolies as a consequence of a process of capital concentration and centralization;
- The merging of financial and banking capital with industrial capital and a tendency toward the separation of ownership and control;
- The prevalence of capital exports over goods exports;
- The formation of international monopolistic cartels that divide the world up among themselves;
- The division of the world between great imperial powers and exacerbation of inter-imperial rivalries.

I will not dwell on the first three characteristics, which seem to be fully confirmed by the evolution of contemporary capitalism.[25] The last two, however, do not appear to have occurred, or be occurring. They therefore demand a closer look.

To understand what has effectively changed since Lenin's time about these two characteristics, we need to recall the infamous thesis of the tendency toward *ultra-imperialism*, meaning the formation of a system of international power ruled by a single global trust. Lenin believed in this thesis. He said so explicitly in his Preface to Bukharin's *Imperialism and the World Economy*: "There is no doubt that the trend of development is *toward* a single world trust absorbing all enterprises without exception and all states without exception" (Lenin, 1915, 3). And in his essay on *Imperialism* he insisted: "Development is proceeding toward monopolies, hence, toward a single world monopoly, toward a single world trust. This is indisputable, but..." (Lenin, 1917, chap. 7).

Lenin harshly criticized Kautsky's "lifeless abstraction" of ultra-imperialism, charging it with "ultra-nonsense." The citation above continues: "but it is also . . . completely meaningless." Here we need to discount Lenin's inclination to hypercriticism if we want to grasp the essential. Kautsky stood accused of employing the notion of ultra-imperialism to console the masses with the fable of permanent peace as the ultimate tendency of imperial evolution, a myth that sought to present a supposed long-run trend as an imminent reality. In this way he tried to hide the true political implication of imperialism: the exacerbation of inter-imperial rivalries and the resulting drive toward war. His was a lifeless abstraction because it lacked any immediate or future practical implications. The explosion of revolution, triggered by the conflicts between empires, would have led to capitalism being superseded before any sort of tendency toward ultra-imperialist world union could be realized. The abstraction was therefore useless, as well as politically dangerous, but in Lenin's eyes it was, however, *not unfounded*.

The thesis of ultra-imperialism contains some fundamental errors and a lucky intuition. I will come back to the errors later. The lucky intuition lies in the observation that due to the competitive process inherent in capitalist accumulation a world order *without irremediable inter-imperial contradictions* would eventually arise: in other words, an economic and political system similar to that of today's world economy. In this sense the "lifeless abstraction" can ultimately be said to have grasped, at least partially, a significant aspect of the current imperial regime.

Lenin maintained that a politically significant effect of imperialism in the "highest phase" is that inter-imperial contradictions tend to be exacerbated. These contradictions are born of the symbiosis between monopoly capital and national power. The big firms seek to make profits by eliminating competition from their markets. To this end they use the nation-state to protect domestic markets from foreign competitors.

But profits can only grow if markets expand. Therefore, partly due to a certain "personal link-up between capital and government," national powers are driven by the needs of accumulation to expand abroad, creating empires that are intrinsically devoted to growth. These empires need to grow because capital wants to accumulate value. Thus capitalist growth *determines* imperialist expansion. However, sooner or later the great empires come into collision. And the system of global equilibriums is incapable of stabilizing into a peaceful division of the world, because the uneven development of national capitalisms continuously alters power relations between them and therefore makes any balance of powers unstable. Hence *inter-imperial contradictions are a result of the national character of monopoly capital.*

To fully understand the significance of this conclusion, we have to reflect upon the relationship between the last two characteristics of Lenin's imperialism. The fourth posits the formation of monopolistic associations that gain control of certain markets or exclusive geographic areas; in other words, the various nations' monopolies create their own markets, which are fairly isolated from each other and protected from the competition of firms of other nationalities. Thus there will be markets dominated by German monopolies, others dominated by British monopolies, and so on. The fifth characteristic implies that the great imperial powers, by putting themselves at the service of those national monopolistic associations, divide the world into special areas of influence. The division into areas of political influence would be a consequence of market divisions. From this viewpoint, the fourth characteristic could not possibly exist without producing the fifth. Therefore, it can be said that *inter-imperial rivalries exist as a result of the rivalries between national monopolies.*

GLOBAL IMPERIALISM

There is no doubt that imperialism maintained these characteristics until the Second World War. But can the instability caused by inter-imperial rivalries be deemed a fundamental characteristic of capitalist accumulation? Or is it true that *capital is intrinsically cosmopolitan*? Here is Marx's (1857–58, 408) opinion:

> Hence, just as capital has the tendency on one side to create ever more surplus labour, so it has the complementary tendency to create more points of exchange; i.e., here, seen from the standpoint of *absolute* surplus value or surplus labour, to summon up more surplus labour as complement to itself; i.e. at bottom, to propagate production based on capital, or the mode of production corresponding to it. The tendency to create the *world market* is directly given in the concept of capital itself. Every limit appears as a barrier to be overcome. Initially, to subjugate every moment of production itself to exchange and to suspend the production of direct use values not entering into exchange, i.e. precisely to posit production based on capital in place of earlier modes of production, which appear primitive from its standpoint.

The same thesis is proposed in Marx's speech "On the Question of Free Trade" and *The Modern Theory of Colonization*. According to this argument, capital exhibits a fundamental tendency: 1) to propagate production based on capital, that is, to expand activities all over the world market; and 2) to propagate the capitalist mode of production, that is, to substitute itself for precapitalist modes of production. It follows that the pursuit of accumulation will urge nation-states to break down any barrier to expansion. Since "every limit appears as a barrier to be overcome," capital will use political power to bring down trade barriers rather than set them up, and to destroy national empires rather than reinforce them. If anything, the great global capital tends to create a single supranational order, insofar as international competition needs to be (de)regulated and imposed upon the nations who resist globalization. This order takes the form of a "world market": an order of markets, not of bureaucratic machinery, regulated by "natural" law and not by constitutions. In order for this tendency to materialize, firms need to have grown enough to be capable of effectively conceiving and planning productive and commercial expansion on a global scale.

It can therefore be said that the imperialism Lenin spoke of, far from being the highest stage of capitalism, was effectively only a transitory phase: that in which the larvae of the big multinational firms have grown within the cocoons of the nation-states before breaking out and soaring off into the world economy when they reached global proportions, which is what British firms had begun to do already in the late nineteenth century. Once the cocoons are broken, inter-imperial rivalries lose their virulence and those that persist, for example, due to the lust for political power of the national ruling classes and the great powers' consequent ambitions of geopolitical supremacy, acquire the significance of "contradictions among the people" of the great capital.

Nowadays those geopolitical aspirations are embodied by certain states, such as the United States, Germany, Japan, Russia, and China, whose ruling classes still play at imperial superpowers. Their actions continuously generate international rifts and political conflicts, which appear as inter-imperial rivalries only because they are interpreted, by both the ruling classes themselves and some Marxist-Leninist critics, from an outdated imperial perspective. Yet, from the point of view of multinational capital, they represent either resistance to be demolished or strong points to be exploited (when convenient) in the short run and overcome in the long run. Big capital can be tactically nationalist on occasion, but strategically it is cosmopolitan. Boeing can ask the U.S. government to implement protectionist policies, but it will want the International Monetary Fund, the World Bank, and the World Trade Organization, as well as the U.S. State Department, to work to erase protectionism in the rest of the world.

The imperialism of the two Bush presidents may have been prompted by a desire to place the rich oil reserves of the Middle East and Central Asia under the control of U.S. oil magnates, and hence may not have been appreciated by the Russian oil magnates. From a broader geopolitical perspective, they may have been seeking to build a new U.S. imperial order, which would explain why they encountered resistance from German and French old-fashioned imperialists. Ultimately, though, it will turn out that their imperialism served to prepare those geographical areas for capitalist penetration. When the American tanks come out, foreign direct investments can pour in: not only from the United States, but also from Germany, China, Japan, and other countries.

The world economic order that capital demands is not an order of great powers, treaties, understandings, and inter-imperial wars, but of *sovereignless global governance*: of governance by markets. There is "world society *without a world state* and *without a global government*" (Beck, 2000, 13), not even the government of a hegemonic state or of a handful of dominant states.

From this perspective it is clear that inter-imperial rivalries are not irreconcilable, nor fundamental; they are not produced by capitalist accumulation. Geopolitical conflicts can be overcome without hampering accumulation, and indeed have to be overcome in order to facilitate it. Of what use would a British or German empire, or even a European empire, be to the big European multinationals, when they are already taking over the world? And, anyway, don't European firms share a fundamental interest with the big U.S. multinationals in removing all *obstacles* to accumulation and all *limits* to the expansion of production and trade? Don't they also have a common interest in overcoming the restrictions deriving from the various states' national policies, when it is this kind of policy that determines those obstacles and limits?[26]

My argument is that today's great capitalists have a *fundamental interest* in overcoming inter-imperial rivalries rather than exacerbating them, even though certain capital sectors of certain nations frequently seek to exploit the outdated imperial ambitions of the political classes. Based on this thesis, I propose a *preliminary definition of "global imperialism"*: *a system of control of the world economy without substantial inter-imperial contradictions.* By "substantial" I mean: resulting from the force that gives economic substance to imperialist ambition, that is, capitalist accumulation.

WHAT GLOBAL IMPERIALISM IS NOT

It is not "super-imperialism." This concept was devised by Mandel (1975, chap. 10) to define a system of international relations and a possible scenario of the prevailing tendency of imperialism—a situation in which the battle between great powers ultimately leads to the predominance of a single world empire on a national basis. Obviously, that nation is the United States. For some observers, this is the situation attained from the late 1990s, following the collapse of the Soviet empire, the crisis in Japan, and the floundering of the European economies.

For Mandel, the establishment of U.S. super-imperialism would imply American capital controlling world capital. This theoretical implication is fundamental from a Marxist perspective, in which the economic movements of big capital determine states' political logic. Not accepting this theoretical implication means conceding that ultimately *the autonomy of the political*[27] is imposed by the process of globalization. This is a good reason why Marxists who criticize, for example, Hardt and Negri's theory on the postmodern monolithic empire[28] should refute the very idea of U.S. super-imperialism. Without the autonomy of the political, there can be no super-imperialism. Indeed, U.S. capital has not gained control over world capital. There are many American corporations among the big multinationals, but also many European and Japanese companies, and the first do not appear to have gobbled up the others, or to be about to. Neither do the processes of neoliberal globalization seem to have increased states' autonomy from capital, not even in the United States.

Nonetheless, various scholars have worked in the wake of this thesis, seeking to explain contemporary globalization as a form of control established by American super-imperialism in the era of its triumph. Among the most refined are the attempts of Panitch (2000) and Panitch and Gindin (2004; 2005). Their contribution is particularly interesting as it highlights the theoretical necessity for assuming the autonomy of the political, which the two authors satisfy by using Brenner's (1986) arguments on the process of "political accumulation." Even Samir Amin (2004; 2012), who previously developed a theory of the "collective imperialism of the Triad" (United States, Europe, and Japan), recently shifted toward a vision of globalized capitalism as the terrain of conquest and supremacy of U.S. imperial power, at least in the sense that the United States is the hegemonic nation and "military head" of the Triad.

Other authors have sought to update Leninist theories by refocusing in a theoretical direction that seems ascribable to super-imperialism.[29] While paying due respect to the thesis of irreconcilable inter-imperial contradictions, which could possibly manifest themselves in the future, they recognize that in contemporary imperialism the commonality of economic interests in the capitalist Center has effectively attenuated the virulence of rivalries between empires. The United States is attributed the role of hegemonic leader of the Triad and true ruler of contemporary imperialism, while the other states are relegated to being either its weak opponents or subordinate partners. In this case the assumption of the autonomy of the political is twisted into a hypothesis of the *supremacy* of the political. The nation-states would be strengthened by globalization, especially the imperial state *par excellence*, whose power would command respect even from its "civil extensions": the international economic organizations, multinational firms, cultural and scientific foundations. Inter-imperial rivalries would in some way be repressed by the overwhelming power of an empire: not because the world capital is united under the command of U.S. capital, but because the U.S. *political* classes have managed to accumulate enough power to control the states and economies of the whole world.

A different and more realistic approach is proposed by authors navigating the waters of *new imperialism*[30] theories, which, for love of precision, I would define theories of *dichotomous imperialism*. While diverging on various issues, these authors have in common a rejection of the concept of super-imperialism, and in particular of the idea that the polity prevails over the economy. They recognize the existence of a drive to expand political power that is distinct from the drive to expand economic power. For Arrighi the state is permeated by a territorial logic, aiming for geopolitical power and seeking to subordinate the accumulation of capital to its own ends, as well as by a capitalist logic, that seeks to extend its control over economic resources and territorial policies. Harvey follows this approach, but tends to attribute the first type of logic to the state and the second to firms (while for Arrighi they both pertain to state policies). Callinicos proposes a similar dichotomy, speaking of geopolitical competition between states and economic competition between capitals. The two logics are self-sufficient, being ascribable to the interests of two different social classes—political and capitalist—but not independent of each other. Harvey suggests their relationship is dialectic, implying both cooperation and rivalry, while for Callinicos they form a relationship of interdependence and interconnection, tending to use each other.

The theories of super-imperialism and dichotomous imperialism diverge on a crucial issue in the interpretation of globalization. According to the first, the establishment of U.S. imperial power has led to inter-imperial rivalries being overcome, as the hegemony and military power of one country have acquired control, either by force or through cooperation, over the interests of the whole world's capitalists and states. According to the second theory, in contrast, inter-imperial rivalries persist and remain of fundamental importance. They are determined by both territorial and capitalist logics. However, authors leaning in this direction find it hard to demonstrate the existence of these super-contradictions. Admitting that the rivalries are not the type to cause the explosion of great world wars, they resort to a more realistic argument: interstate geopolitical rivalries still spawn conflicts, even though these generally take the form of currency and trade wars.

Some theorists of dichotomous imperialism tend to force the reasoning in the opposite direction from that of super-imperialism, twisting the notion of the autonomy of the political toward a hypothesis of the supremacy of economic forces. For Callinicos (2007, 541), in contemporary imperialism "interstate competition became subsumed under that between capitals." This hypothesis clearly enables proponents to continue speaking of *capitalist* imperialism from a neo-Leninist perspective and claim that inter-imperial rivalries are ascribable to competition between capitals. Yet the arguments for such a conclusion and the hypothesis it is based on are unconvincing. Can trade and currency wars between states have the same virulence and the same devastating effects as the inter-imperial contradictions that Lenin spoke of? Could they really lead to the explosion of a great world war and consequently to proletarian revolution?

My impression is that the theories of dichotomous imperialism are plagued by a dilemma. They are fairly convincing when they argue in favor of states' political logic being subsumed under the economic logic of capital, but then they have to give up the idea that inter-imperial contradictions are irreconcilable. These theories can also be convincing about the existence of bitter inter-imperial rivalries, but only if they are attributed to the purely political logics of the nation-states' ruling classes. Thus, in an attempt to salvage the Leninist theory of irreconcilable inter-imperial contradictions, these theories distance themselves from Lenin on the far more important issue of the predominance of capitalist interests over those of the political classes.

In the history of capitalism, only under mercantilist imperialism (sixteenth to eighteenth centuries) have political interests shown a clear predominance over economic ones. This is certainly not what is happening in the current globalization. Even if some states in the North of the world are seeking to hold out against the predominance of globalized capital by adopting economic and commercial policies that could be defined as *neo-mercantilist*, the capitalist logic of "markets" effectively condemns those policies to failure in the long run, as I shall argue in chapter 6.

Let's return to the category of *ultra-imperialism*. In Kautsky's and Lenin's versions this is a completely different form of control from super-imperialism. Lenin's acceptance of the thesis on the tendency toward ultra-imperialism is not incidental, nor is it an oversight. It was rendered necessary by the conviction of an inexorable drive toward monopolistic concentration. If firms continually grow in size and market power, and tend to organize themselves into maxi-cartels, sooner or later a single world trust, or something similar, will be formed. However, the inter-imperial contradictions will be heightened in the "highest phase" and will put a stop to that tendency by bringing about revolution. But we might ask: what happens if the inter-imperial contradictions do not explode in a great war that triggers world revolution? Obviously the highest phase becomes a transitory phase, after which ultra-imperialism will take over. This is why some Leninist scholars interpret contemporary globalization as the process of realization of a form of ultra-imperialism: an interpretation that is entirely plausible from a Leninist perspective.

Looking at reality, though, can we really believe that globalization tends to generate ultra-imperialism? My answer is negative. No tendency toward the formation of a single capitalist world trust has been observed. As I have already noted, the theory of ultra-imperialism contains some errors, the most significant of which lies precisely in the conviction that the progressive concentration of capital on a global scale can lead to the formation of a single cartel. In reality, competition is an essential component of the process of capitalist accumulation. The size of a firm can increase indefinitely and profits can take on the characteristics of monopoly rents. Yet a situation in which the world economy is dominated by a single cartel will never arise, precisely because of the uneven development caused by technological competition. In fact, the accumulation of capital on a global scale brings about not only an increase in the size of firms but also a multiplication of their numbers, making the formation of a single maxi-cartel ever more unlikely. In 1976 there were about 11,000 multinationals. By 2010 there were 103,788 (UNCTAD, 2011).

However, Lenin did not fall for the other mistake of the ultra-imperialism theory—the opinion that realization of the tendency would have reduced the disparities and contradictions of the world economy. He maintained that these would have been heightened. The question is: which *disparities* and which *contradictions*?

It is now possible to update Lenin's thesis: the contradictions exacerbated by the evolution of imperialism *do not* depend on inter-imperial rivalries. Rivalries certainly continue to exist, but they have lost the explosive nature they had in the era of colonial imperialism. The contradictions intensified by globalization are those caused by antagonism between workers and capital on the one hand, and by the disparity between the Center and Periphery of the world capitalist system on the other. In fact, just as accumulation feeds on surplus value, global accumulation feeds on global surplus value. Multinational firms invest where they earn most. Capital exports from the North to the South, in the form of both direct investments and portfolio and speculative investments, are justified by the profit goal and therefore imply the re-importation of profits. In the long run, the net flow of value between the Center and the Periphery is positive for the Center, as I will show in the next chapter. This means that the increase in income inequality between the North and the South of the world is an intrinsic upshot of the logic of capitalist accumulation and exploitation on a global scale. Moreover, the increased exploitation of the Periphery by the Center in contemporary globalization also contributes to increasing the exploitation of the working classes in advanced countries.

There is another reason why the thesis of ultra-capitalism is unconvincing. Mandel highlighted one of its political implications: the creation of a "supranational imperial world state." If there are no more inter-capitalist contradictions because all capitals are unified under the command of a single immense trust, national rivalries should be controlled by the actions of a single world-state. This state would guarantee the peaceful political rule and economic control of the world on behalf of the capital. Where, then, is this ultra-state? Certainly not in the United Nations.

Among contemporary scholars, those who come closest to a theory of ultra-imperialism are Sklair (2001; 2002) and Robinson (2004; 2005),[31] but not for the reason put forward by Callinicos (2007, 535), which is because they maintain that today's globalized capitalism works along transnational rather than national lines. If anything, this is one of their more sound assessments. Less understandable is their tendency to anthropomorphize "transnational capital."

On the one hand, Sklair and Robbins (2002, 84–85) propose the idea that the "Transnational Capitalist Class" (TCC) is organized into fractions that fulfill complementary functions to integrate the whole; on the other, they suggest that the TCC would be governed by a sort of secret central committee, "one central inner circle that makes system-wide decisions," even if "there is, as yet, insufficient evidence to demonstrate the existence of an effective global inner circle for the TCC, global system theory predicts that one exists and that it operates to give a unity to the diverse economic interests, political organizations and cultural and ideological formations of those who make up the

TCC." These ideas have recently been developed by Sklair and Miller (2010, 484) in a thesis according to which the function of integrating the whole is fulfilled by a "state fraction" of the TCC composed of "globalizing state and interstate politicians and officials."

Robinson (2005, 7) goes even further. Stretching Gramsci's concepts of "hegemony" and "historical bloc," he hypothesizes that "the TCC has been attempting to position itself as a new ruling class group worldwide and to bring some coherence and stability to its rule through an emergent TNS apparatus." The "TNS" is the big "transnational state." Obviously, caution is called for here, and in fact two years later Robinson (2007a, 17–18) adjusts his view: a TNS apparatus is currently only "emerging" and can be seen in an incomplete form in the meetings of the Trilateral Commission, the World Economic Forum, the G7, the WTO General Council, and similar organizations. Nonetheless, a "transnational institutional structure has played an increasingly salient role in coordinating global capitalism and imposing capitalist domination beyond national borders." At any rate, the TNS would only be an instrument of the TCC. The real historical protagonist is the TCC itself, the group that exercises leadership and imposes its project upon the world. It does so by creating an ideological hegemony and a historical bloc involving the "new middle classes, highly paid workers, and cosmopolitan professionals" (Robinson, 2005, 7).

Rather than to Gramsci, it seems to me that we should refer to Kautsky if we are to believe that the global empire is governed by a central committee of the world's bourgeoisie. If we admit the idea of a growing trustification of capital, we could surmise that the central committee is controlled by the cartel that unites and organizes the interests of monopoly capital. But who believes that this is what is happening with contemporary globalization?

Certainly not Ellen M. Wood (2002; 2003). While granting that multinational capital in the era of globalization has achieved universalization, meaning that it has fully established its power on a global scale, Wood does not believe we are now in the presence of a global imperial order capable of doing without the nation-states. She recognizes that capitalist rule needs states' power to regulate labor and maintain the subordination of the Periphery to the Center, but denies that these functions are fulfilled by a single national or transnational state. U.S. military and financial power has not led to American super-imperialism, nor to the elimination of rivalries between states. Nonetheless, inter-imperial conflicts have now lost the destructive nature they had in Lenin's times and easily let themselves be settled under America's leadership, as long as that leadership is functional to globalized capital interests.

WHAT IS GLOBAL IMPERIALISM?

If it is true that in the capitalist mode of production the state ultimately serves the needs of capital, then we can propose a second definition of global imperialism: *a system of international relations in which state policies are forced to remove the obstacles that national agglomerations place in the way of the process of accumulation on a global scale.*

By globalizing, capital frees itself of political dependence on the nation-state. It acts in the first person,[32] or rather plays the roles of many leading actors. In order to assert its control over the subjugated countries, capital makes use, above all, of modern communications and transport. These instruments have turned out to be far more incisive and effective than the Gurkhas and the French Foreign Legion. It also uses the markets that grow in the networks created by these instruments. Through the networks, big capital builds and manages its imperial power structure in the process of value creation. *The fundamental coercive structure of global imperial rule is that of production itself. Its administrative structure is the organizational apparatus of multinational corporations.*

One important difference between contemporary imperialism and that of the nineteenth and twentieth centuries is the way in which big capital relates to peripheral economies. Colonial imperialism penetrated underdeveloped countries without substantially changing their modes of production, leaving them to languish in their precapitalist economic and social structures and mostly limiting itself to extracting raw materials.[33] In some cases settlers were brought from the Center and peripheral capitalist areas were built, which still remained rather circumscribed. In nineteenth- and twentieth-century imperialism opposition between the Center and the Periphery mainly took the form of a systemic difference between industrialized capitalist countries and nonindustrialized precapitalist countries (Amin, 2002, 17). Global imperialism instead pervades the whole world through capital and renders everything its own. Capital exports itself through the export of investments, finance, and goods. Although there are still quite a large number of peasants remaining in the world, today the capitalist mode of production has become global, and few vestiges of uncontaminated precapitalist "backwardness" remain.[34] This brings us to a third definition: *global imperialism is the globalization of the capitalist mode of production*.

The methods of imperial *exploitation* also change accordingly. First, the mechanism of unequal exchange is reinforced. Then the use of military force changes in nature. These two mechanisms of exploitation and domination are indeed important, but they have become secondary to three other mechanisms, which I shall only list here, intending to come back to them in the next chapter:

1. The use of wage workers by capitalist multinationals to extract surplus value;
2. The use of finance to expropriate surplus value and wealth;
3. The use of labor, goods, and capital markets to place the workers in every country in competition against workers in all other countries.

The process of unequal exchange is becoming increasingly effective, as its mechanisms become more complex and refined. One of them is prompted by productive specialization.[35] The countries in the South of the world that export commodities to the North face unfavorable terms of trade due, above all, to their low wages. This effect could be compensated by low productivity. But one of the consequences of globalization is that labor productivity tends to increase rapidly in the countries of the Periphery, which further deteriorates their terms of trade. Moreover, the World Bank and International Monetary Fund systematically drive the countries in the South of the world to increase their output of agricultural products and raw materials for export. These countries comply, increasing the availability of commodities and consequently reducing their *market* prices, which helps exacerbate the effects of the downward trend of *production* prices. These mechanisms of unequal exchange are strengthened under the global imperialism of multinationals.

Other mechanisms derive from the neo-mercantilist policies of the states in the North of the world. For example, some insist that the states in the South lower their trade barriers, as well as their social and environmental dumping. At the same time, however, the Northern states tend to protect (among other things) their own agricultural sectors, raising their farmers' incomes. This depresses the demand for food and raw materials produced in the Southern countries and weakens their terms of trade. Another perverse consequence of neo-mercantilism lies in the tendency of advanced countries to protect their processing industries through tariff-escalation. For example, relatively low tariffs are applied to imported green coffee, cocoa beans, oilseeds, and raw jute, while higher tariffs are applied to imported roasted coffee, cocoa powder, vegetable oils, and jute cloth. This pushes many countries in the South toward a specialization that exacerbates unequal exchange.

There is also a powerful macroeconomic mechanism of unequal exchange that affects the least developed and some developing countries. Many of these nations have to deal with chronic balance of payments deficits and therefore systematic pressure to depreciate their currencies in relation to the dollar and the euro. This is detrimental to their terms of trade for all products exported, which explains why certain developing countries fail to make much progress toward industrialization.

Lastly, two particular mechanisms of unequal exchange also affect emerging countries. In order to get exports to drive their growth, these nations strive both to maintain low wages and to attract foreign direct investments and technology transfers to increase their labor productivity. Their goods consequently become highly competitive, which is another way of saying that their terms of trade with advanced countries are systematically unfavorable. The governments of emerging countries also adopt currency policies aimed at maintaining low exchange rates with the dollar, euro, and yen, which further deteriorates their terms of trade.

Now let's look at the use of military force as an instrument of imperial penetration. Though it has certainly not disappeared in contemporary globalization, its function has changed. Today military force essentially serves to open up markets and counter the political resistance of rogue countries (such as Iraq, Afghanistan, Iran), as well as to protect the respectable states (such as Israel, Pakistan, and Saudi Arabia). The difference between these two types of states, apart from which side they take in the global war on terror (which I will come to in the next chapter), lies in the strength of their cultural and political resistance to opening up their markets. From this perspective, which flag the Western forces of "freedom" and "democracy" fight under is quite irrelevant. Whether starred and striped, crossed, or tricolored, they all work to achieve the interests of global capital, and not those of a single nation.

In closing this section, I need to make a few points about the problem of the differing degrees of development in the peripheral countries. The forms of the multinational corporations' investments in these countries vary according to the extent of their infrastructures, type of culture, and natural resource endowment, as well as the quality and skills of their workforce. Thus the dominated countries can be divided into various groups.

On the basis of their *productive structure*, there are:

- *Nonindustrialized* countries, characterized by the mass exploitation of natural resources through the introduction of monocultures and the destruction of traditional methods and units of production;
- *Partially industrialized* countries, in which low-cost consumer or intermediate goods are produced and simple technologies are used;
- *Industrialized* countries, in which technologically advanced but standardized production is located (machine tools, cars, computer parts, etc.).

On the basis of their *growth dynamics*, there are:

- *Underdeveloped* countries (about fifty nations in conditions of "extreme poverty," mostly in Africa)[36] that experience processes of absolute impoverishment, with low GDP growth and sometimes even negative per capita GDP growth;
- *Developing* countries (some Latin American, Eastern European, and Arab countries), characterized by processes of relative impoverishment, with GDP per-capita growth not high enough to reduce the gap with advanced economies;
- *Emerging*[37] countries (various nations of the Far East, Latin America, Eastern Europe, and a few African ones), which have managed to launch processes of intense capitalist accumulation—mainly by breaking some of the most fundamental rules of neoliberal globalization and frequently resorting to protectionism, dumping, and industrial and exchange rate policies—and therefore reduce the gap with the Center of the empire.

As for impoverishment, it cannot be fully understood in terms of "absolute" poverty. It needs to be studied as a class phenomenon, as the impoverishment of exploited classes. Nowadays it affects all countries, whether underdeveloped, emerging, or advanced. And it is true that in every country, due to global imperialism, "the wealth of the nation is once again, by its very nature, identical with the misery of the people" (Marx, 1867, 938). The increased inequality of income distribution is in fact a consequence of the expansion of global capitalist exploitation.

The countries in the South are almost all penalized, to some extent, by the technological gap with the dominant countries, and by their structural differences in labor productivity. Thus the multinationals invest in them only if their wages are modest enough to guarantee low labor costs and high competitiveness. And as a large industrial reserve army is an essential condition for the maintenance of low wages, in these countries unemployment and underemployment are rife. In other words, it is not so much absolute poverty in developing countries

that merits investigation, but rather the poverty of workers and especially its economic functionality.

In effect, this poverty fulfills more than one beneficial purpose. Not
only does it permit exploitation in countries with low productivity, it
also serves to enhance labor exploitation in advanced countries. On the
one hand, the competitiveness of goods produced in dominated countries helps reduce employment in advanced countries; on the other,
migration from the South increases the labor force in the North. Both
processes contribute to swelling the reserve army, and therefore keeping down wages, even in the Center of the empire.

This gives rise to a completely new phenomenon. In today's global
imperialism the exploitation of dominated countries is also conducive
to increasing exploitation in the imperial Center. Indeed, inequality in
income distribution is known to be escalating even in rich and super-
rich countries. To a greater or lesser extent, this phenomenon involves
the entire working class.

All this provides a useful clue to the identification of the revolutionary forces. I don't wish to deal with this problem here. I will limit myself
to observing that global imperialism, far from making class conflict out-
moded, exacerbates it, intensifies it, and, above all, globalizes it. As a
tendency, it unifies it. And it is the typical conflict of the capitalist mode
of production: the class struggle between capital and labor, between
global capital and the international proletariat.

An *Imperium maius* Without a Sovereign

The problem is: if exploitation requires a power structure, how can
global exploitation be achieved? At a microeconomic level, factory
hierarchy is necessary for exploitation within the production process.
The nation-state is necessary to maintain social control over the lower
classes, to provide the political conditions for exploitation. It will
therefore be necessary to set up some kind of global power structure to
ensure exploitation on a global scale. A global empire will be needed,

the term "empire" being understood in the Latin sense of *imperium,* a set of power prerogatives.[38]

The novelty lies in the fact that the global nature of imperialism, its tendency to surpass national limits to capitalist accumulation, makes it impossible to use nation-states in the same way as under the nineteenth- and twentieth-century empires. Colonies no longer exist. Nonetheless, global capital needs to control the nation-states and govern their politics, not only in the South of the world. In other words, the theoretical difficulty lies in the fact that though global imperialism would seem to require a thinking and ruling head, it is an intrinsically headless structure. Or rather, as we shall see below, it is a structure with many heads.

Aside from the more general reasons for perplexity concerning the theories of U.S. super-imperialism, as mentioned above, I insist that it would be mistaken to believe that global *imperium* can be achieved by the imperialism of a single nation. Nowadays, observing the way in which the United States continues to pose as sheriff on the world stage, it is particularly easy to fall into such a mistake. But this view tends to focus on military power alone, while control of the world economy requires other, completely different, instruments of power. In effect, it would imply controlling the creation of international currency, international financial flows, national monetary and fiscal policies, the protection of property rights beyond national boundaries, lowering trade barriers, creating infrastructures for accumulation on a global scale, opening markets and commodifying goods and services—all things that cannot be done by U.S. Marines, and all things that require far more complex instruments of world control and governance than the Pentagon could even imagine.

Nowadays, we "have a system of global *governance* but without a global government" (Stiglitz, 2001, 5). So, how does governance of the global empire work? It works, like an "organic" process, on the basis of laws that appear to be "natural." Recalling and contradicting Hardt and Negri, I would say that the *imperium* "somehow rises up spontaneously out of the interactions of radically heterogeneous global forces, as if this order were a harmonious concert orchestrated by the natural and neutral hidden hand of the world market,"[39] but that it is controlled by the hands—anything but invisible and neutral—of the world "market." There is no central mind, no world-state or super-state that commands the whole process. Instead, there is a multitude of centers of *governance*. Some are international organizations—the World Bank, International Monetary Fund, World Trade Organization, NATO, UN. Others are the central banks of national governments, above all the Federal Reserve and the European Central Bank. Yet others are the governments of the main capitalist countries themselves.

Lastly, the most important are the myriad governance centers that pass for the so-called market. Here we must be careful: "The market is sovereign" is a metaphor. The market is not a decision-making body or a legal person. It is sovereign in the sense that the economic agents operating within it, those that *make* the market, are sovereign. Among these, the multinational firms stand out as they manage to win over the actors endowed with formal political sovereignty, despite not possessing any themselves.

All the various international decision-making centers interact in complex relationships of competition and cooperation. They contribute in different ways, without anybody having planned it, to rendering the laws of accumulation (those regulating multinational capital's exploitation of the planet) both effective and stringent. We should not be fooled by the organic or "natural" character of this type of governance. There is nothing really natural about it, as it remains a form of governance based on intentional actions. The point is that these agencies of governance, be they national or supranational, are not accountable to any constituent political subjects, such as the citizens of the world or even only those of some great countries. Instead they answer to the laws of accumulation, which appear not to depend upon human will.

In such a system of world governance, the markets constrain states and, insofar as states should be accountable to citizens, they empty democratic institutions of any deliberative power, transforming them into simple apparatuses for the formation of consent and repression of dissent. They turn the heads of government into the Gauleiters of a multinational capital dictatorship, forcing them to implement the "structural reforms" necessary to globally level out the cost of labor and tax pressure on firms, as well as policies protecting citizens from the negative externalities produced by capitalist accumulation. In foreign policy they push states to promote the opening of all markets to the penetration of multinational capital and to discipline recalcitrant countries. In this way they tend to establish a *sovereignless global governance*.

The mechanisms of "sovereignless governance" acquire the form of feedback processes that, taken together, work as automatisms capable of stabilizing the "social balance" of world domination and exploitation. They are proper disciplinary mechanisms, of which at least four, which I will call commercial, financial, terrorist, and ideological disciplines, are worth describing and explaining. The next chapter is dedicated to this.

3. Governing the Global Empire

Imperium superat regnum.
—MARCUS A. AURELIUS

The market is sovereign.
—LUCA C. MONTEZEMOLO

In this chapter I seek to substantiate the idea that the global empire governs the world without the need for a sovereign political authority. Accumulation entails the capitalist mode of production penetrating all geographic areas. It also triggers certain disciplinary mechanisms, which result in the Peripheral countries and the world's proletariat being subjugated to and exploited by multinational capital. I will describe four of these mechanisms and discuss commercial, financial, terroristic, and ideological discipline. The key idea is that these mechanisms are organic. They seem to be governed by a "blind law of nature."

Marx grasped capital's drive to globalize and understood the essence of contemporary globalization, namely capital's tendency to govern the world through the market. Globalization is, above all, the expansion of the world market. And the market operates through the "law of value." This is a law of competition among capitals, which pushes market prices toward production prices and rates of return toward uniformity. It is one of the fundamental laws of capitalism, and it determines the "social balance" fit for this mode of production.

The disciplinary mechanisms that govern equilibrium emerge not as a consequence of policies or central planning, but as the result of a multiplicity of uncoordinated actions by myriad economic and political actors, each of which ignores the broader effects of his decisions. And although each of them, above all the multinationals, have the internal power structure of hierarchical organizations, the world order they contribute to creating has a market or network structure. Circulation of the goods, financial assets, capitals, information, and ideologies that govern the world capitalist system takes place through trading within this type of structure. Military discipline is the exception, as it is obviously carried out by hierarchical structures. But, as we shall see, even military discipline involves a feedback mechanism with the characteristics of an "organic" reaction.

Before expounding the theory, I need to indulge in a methodological digression. When a global collective action materializes, such as a wave of panic in the financial markets, the bailout of a crisis-stricken country by the IMF and WB, or a war for freedom against a rogue state, the various decision-makers may pursue different goals, not only having different ends from one another, but sometimes having several different aims each. The governments of the various belligerent countries may have been prompted to wage war in Afghanistan, for example, by different reasons, and likewise the U.S. president, secretary of state, Pentagon, CIA, multinationals, oil companies, and the like, may have had different motivations for their country's actions. At the end of the war some goals will have been achieved, others not. Some decision-makers will be satisfied, others frustrated. It goes without saying that the effects of actions can be explained in different ways: the victory of freedom and democracy, the achievement of control over oil pipelines, the punishment of Islamic terrorists, the expansion of American imperial power, the preparation of a territory for penetration by multinational capital. And each of these will have elements of validity.

However, anyone seeking an explanation that really grasps the heart of the matter cannot simply stop at a list of more or less superficial observations. Among the many possible causes, the fundamental ones need to be identified, that is, those ascribable to the role and aims of the *dominant* actors within the collective action. Then it has to be seen whether the action effectively contributed to attaining the goals. If they are determined by the *common interests* of many actors, and if the numerousness of the actors and the opacity of their intentions makes it difficult to pinpoint individual motivations, the explanation may take on the guise of an ostensibly holistic justification: the action produced results that were "functional" to the achievement of common interests, therefore those interests should be referred to as the fundamental cause of the phenomenon.

To remain with the example above, multinational capital's interest in wars of liberation against rogue states is an interest in opening up markets and removing all obstacles to the free movement of capital and goods. The fact that only a handful of managers have said so explicitly is of no importance. And it would be difficult to trace all the flows of information and all the types of economic and political pressure exercised by the various firms on belligerent governments. But this is not necessary, as long as it makes sense to attribute common interests to them. What counts is that they all share the same type of interest and could all plausibly have had the same aim, and that they ultimately achieved their common goal.

Note that, despite appearances, this type of explanation is not functionalist, since the main causal nexuses have been identified. Nor should the use of a linguistic simplification referring to a collective subject (multinational capital) permit a lapse into holistic mysticism. In fact the "actor" must be seen as a group of autonomous entities (the multinational corporations), which are deemed to have effectively acted, with the lobbies, political influence, corruption, funding, and mass media, as individual agents. And the results of their collective actions may go beyond the intentions of some decision-makers. This is not a problem; indeed, it is to be expected when studying such a complex phenomenon.

Now, in order for global markets to work effectively as disciplinary mechanisms certain actions of central global governance are required anyway. These actions constitute the presuppositions of the market. In particular, if globalization is to serve the process of accumulation, international currency needs to be produced in ever greater quantities so as to sustain continual growth in the volume of real and financial transactions. Effective demand also needs to expand, and consequently there needs to be at least one big economy capable of driving exports and production in all other countries via its imports. Lastly, in order for wars to subdue the resistant countries of the Periphery without heightening rivalries between advanced countries, the armed forces of a dominant state need to have developed sufficient power to suppress any outdated imperial ambitions on the part of other countries.

So far, the United States has managed to play the roles of global banker, growth-driver, and sheriff thanks to its greater size in relation to all other economies. The vastness of the U.S. economy has created a certain synergy between fiscal, monetary, and war policies, so that the pursuit of each of the three functions has facilitated realization of the others. The huge weight of U.S. GDP in global production has allowed the government to implement expansive fiscal policies without being overly hampered by external constraints. Besides, these constraints have been partly mitigated thanks to the U.S.'s capacity to finance its own trade deficits by issuing the key international reserve currency. Under these conditions, its expansive fiscal policies result in the creation of aggregate demand for the rest of the world. Moreover, the possibility of limitlessly expanding the money supply has allowed it to monetize national debt and maintain low debt service costs. Lastly, the ability to implement expansionary fiscal policies through deficit spending has allowed it to meet the enormous military expenditure necessary for playing the role of global sheriff.

However, the United States' size advantage has been shrinking over the years, as other countries have continued to grow. Nowadays U.S. economic dominance is in decline, partly due to globalization, and Washington appears to be losing its ability to fulfill the function of global banker and growth-driver effectively. We are probably in the midst of a transition toward a new system of international relations, which is being accelerated by the current crisis. It cannot be ruled out, as I shall argue in the final chapter, that the three functions of central governance will be fulfilled differently in the near future.

THE "LAW OF VALUE"

In the third volume of *Capital* (1894, 1020) Marx states:

> In this quite specific form of value, labour is valid only as social labour; on the other hand, the division of this social labour and the reciprocal complementarity or metabolism of its products, subjugation to and insertion into the social mechanism, is left to the accidental and reciprocally countervailing motives of the individual capitalist producers. Since these confront one another only as commodity owners, each trying to sell his commodity as dear as possible (and seeming to be governed only by caprice even in the regulation of production), the inner law operates only by way of their competition, their reciprocal pressure on one other, which is how divergences are mutually counterbalanced. It is only as an inner law, a blind natural force vis-à-vis the individual agents, that the law of value operates here and that the *social balance* of production is asserted in the midst of accidental fluctuations.

It is through the law of value that markets assert the "social balance" most conducive to capital accumulation. In *Results of the Immediate Process of Production* (1863–66, 1038) Marx clarifies:

> *Productivity of labour* in general = the *maximum of profit* with the *minimum of work*, hence, too, goods constantly become cheaper. This becomes a *law*, independent of the will of the individual capitalist. And this law only becomes reality because instead of the scale of production being controlled by existing needs, the quantity of products made is determined by the constantly increasing scale of production dictated by the mode of production itself. Its aim is that the individual product should contain as *much unpaid labour as possible*, and this is achieved only by *producing for the sake of production*. This becomes manifest, on the one hand, as a law, since the capitalist who produces on too small a scale puts more than the socially necessary quantum of labour into his products. That

is to say, it becomes manifest as an adequate embodiment of the *law of value* which develops fully only on the foundation of capitalist production. But, on the other hand, it becomes manifest as the desire of the individual capitalist who, in his wish to render this law ineffectual, or to *outwit it* and turn it to his own advantage, reduces the *individual* value of his product to a point where it falls *below* its socially determined value.

Marx was not only the first to theorize globalization as an inherent tendency of the capitalist mode of production. He was also the first to understand *the fundamental law of regulation*, the law with which the empire of the Hydra imposes the "social balance." This is the "law of value," or *the market process.* Competition ensures that production is organized and workers used as efficiently as possible: maximum labor productivity means maximum production with minimum labor inputs.[40] The market generates the only "social balance" fit for the capitalist system. Its "law of nature" imposes itself "blindly"—that is, without the need for constitutions, parliaments, central planning, or an imperial sovereign. In order to work, it only needs the myriad lesser "sovereigns" who govern firms pursuing maximum profits. These sovereigns push for global expansion, also to take advantage of scale economies. In fact "the quantity of products made is determined by the constantly increasing scale of production. . . . Its aim is that the individual product should contain as *much unpaid labour as possible.* . . . The capitalist who produces on too small a scale puts more than the socially necessary quantum of labour into his products." On the other hand, "the desire of the individual capitalist [to reduce] the *individual* value of his product to a point where it falls *below* its socially determined value" has the effect of stimulating technological innovation.

The ideal form of capitalist regulation is *sovereignless global governance.* The blind law of nature Marx speaks of works on the basis of the free movement of capital (including the output of production, or what Marx called "commodity capital"). The pursuit of maximum profits continuously induces capitalists to perform arbitrage operations, investing in the places and sectors in which rates of return are higher and disinvesting from those in which they are lower. This process brings about a tendency toward a single price for each good and asset on the one hand, and a tendency toward uniform rates of return on the other.[41] For the law to work well, not all productive requirements need to be perfectly mobile; it is sufficient that capital is. If workers are not fully mobile, for example, capital can move to seek out cheaper labor. Thus wages also tend to become uniform.

In the reality of contemporary capitalism, however, this uniformity is far from being achieved, and for many reasons. First, markets are not perfectly competitive (as Marx assumed they were, following Smith and Ricardo). But this doesn't change the essence of the matter. It just happens that, with oligopolistic competition, profit rates tend to converge toward a structure that also reflects the balance of market power between firms, besides production costs. In fact, differentiated oligopoly prevails in manufacturing sectors: big corporations make the prices and determine their own profit rates; smaller firms take the prices and accept lower profits; so a nonuniform profit structure prevails that is rather stable and reflects the distribution of market power.

Second, technology differs from one country to another so that, as labor is not perfectly mobile, wages may be higher in more technologically advanced countries. However, capital mobility will induce technology transfers, resulting in reduced productivity and wage differentials. Of course, as long as only a few nations lead technological innovation, wages will still vary from one country to another.

In any case, a convergence of unit labor costs (the ratio of wages to productivity) will arise. Firms try to minimize costs, the main component of which is labor. The convergence of labor costs results in an international leveling to the bottom, that is, in a maximization of global exploitation, and this is the social balance that really interests capital.

Third, transport costs make it difficult to ship some goods in such a way as to level out their prices internationally. Yet technological progress tends to continually bring down this kind of cost. Fourth, some goods, including many services, are not transferrable and thus cannot have a uniform international price. Many of these (such as education and health care) have not yet been completely commodified, which is why they do not have uniform world prices. Fifth, there are extra-economic factors, institutions, organizations, and politics that work to alter the way the "law of value" functions. Commercial and monetary policies can counter the tendency toward a single price. Legislation and trade union power can prevent excessive cuts in wages and excessive increases in exploitation. Fiscal policies can redistribute income among social classes. Environmental policies can boost production costs.

Generally, the market generates a tendency toward uniformity of returns and prices, while political and institutional factors can produce countertendencies. Some of these, like the oligopolistic structure of industrial markets, are permanent. Others are not, and it is over these that an incessant war between the market and politics, or between multinational capital and noncapitalist organizations, is fought.

Capital won a decisive battle in this war in 1995, when the World Trade Organization was established with the goal of removing trade barriers and promoting the free movement of capital. Since then, the states, as well as political and trade union organizations, have experienced one defeat after another, while capital has gained ever more ground; for example, by forcing states to commodify public services and commons. Whereas political actions tend to lead to inefficient production in the form of high wages and low profits, capital flight, investment relocation, offshoring, and especially crises tend to restore the right "social balance."

Hence capitalist competition works not only through incentives and disincentives: high profits to those who produce efficiently and losses to those incapable of doing so. It also works by meting out punishments (Beck, 2000, 4) to those who seek to obstruct the mechanism. In a globalized world in which states and political organizations are immobile and capital is mobile, capital ultimately lays down the law. Institutions have to adapt, unless they want to experience the negative consequences of market discipline. This is the essence of *sovereignless global governance*: once the free circulation of capital has been established, sooner or later the blind law of value succeeds in disciplining even political actors.

Commercial Discipline

It should be stressed that *oligopolistic competition*, a process in which firms enter into both competitive and collaborative relationships (Chesnais, 1998–99), prevails in global industrial markets. This kind of competition functions through innovation, marketing, product differentiation, and advertising rather than through price wars. It also manifests through the struggles for corporate control, the merger and acquisition processes by which big concerns try to appropriate the capital of their rivals to build market power.

Success demands large dimensions. Small firms do not have sufficient quantities of capital to finance non-price competition, whereas big corporations enjoy the advantages of increasing returns to scale, technological progress, and market power. Moreover, firms using advanced technologies need to employ specialized labor and technical and scientific staff with high-level skills. This requires the existence of social economies, that is, highly developed social and cultural environments of the type encountered in advanced countries, and nowadays taking shape in emerging countries too.

For all these reasons, the countries of the imperial Center, in which the governing bodies and research divisions of the big multinationals are based, and where profits are collected, enjoy a systematic advantage compared to most Peripheral countries, despite the enormous wage differentials. Research is performed in the North, and its results are not easily accessible to the countries of the South, both because they have to pay high royalties and because industrial applications require the social economies that most developing countries lack.

These countries are therefore compelled to specialize in the production of commodities, basic manufactured goods, components, and standardized consumer goods, and pay lower wages than in the North, as well as providing inferior working conditions. This type of production specialization and income distribution does nothing to favor investment in human capital or to develop a culture of research and innovation, and consequently cannot help reduce the technological gap. Thus many countries of the South fall into a technological "gap trap": their sluggish productivity growth is caused by social and cultural backwardness (from the point of view of capital), which in turn is exacerbated by economic backwardness due to the gap.

This is not all: due to their technological backwardness, commodity-producing countries are afflicted by another trap. Liberal ideology claims that all countries specialize in exporting the goods they are best equipped to produce—those for which they enjoy a comparative advantage. Thus developing countries should orient themselves toward the provision of raw materials and foodstuffs, a choice that was effectively made for them centuries ago by colonialist countries and is continuously reaffirmed by the modern multinationals.[42]

Development in the Periphery is driven by exports. But the trend of the relative demand for commodities in industrialized countries is diminishing, albeit through long fluctuations. The reasons are multiple: the declining importance of heavy industry in advanced economies, the growing importance of sectors producing intangibles, the substitution of traditional raw materials with new synthetic products, improvements in recycling techniques, increased consumption of luxury goods, and state subsidies on agricultural production in industrialized countries.[43] The main consequence is that the real price of commodities (defined as their ratio to that of products exported by advanced countries) has exhibited a century-long decreasing trend. It shrank by an average of 0.6 percent per year in the twentieth century, and in the 1990s alone it was more than halved.

Faced with a systematic downward drift in their terms of trade, commodity-specialized countries produce increasing volumes of exports but receive decreasing values for them; they export their goods to the North at ever lower prices to import industrial goods at ever higher prices. Later I will explain how such a tendency contributes to activating another deadly trap—that of foreign debt. For the moment, I will provide a preliminary and general conclusion on how this mechanism of underdevelopment works. By exporting their products, many commodity producers are simply not able to generate the systematic current account surplus necessary to launch a real process of industrial takeoff, and are therefore condemned to remain trapped in their specialization.[44]

Moreover, the most profitable types of production in developing countries are often controlled by the big multinationals and by international trade brokers, so that most of the profits are seized by corporations that import them into the North of the world. It is calculated, for example, that no more than 12 to 13 percent of the price of a kilo of bananas or coffee returns to the producing country: the rest goes to the Center of the empire.

Although various economies in the South have a high rate of exploitation of their workforce, they fail to hold on to all the surplus value they need to trigger industrial takeoff. Understandably, the big multinationals continuously press the countries of the South to remove trade barriers and liberalize their markets. In other words, commercial discipline regulates relations between the countries of the imperial Center and many less developed and developing countries in such a way as to systematically redistribute surplus value in favor of the Center.

Commercial discipline also regulates relations between advanced and emerging countries. The latter need to import capital to support their processes of industrial takeoff. Hence they have to provide the big multinationals of the North with incentives to invest, which they do by keeping wages and workers' legal protection low, privatizing public companies, reducing tax pressure on firms, neglecting environmental protection policies, and creating financial markets in which the big banks and institutional investors can speculate and multinational industrial firms carry out mergers and acquisitions.

In this way, emerging countries achieve the high rate of accumulation and technology transfer necessary for modernization. Industrial employment rises but real wages grow less than labor productivity, and capitalist exploitation spreads. Furthermore, the expansion of capitalism in emerging countries is favored not only by foreign direct investments, but also by the growth of exports. The goods they produce at low prices have to face a lack of domestic demand (given the low wages), but are exported to the rich markets of advanced countries. An adverse consequence of this boost to development is a systematic deterioration in the terms of trade. China's terms of trade, for example, decreased by 1.3 percent per year in the period 1980–2008. In the

United States, on the other hand, the terms of trade improved by 0.1 percent (Krugman, Obstfeld and Melitz, 2012, 154). This means that unequal exchange also enables the capitalists of the imperial Center to lay their hands on part of the large and growing surplus value produced in emerging countries.

Goods exported by these countries to the North compete with goods produced at higher costs by local firms, which are induced to react by offshoring and relocating investments. This reduces industrial employment in advanced countries and weakens trade unions, so that real wages stagnate here too and exploitation increases. What's more, to counter the outflow of capital and attract foreign direct investments themselves, the governments of advanced countries are prompted to cut taxes on businesses and wealth. Then, to avoid excessive increases in budget deficits and public debts, they increase taxation on wages or they reduce public spending, so that workers are hit by a further reduction in their overall income and social rights. Not only nominal wages, but also real take-home pay, pensions, and social welfare provisions tend to be impaired.

In other words, in contrast to nineteenth- and twentieth-century colonial imperialism, the unequal exchange through which the imperial Center now exploits the Periphery does not generate significant labor aristocracies in the North.[45] The increasing surplus value extracted from the South flows only into the pockets of the big capitalists, thus contributing to increasing income inequalities even in the North. By placing the workers of every country in the world in competition with those of all other countries, commercial discipline exacerbates the exploitation of workers worldwide.

It is understandable why big capital constantly presses for the demolition of all barriers to the free movement of capital and goods. Capital loves freedom—and the sense of fraternity that freedom engenders—not for fortuitous reasons, but out of principle:

> Gentlemen! Do not allow yourselves to be deluded by the abstract word freedom. Whose freedom? It is .., the freedom of capital to crush the worker.... The brotherhood which free trade would

establish between the nations of the Earth would hardly be more fraternal. To call *cosmopolitan exploitation* universal brotherhood is an idea that could only be engendered in the brain of the bourgeoisie. All the destructive phenomena which unlimited competition gives rise to within one country are reproduced in more gigantic proportions on the world market. (Marx, 1848, 1)

FINANCIAL DISCIPLINE

In the 1970s, many developing countries found it convenient to get into debt, as interest rates were low and the prices of raw materials rising. They thought it would be easy to finance industrialization, strengthen national armed forces, and enrich the ruling classes at low cost. What's more, they were confident of their ability to repay any debts with growing revenues from the export of raw materials. And so the foreign debt of the South of the world rose enormously.

In the 1980s, however, things changed.[46] In October 1979 the *Volcker shock*, triggered by the decisions of the then chairman of the Board of Governors of the U.S. Federal Reserve, dramatically raised interest rates and reduced the money supply. Then Reagan's rearmament costs, together with a lethal cocktail of expansionary fiscal policies and restrictive monetary policies, dragged the whole world toward a marked interest rate hike. At the same time, the restrictive policies adopted by many advanced countries in response to the inflationary spiral triggered by oil price shocks led to a slowdown in world production and trade, and this resulted, among other things, in reduced global demand for commodities. The prices of raw materials dropped while those of industrial goods were skyrocketing, and the South saw its terms of trade plummet.

Many developing countries had to face increasing interest rates on their debts and shrinking revenues from their exports: in other words, a rise in the cost of debt just as their ability to pay was weakening. Thus they were compelled to apply for new loans only to pay the interest on old ones.

IMF assistance exacerbated the problem. The fund granted loans on the condition that the indebted countries accept its structural adjustment programs, which usually included pay reductions, public spending cuts, currency devaluation, higher interest rates, and the increasing exploitation of resources for export. These policies were, and are today, not the product of particularly evil minds, but the result of an inflexible accountancy-based vision of money management: whoever lends money wants to know that the debtor is capable of repaying it. When the loan is also granted in the interests of the creditors, which are mainly banks of the imperial Center, the precautions taken by the international bodies become easier to understand.

The IMF's structural adjustment programs aim, above all, to reduce consumption, and therefore the imports of indebted countries, and possibly to boost their exports. This should create a current account surplus with which to generate the funds necessary to repay debts. Except that when this solution is imposed upon many countries, the overall effects may be adverse. Reducing many states' imports leads to a reduction in all states' exports, which magnifies the effects of the demand slowdown in advanced economies. The greater availability of goods exported by the South brings down their prices even further, and this may be detrimental rather than beneficial to their balance of payments. Many Peripheral countries are unable to increase their volume of exports, and when they can they see their revenues shrink all the same.

Now, how can a family repay its debts when it cannot do so with its flow of income? It will have to use its capital and sell the family jewels. This is what the Brady Plan boiled down to. The plan was proposed by U.S. Treasury Secretary Nicholas Brady in the late 1980s as a solution to the developing countries' debt crisis; it was enacted in the 1990s. The credits of private banks were partially converted into long-term bonds, but not before undergoing a haircut in their value and/or a reduction of interest rates. The bonds were guaranteed by the IMF, the WB, and the U.S. Treasury. These institutions also granted new loans to developing countries, thus providing them with the liquidity required to repay part of the debt to the private banks. Another part was repaid through a more tortuous route. The banks sold allotments of the bonds on the secondary market at discounted prices. The big multinational companies who bought the bonds converted them into the national currencies of indebted countries, meaning that these would be able to repay their debt with national real assets. As a result, the private banks limited their credit exposure while the big manufacturing multinationals were able to buy up the firms and natural resources of indebted countries at knockdown prices. Part of the debt was repaid by transferring the ownership of firms through the *debt-equity swap*, and the surrender of vast reserves of natural resources was attained through the so-called *debt-nature swap*.

Actually, this mechanism of expropriation was not really invented by Brady, as his plan merely sanctioned and regulated a market mechanism that already functioned in the same way: the banks sold their credit on the secondary market at low prices, the manufacturing multinationals bought it, and then used it to buy up pieces of indebted developing countries. This is a prime example of the process of "accumulation by expropriation" (Harvey, 2003, 49) that global capital manages to realize using the market rather than gunboats.[47]

During the 1980s and early 1990s, flows of capital from the South to the North to service the former's debt exceeded the flows of international investment from the North to the South. Many poor countries financed the rich countries. To do so they had to "tighten their belts," meaning further impoverishment. At the same time a growing share of Southern countries' resources came into the possession of the multinationals. Many developing countries were forced to undersell, to sell parts of their wealth at knocked-down prices.

The debt trap generates a sort of long cycle of foreign debt. There are phases in which foreign investments in the subjugated countries increase (the 1920s, 1950s, and 1970s), followed by phases in which the problem of debt repayment explodes. In the 1990s the flow of foreign investments to the South began to increase again, due especially to lower interest rates in the North. This time much speculative capital was involved and produced devastating effects, such as the currency crises in Mexico (1994), East and Southeast Asia (1997), and Argentina (2002).

Credit discipline is an inescapable trap, regulated by pure and simple market logic. There is no need for an imperial tyrant to set it up and make sure it works properly. All that is required are speculators, and the accountants of banks and international organizations. The countries trapped can escape by agreeing to submit to processes of systematic impoverishment and exploitation, but some of them daringly refused to pay at least part of their debt, sometimes without catastrophic consequences.

The IMF does not have sole responsibility for maintaining this trap. It is assisted by the "financial markets," that is, the big multinationals operating in the financial sector. Besides, modern manufacturing companies have also vastly expanded their finance management divisions and operate by continuously shifting capital between industrial production and speculation. But especially important are the great universal banks. The world financial markets are dominated by about ten maxi-banks and about twenty banking multinationals of "lesser" dimensions, as well as myriad other financial institutions and institutional investors (Morin, 2006).

Multinational financial corporations also operate in conditions of oligopolistic competition.[48] While often acting in collusion, they also compete in attempts to influence governmental monetary, commercial, fiscal, and industrial policies, especially in the privatization of public companies. When investing in financial markets, they are not normally able to *oligopolistically* influence the prices of securities. However, given their size, and given that over-the-counter markets are rather thin, any variation in their expectations has macroscopic repercussions on the quotation of derivatives and other financial assets. And when their expectations change, herd-like, as occurs with speculative bubbles and financial crashes, they "make the market."

Speculators play a key role in implementing financial discipline on a global scale. When a developing country has a "structural" deficit in its balance of payments, or when it experiences a prolonged outflow of capital, speculators can expect a currency devaluation. This kind of expectation has a high capacity for self-fulfillment. If everyone sells the Argentine peso because they expect it to be devalued, it will effectively be devalued as a simple consequence of the increased selling. Capital will take flight from Argentina, which will further exacerbate its balance of payments problems. Devaluation will also increase the value of imports, and the current account deficit could deteriorate. Current account deficits may not be exactly "structural" at first, nor particularly serious. However, if the speculators are convinced they are, they will become so.

There is an additional cause of the relative impoverishment experienced by many countries of the Periphery when they are targeted by speculative attacks. Developing and less developed countries are guilty of an inexpiable "original sin" (Eichengreen and Hausmann, 1999; Rajan and Tokatlidis, 2005): given the weakness, marginality, and riskiness of their economies, they are incapable of borrowing in their own currencies but accumulate debt in dollars or other advanced country currencies. Consequently, depreciation of their exchange rate increases the net value (in national currency) of their foreign debt. In other words, a speculative attack leading to a currency crisis impoverishes the country attacked because it increases the quantity of national resources necessary to repay a debt that has been revalued.

The opposite happens in advanced countries. For example, most of the foreign assets held by the United States are foreign currency–denominated, while almost all their liabilities (95 percent) are dollar-denominated. Hence, if the dollar is devalued, the value of U.S. assets increases without the value of its liabilities increasing. Depreciation in itself brings about an automatic transfer of wealth from the rest of the world to the United States. Euroland also enjoys this advantage.

Among the causes of the financial crises that hit industrialized countries of the Periphery in the 1990s is the liberalization of capital flows in situations where a strong *demand* for capital to sustain growth exposed those countries to an increasing credit risk. Liberalization processes are undoubtedly responsible for the financial fragility of developing countries, but the problems do not stem exclusively from the conditions of *demand*. De Cecco (1999, 129–42) pointed out that the conditions of credit *supply* may be even more important. Interest rate hikes in the United States and Europe, for example, can cause a crisis in a country of

the South, as they induce the big multinational banks to disinvest from
the South and move their capital toward the Center of the empire. This
increases the risk of currency depreciation and local bank and industry
bankruptcy, and may prompt other financial outflows, thus triggering
speculation.[49] A currency crisis of this type broke out in many emerging
and developing countries in May 2013, after Ben Bernanke's declaration
that the U.S. Federal Reserve was planning a tapering of quantitative
easing. The simple intention to raise interest rates in the imperial Center
was perceived by speculators as a threat against Peripheral countries,
and capital flights caused striking devaluations there.

The victory of speculation in the crises of fragile countries is not
without real effects. As a consequence of devaluation, the "country risk"
rises and interest rates soar. They may soar even further if the governments seek to resist, for example, by attempting to defend exchange rate
stability by shrinking the money supply. Moreover, measures could be
implemented to limit public spending in order to improve the balance
of payments. This type of policy triggers economic recession. In short,
while the speculators get richer, the countries preyed upon get poorer.
Speculative capital gains are the price paid for the lesson learned.

Speculation plays a decisive role in disciplining national economic
policies. It accelerates processes of adjustment by punishing the
"wrong" policies. It often tames recalcitrant governments by anticipating the recommendations of the IMF. Indeed, the discipline imposed
by speculation can be more effective than that of the IMF, as it can act
ante factum, whereas the IMF mainly intervenes *post factum*.

Now we have a better understanding of which "contradictions" tend
to be heightened by capitalist development on a global scale. They
are the disparities between the North and the South, between dominant and dominated capitalism on the one hand, and the opposition
between profits and wages, between capital and workers on the other.
We can also see that the global rise in income inequalities observed
over the last twenty years is not an anomaly, nor an incidental event. It
is a systematic tendency caused by global exploitation.

Understandably, many Peripheral states react badly. Some countries
have assimilated the logic of capital accumulation, while refusing to

fully comply with free trade rules. Not long ago these countries were considered *opportunist*. Nowadays, more benevolently, and in consideration of the economic power they are gaining, they are called *emerging*. They have not demolished all trade barriers, nor have they completely liberalized capital movements, and they still practice some industrial, currency, and commercial policies. Some of the countries that have chosen this path have managed to launch effective processes of industrial takeoff, sustain high growth rates, and reduce poverty. They have also succeeded in reducing the income gap between them and the North. These countries joined the WTO only after having industrialized. The prime example is China.

The global sheriff and its acolytes can employ various forms of discipline against opportunist countries. With the most powerful emerging countries, such as China and India, they implement a policy of co-optation into the circle of great powers, so that the G7 has gradually expanded to become the G20. They also seek to negotiate exchange rate policies with these countries and use international organizations, such as the WTO and the WB, to buy their conformity to the rules of free trade. A heavier hand is used with the weakest countries, sometimes decreeing economic sanctions with the aim of impeding industrial development, or seeking to destabilize the country to bring about a change of political class.

But the most effective tool remains speculation. The hyenas of the financial markets wait patiently, ready to pounce as soon as an opportunist country shows signs of weakness. At the first hint of balance of payments difficulties, the international speculation trap is sprung, with capital outflows and the sudden stop of foreign portfolio investments. This is the explanation behind various crises of the 1990s. It needs to be pointed out that there is no evil mind planning all this. Speculation is controlled by no one. It is an organic, spontaneous reaction. It is also complex, involving many decision-makers acting independently to pursue different goals. Yet the whole process objectively results in punishment.

As for the big international organizations—the IMF, WB, WTO— it is true that they are dominated by advanced countries,[50] but their disciplinary actions are determined more by the logic inscribed in their statutes and in the ideologies of their directors than by the political action of the dominant countries.

DISCIPLINE THROUGH TERROR

Besides the opportunists, there are other, more evil, countries: those that have reacted to global exploitation with an attempt at regressive flight from capitalism. They have rejected "Western" culture and turned to the fundamentalist exaltation of traditional religious values, in the typical reaction of the fox to the sour grapes. These are the recalcitrant countries. The technical term for them is "rogue states."

Quite another disciplinary mechanism is used to deal with these states. The influence of speculation and the WTO are limited in such countries, as "capitalist" values have little relevance. Here the discipline of terror, war, and devastation is put into practice. In this case the decision-makers act as part of a rather complex political process, based on a sort of positive feedback of the collective psychology. Political repression and economic impoverishment induce substantial layers of the resistant population to support fundamentalist and anti-capitalist political groups, some of which practice terrorism. This, in turn, prompts "civilized" countries to react with war, mainly against, but sometimes in alliances with, the fundamentalist groups. Then U.S. and Western pushiness prompts terrorist reactions in return (Layne, 2009). As the feedback is positive, the effect is destabilizing, and the process inevitably culminates in a final day of reckoning in which good triumphs over evil. Afterward, the tanks can be withdrawn, the markets opened, and oil pipelines built.

Another point that needs to be clarified about the meaning of military intervention in recalcitrant countries concerns the role of the global sheriff. As I observed in the previous chapter, it would be an error to believe that the modern global *imperium* represents the triumph of a U.S. national super-empire. In reality, power is in the hands of multinational capital, and therefore of the advanced countries as a whole. This can be seen in the fact, among others, that U.S. military interventions are supported and complemented by the armed forces of other countries of the imperial Center. It can be understood even more clearly if we observe that such interventions aim to pursue the collective economic interests of multinational capital. They are directed, for example, toward countries that control vast energy resources or strategic trade routes, such as Iraq, Libya, and Afghanistan. In other words, the global sheriff acts on behalf of multinational capital. Obviously, interstate rivalries still exist. Neo-Gaullist France, "Democratic" Germany, or "Communist" China can spark frictions. But these contradictions are not fundamental, being caused by ideological relics and old-fashioned imperial political ambitions, and are more or less easily resolvable. They are certainly not the sort of inter-imperial rivalries that could be expected to put an end to capitalism.

As for the political approach to military intervention, it seems to be based on the "sheriff-and-posse" model (Haass, 2002, 93; Foster, 2003, 7). Just as the sheriff of the American West gathered together a group of armed citizens to hunt down Indian rebels, today's sheriff of the Far East gathers together a group of armed nations to discipline the wayward Arabs.

The intentions declared by the principal political decision-makers may not always reveal the sense of their actions within the global imperial system. Bush may have been genuinely convinced, let's say, that he was bringing freedom to Iraq. He was not perturbed by those who pointed out his oil interests, as well as those of his ministers and the lobbies who put the words in their mouths. After all, pursuit of the two ends, freedom and profit, can lead to the same result. And certain particular interests may be fulfilled in the process. Yet what really counts is that Bush ultimately contributed to achieving an aim that may not have been at the top of his list: Bush brought real freedom to Iraq—the freedom of movement for global capital, though the effects of the war on Iraq seem to preclude this result for a long period of time, and the political climate might not be to capital's liking for the moment.

Observing the immense military power exhibited by the Bush and Clinton administrations, we may easily be led to believe in the theories of American super-imperialism. Still, as Arrighi (2005, 57) observed, the United States today is practicing a form of rule without hegemony. The power it flaunts is mainly military, whereas its economic and political influence continue to decline. The result is that, aside from what the Pentagon says, U.S. military action is effectively a service provided in the interest of all multinational capital. Its military power results in a public good (Serfati, 2004; Callinicos, 2005; Mandelbaum, 2005) enjoyed by the whole economic clique of the North.

The fact that many states have conformed to the sheriff-and-posse model of intervention suggests a certain political awareness of the common nature of the interests at stake. This commonality of interests need not be expressed in an ideology of imperialist solidarity or give rise to a supranational military organization. There is no incentive to free ride vis-à-vis the service provided with the deployment of U.S. armed forces, simply because the big multinationals have an immediate economic interest in the military involvement of their respective countries of origin, as special investment opportunities lie behind every national armed force. It seems that in international peacekeeping missions, the realization of a public good (opening markets to free trade) goes hand-in-hand with the production of a private good (investment opportunities), so that individual states often find themselves acting as the agents of certain particular multinationals.[51] This is why there is no need for a supranational army. The armed forces of the nations in which the strongest corporations are based are enough.

War is obviously not a market process and does not involve the exchange of goods. Nonetheless, in one aspect the discipline of terror recalls a practice of marketing, if not of markets. The destructive acts of terrorist groups and armies have the purpose of gaining control not only of the land, but also of the people, by winning over minds. Wars of terror are also ideological wars, which use the destruction of structures and the massacre of civilian populations for the purpose of persuasion. Shows of strength and of power over life and death play a significant psychological role in convincing populations to accept the situation, or rather the winner's interpretation of it. In this sense the "marketing campaigns" carried out through subversive groups' acts of terror and

the "surgical" strikes of liberating forces are more effective if, "by acci-
dent," they also impact on civilian populations.

The most potent disciplinary tool is also the most subtle—that which
works on the human mind. Understanding how it works may be of use
to avoid being dazzled by conspiratorial or anthropomorphic visions of
the empire.

Modern neoliberal thought is anything but a *pensée unique*. It is characterized by so many facets, differences, and contrasts that it would
be rash to try to condense them into the form of a systematic theory.
We could ask what philosophical relationship there could be between
Hayek, Friedman, Nozick, Coase, Buchanan, and many others. Yet they
do have something in common, and it is possible, by identifying a sort
of lowest common denominator of the various schools of thought, to
broadly define the core of contemporary neoliberal theory. I will do
this by outlining two of the most important tenets upon which it is
based and some of their political corollaries.

Tenet I: *Market Efficiency.* The market allocates resources
                  efficiently as actions are moved by self-interest and reg-
                  ulated by competition. The public sector is inefficient
                  because it does not operate under a market regime and
                  is not guided by profit.

Corollary I.1: State-owned companies must be privatized.
Corollary I.2: Taxation must be the least progressive possible.
Corollary I.3: Barriers to the free movement of goods and capital
                  must be removed.

Tenet II: *The Efficiency of Money.* Money mediates exchanges
                  and allows savings to be transferred from savers to
                  investors. Financial markets enhance this type of effi-
                  ciency because they accelerate the process of adjusting

demand and supply. They are also capable of self-regulation through competition and by virtue of agents' rationality. Public intervention in the economy can jeopardize this efficiency as it can cause excess money supply and generate inflation, which, by redistributing wealth from creditors to debtors, discourages saving.

Corollary II.1: Financial markets have to be deregulated.

Corollary II.2: Public budgets should be balanced.

Corollary II.3: Central banks must act to ensure monetary stability.

Both these tenets are unfounded, but I am not about to prove that here.[52] Nor do I intend to describe the mass media processes through which an ideology based on plain lies can become hegemonic. What I want most is to show how all decision-makers through whose actions the *imperium* operates always make the right decisions spontaneously—if they trust in those tenets.

The various corollaries form the basis of the policies pursued by the big international economic bodies. Most WB funds, for example, are granted to developing countries as long as they serve to support private investments. Those of the IMF are granted to countries in crisis, under the stipulation that they are used to create market conditions that foster accumulation. As for the WTO, candidate members are required to privatize state-owned companies and demolish trade barriers. This, it is claimed, stimulates investment and the inflow of foreign capital and therefore sustains growth. Free trade is the main route to industrial takeoff. No mention is made of the fact that all the major advanced countries launched their own takeoffs with the use of protectionism![53]

Corollaries II.1, II.2, and II.3 serve to disarm national governments. If the central banks have the primary task of keeping inflation under control, they should be as independent as possible of governments, so the latter cannot use monetary policy to finance public spending and regulate the economy.[54] On the other hand, the need to balance the budget means that governments can no longer use even fiscal policy effectively. Nor can national governments engage in discretionary economic policymaking. They must leave it to the market, otherwise they may contribute to compromising economic efficiency. For example, the movement toward full employment could raise the cost of labor, as well as swelling public budget deficits. When these need to be reduced, it is better to do so by avoiding tax increases, especially on wealth and business, which could discourage individual economic enterprise and investments. It would be better to reduce public spending by down-sizing the "bureaucratic apparatus" of the state, which is nothing but detrimental to the market economy. Better still, public debt should be brought down by privatizing companies and commons.

Now, try putting these "ideas" in the heads of the speculators. If a government wishes to use economic policy to take care of unemployment, for example, by increasing public spending and/or the money supply, it can only lead to disaster. It will drive up inflation and cause public investment to crowd out private investment, as well as bring about excessive growth in consumption and imports. The current account will be pushed toward structural deficit and the national currency toward devaluation. As soon as the financial "markets" begin to suspect such a decline toward socialism, financial discipline will be unleashed. Often the government will not even have to implement these dangerous policies; it is sufficient to announce them. Speculation on the country's currency or sovereign debt will render them ineffective even before the feared structural conditions arise. Thus, the government will learn a hard lesson. In other words, either the government behaves as the markets wish or the markets will force it to behave as they wish.

I define acceptance of the ideology encapsulated in these two tenets as "ideological allegiance to the multinational capital standpoint." The allegiance of the managers of the main national and international political and economic bodies and the biggest financial operators is of fundamental importance. These people have to make crucial decisions in order for the "natural" laws of accumulation to function effectively. And their decisions must be made autonomously.

In a world as complex as today's, the subordination of politics to the needs of accumulation cannot simply be explained by assuming, like Lenin, the existence of a "personal link-up between capital and government," or by maintaining that the "Transnational State" serves the "central inner circle" of the "Transnational Capital Class" (Sklair and Robbins 2002, 84–85). Then, how would we explain that practically all those who make significant decisions make them in a way that favors the accumulation process? We cannot seriously expect the managers of the IMF, WTO, WB, Federal Reserve, and European Central Bank to take orders from "Mr. Capital" via the U.S. State Department, can we? The point is that they don't actually take orders: they know what to do. And they know because they have sworn allegiance to the ideology of multinational capital.

In this sense, the ideology is not a mere distortion of reality without any tangible effects. Rather, it is a world vision in which scientific rhetoric and subtle lies are closely combined in order to justify the political choices necessary to make the whole system work. Then the effectiveness of policies is assessed on the grounds of their ability to at least partially fulfill the theoretical expectations. In short, a relationship between theory and practice in which this fulfills that and that justifies this.

How does ideological discipline function? How do the right people choose the right ideological allegiance? Through a mechanism—call it "the persuasive power of power"—that operates through punishment and co-optation.

As to punishment, think, for example, of how many would-be Ceausescus of the European left converted to neoliberalism after his unhappy end. And think of how many Middle Eastern petty dictators and how many Islamic fundamentalists are undergoing the same conversion following the liberation of Iraq, Afghanistan, and Libya. The mechanism works on the terrorist principle of "punish one to educate them all." Punishment need not be so violent as with Saddam and Gaddafi, but sometime it can be even more so.

Dissenting personalities can occasionally succeed in obtaining positions of significant responsibility. Then they are taken care of by firing. Two revealing examples are those of Joseph Stiglitz, a Keynesian chief economist at the WB who dared to criticize IMF policies, and Dominique Strauss-Kahn, a socialist and Keynesian chairman of the IMF itself, who tried to radically reform the institution. The former was sacked; the latter was ruined by a sex scandal. We do not know how many economists have learned the lesson.

Co-optation, on the other hand, occurs in the form of tournaments in which those aspiring to certain positions of power show off their skills, abilities, and convictions. These tournaments are effectively markets for allegiance and can take on the most diverse forms, starting with competitive exams. They are often more subtle, such as an academic career[55] in the right universities with the right publications, or political militancy in the right parties and with the right programs.

To conclude, ideological discipline also works through a feedback mechanism. Although somewhat complex, the mechanism can be easily understood by reducing it to its simple core. The power structure within which crucial decisions are made selects its own staff: it co-opts the individuals who have chosen the right ideological allegiance and excludes the others. The personnel thus selected then gain strong income, power, and prestige interests in the maintenance and proper functioning of the structures in which they work. In turn, the personnel's ideological allegiance leads to the right decisions being made, decisions that contribute to the proper functioning of "free markets." Power stimulates ideological allegiance; ideology consolidates power.

4. Multinational Corporations and Nation-States

> The Hydra had a prodigious dog-like body, and eight or
> nine snaky heads, one of them immortal; but some credit it with
> fifty, or one hundred, or even ten thousand heads. . . . In vain did
> [Heracles] batter at its heads with his club: no sooner was one
> crushed, than two or three more grew in its place.
> —Graves, 1960

Together, the multinational firms represent the Hydra of the global empire. Like the mythical creature's multiple heads, their numbers grow at an exponential rate. In 1976, there were 11,000 of them, with 82,600 foreign affiliates. By 2010, the heads were 103,788 and the foreign affiliates 892,114 (UNCTAD, 2011). Many of them are relatively small organizations, "pocket" multinationals operating in no more than two or three countries. But others have the dimensions of full-blown states.

When I said that the *imperium* is sovereignless, and that it works through the market and autonomous decision-making centers, I did not mean that all the economic actors have the same power and operate as if the markets were perfectly competitive. I specified that the multinationals stand out among the various actors involved. In fact, the so-called deregulated markets are effectively regulated, directly or indirectly, by the big capitalist firms (Amin, 2002, 6). Multinational capital is the real *dominant actor* in globalization, in the sense that it regulates the process in the pursuit of its own ends and seeks to subordinate all other actors to ensure that they serve its own interests. However, it is not a holistic subject; it does not pursue collective goals through an idea, a project, or a capital plan. It comprises tens of thousands of individuals moved by their own ends and interests. But, like the heads of the Hydra, which all act independently of one another, each contributes to the triumph of their common body. The capital body grows and stretches its coils around the whole world thanks to the action of myriad individual firms.

The big multinationals are increasingly establishing themselves as the only truly international *organizations*, the only *hierarchical* structures that exert the *power of command on a global scale*. The nation-states, however big, do not enjoy this prerogative. Their hierarchical power is exercised within national boundaries, or at most within military bases abroad, but never over a truly global population. The big international organizations (IMF, WB, WTO) are in charge of finance and trade-related functions that are ancillary to production. Moreover, even if they operate in a cosmopolitan context, they do not have hierarchical power structures that allow them to directly govern people and resources on a global scale. The big multinationals, conversely, do, and are in control of the productive process. This is why they are, and will increasingly be, the true dominant actors of the global empire.

The most important development generated by the multinationals' success is a systemic effect emerging from individual companies' separate actions. When one of them negotiates with a state or national trade union to obtain special treatment in view of a foreign investment, it uses the threat of investing elsewhere as a deterrent. All of them do the same, the upshot being that states and trade unions are forced into a global competition that places them in a weak position. For their part, the states and trade unions fail to create competition among multinationals, since national institutions and trade union organizations do not enjoy international mobility, and the prize at stake is the localization of investments, which is controlled by the multinationals. In this way, *every single firm, by pursuing its own interests, serves the fundamental interests of all multinational capital.*

The effect of systemic power is then enhanced by financial markets, in which short-term capital movements are unleashed. Also in this case, the interests of individual firms (industrial and financial) dictate which direction portfolio investments and currency flows will take. This exposes states to fierce competition, which limits their ability to determine the cost of financing their debts, interest rates, and public spending levels. Again, the effect is asymmetric: the markets lay down the law to states, forcing them to compete to attract portfolio investments, whereas the states are incapable of laying down the law to international financial operators, precisely because the latter enjoy the advantages brought by the free movement of capital.

Such devastating systemic effects were placed under relative control by the Bretton Woods agreement. The gold exchange standard, the fixed exchange rate system, and control over international capital movements functioned relatively well in safeguarding the states' power of command and the interstate cohesion upon which postcolonial imperialism was based from the 1950s to the 1970s. The demise of these three regulatory instruments created the financial conditions for the relationship of supremacy between states and capital to be overturned. The birth of the WTO then provided the commercial conditions.

Here is another way of defining *the essence of global imperialism*: the liberalization of capital and goods movements on a global scale has caused individual firms to pursue their own ends to produce a systemic effect, thanks to which multinational capital now enjoys a position of supremacy over states, international bodies, political institutions, and, in particular, workers' organizations.

THE HEADS OF THE HYDRA

Multinationals differ from national firms because they expand throughout the world by exporting not only goods, but also capital. Foreign direct investments (FDIs) have grown rapidly over the last sixty years and experienced an upswing in the second half of the 1990s, following the creation of the WTO. The ratio of FDI *stock* to global GDP was 4.4 percent in 1960, 9.6 percent in 1990, and 30.3 percent in 2010. The majority of this capital, 82.3 percent, comes from advanced countries, and is mostly (65.3 percent) located in advanced countries (Ietto-Gillies, 2012, 15). But a look at FDI *flows* clarifies what has been happening more effectively: those incoming toward the Periphery (emerging, developing, less developed, and transition countries) grew rapidly, beginning in the mid-1990s and overtook FDIs toward advanced countries for the first time in 2010, when they reached 52.7 percent of the total (UNCTAD, 2012). Capital movements toward the South have been increasing constantly, especially for the purpose of mergers and acquisitions. In the period 1986 to 1990, each year 8.3 percent (annual mean) of cross-border mergers and acquisitions targeted firms in the South. Between 2001 and 2005, this percentage rose to 24.3 percent (Brakman, Garretsen, and van Marrewijk, 2006, 15).

On the other hand, with the explosion of the great crisis, the values of companies in advanced economies shrank drastically, and the multinationals of emerging countries, especially China, were able to go shopping for corporate control at fire-sale prices. Their *brown field* foreign direct investments soared worldwide.

According to some forecasts (World Bank, 2013a), South-South capital flows will increase rapidly in the coming decades, and the percentage of global investments toward developing countries will triple by 2030, to the extent that sixty cents of each dollar invested in the world will go to developing countries. China will count for 30 percent of all investments, India 7 percent, and the United States 11 percent.

Most big multinationals have their parent companies in advanced countries. In 2011, according to *Fortune*, of the 500 biggest multinationals 164 were based in Europe, 133 in the United States, 68 in Japan, 61 in China, 14 in South Korea, 11 in Canada, 8 in Australia, 8 in India, 7 in Brazil, 7 in Russia. Today's biggest multinationals, especially the European and Japanese ones, were founded in the 1960s and 1970s. Their expansion in the world markets became impressive from the 1980s onward.[56]

The forces that push firms toward international expansion are many and merit at least a brief exposition. I have no intention of proposing the umpteenth theory of internationalization here. There are already so many on the market that scholars are spoiled for choice. Moreover, the phenomenon of internationalization is so varied and complex that it cannot be fully grasped by any one theory. Therefore, in this section I will only give a schematic outline of the main factors behind the big firms' propensity to expand their production to the global scale. Putting together somewhat heterogeneous results, I will draw on the contributions of many scholars who have carried out research on multinationals over the last half-century.[57] Then again, I can't avoid mentioning that my principal theoretical reference remains Stephen Hymer (1976; 1979): not only because he was the first scholar to develop a realistic theory of internationalization, and not even because his research is based on a criticism of orthodox theory, but above all because his ideas have inspired and continue to inspire all subsequent research. For Hymer, the big multinational corporation is a productive organization that uses the power of *control* to make profits and accumulates it to expand: the power of command over labor to enhance exploitation, market power to pump up monopoly profits, and political power to influence states. Based on this approach, subsequent research has detailed various factors that push firms toward global expansion.

Firms are productive organizations that make profits above all by exerting *control*[58] over internal resources. These resources are of two main types: intangible and tangible. The first comprise various forms of knowledge, the second a set of physical production requirements, including labor. The first determine the dynamics of productivity, the second the dynamics of cost. Profits derive from the efficient use of *knowledge control* and *cost control*.

Knowledge is composed of the company's specific competences in production, organization, commerce, marketing, and research. This is generally a form of capital that cannot be sold without losing value, though its use can be expanded internally without increasing its cost. Controlling knowledge ensures that economies of scale and scope can be implemented. Dynamic economies of scale, determined by innovation and learning by doing, are particularly important. Knowledge is a public good within a firm, in that its use can be extend at zero or very low marginal costs. On the other hand, expanding its use boosts labor productivity and therefore profitability. This makes it advantageous to increase production and enlarge the size of a firm. When a firm has established itself in a national territory and its market share can grow no more, it becomes difficult to increase its size without expanding abroad. However, international expansion could be based solely on the export of goods; the resulting increase in production would cause the firm to grow in size anyway. Thus, *which reasons prompt a firm to expand through foreign direct investments besides exports of goods?*

As for *costs*, a firm's advantages derive from the fact that its hierarchical control of labor allows it to plan production rationally and therefore minimize the costs of production requirements. Some of these costs are fixed, so that expanding the scale and scope of production also brings profit opportunities. Here again we can ask: *What prompts a firm to take advantage of decreasing costs by expanding production abroad other than increasing exports?*

The two questions boil down to one problem: given that increasing national production brings advantages, what are the *disadvantages of not internationalizing?* If these disadvantages exist and outweigh the advantages, we have found an explanation. Until the 1990s, most research moved in this direction. Control of knowledge and costs made internal expansion advantageous. Hence there must be limits to expansion that are external to the firm and its national market, limits that the firm can only overcome by internationalizing.

In the new millennium, however, another approach has emerged. Observing the upswing in the process of internationalization at the end of the previous century, some scholars began to probe whether there were *advantages to internationalization* independent of those produced by internal control, advantages that result not from overcoming international obstacles to expansion, but from the international expansion itself. Various answers were found through reflection on the consequences of the liberalization of capital movements that followed the birth of the WTO, and especially on the consequences of certain agreements (GATS, TRIMs, TRIPs) that favored the international expansion of production.

The reasons for internationalization can be summarized into four types, as shown in Table 1.

TABLE 1: Reasons for Internationalization

	Control of Knowledge	*Control of Costs*
Overcoming Disadvantages of Non-Internationalization	Defense of Monopoly over Knowledge	Reduction of Commercial Costs
Exploiting Advantages of Internationalization	Expansion of Knowledge	Building Bargaining Power

Type A reasons:

1. A first reason emerges if we reflect upon the fact that the knowledge owned by a firm constitutes a sort of monopoly power. If the firm externalizes its knowledge, for example through franchising and licensing, it exposes itself to the risk of imitation. What was previously a public good within the firm is placed at the disposal of other firms, which can capitalize it to create incremental innovations or pseudo-innovations, from which the parent company can be excluded. Hence, to safeguard the control ensured by intellectual property rights and specific competences, multinationals can opt to make *green field* investments in foreign markets. They can also seek to absorb companies that more or less legally imitate their patents or trademarks, production, and business methods, or the products themselves: thus they make *brown field* investments abroad, buying out local firms. Publicly owned companies, previously established by governments with a view to substituting imports, are particularly appetizing.

2. Many firms use control over specific knowledge to expand abroad with direct investments in order to implement *oligopolistic strategies*. They may, for example, seek to gain significant market shares abroad to the detriment of a competitor that produces substitutes of its products and could endanger the economic value of its knowledge. Or they may attempt to penetrate the market of a foreign competitor in retaliation for its penetration of their preferential markets.

Alternatively, they can try to divide up the world markets, colluding with certain competitors to avoid competitive wars of innovation and product differentiation, which tend to devalue a company's intangible capital. Car producers, for example, have been particularly active in this form of oligopolistic war.

Type B reasons:

1. One reason that can prompt the internationalization of production lies in the fact that an exclusively export-based growth strategy can be rendered burdensome by *transaction costs* and other similar expenses, such as those for transportation, collecting external information, agency, and distribution costs—all elements over which a firm does not have the advantage of control. A foreign direct investment strategy can serve to minimize these costs by reducing market transactions. This is another important reason for the internationalization of car producers, whose transport costs are heavy.

2. Costs can also be generated by the tariff and non-tariff barriers with which many countries seek to defend their national industries, and by the currency policies with which some seek to enhance the competitiveness of their own products. The creation of foreign branches serves to reduce this type of cost. If a country has high trade barriers and/or a systematically undervalued exchange rate, it may be more convenient for multinationals to export capital rather than goods to it.

Type C reasons:

1. Company-specific knowledge includes a particular type that can be defined as *learning skills*. These comprise the practices, techniques, and routines through which new information is acquired and innovations developed. Firms operating in global markets need to acquire knowledge about customers, suppliers, habits, and customs, and the laws and regulations in force in different places. They may therefore find it advantageous to open branches in end markets and source markets in various parts of the world, as the direct contact generated can help them acquire and process the information they need. In such cases companies employ the *learning skills* gained in

a certain location or in the parent company to build knowledge in new countries. For instance, Ferrero, which produces Nutella and other chocolate products, expanded abroad and collects information on local tastes, habits, and laws.

2. As innovation is a fundamental instrument of competition, firms seek to accumulate technological know-how by implementing oligopolistic strategies to take over the most innovative firms. For this purpose, they use brown field foreign direct investments, with which they acquire know-how developed by foreign firms operating both upstream and downstream of their own production process. A multinational may also decide to take over a company with which it had a previous *franchising* or *licensing* relationship if it discovers the company has managed to develop useful incremental innovations based on its patents. Lastly, a multinational may decide to take over a competitor in a local market if it wants that company's know-how. Multinationals sometimes decide to undertake *joint ventures* with rivals if they believe they can increase their technological knowledge by pooling complementary competences. Often, especially in emerging countries, governments request the introduction of joint ventures with multinational companies in order to trigger and take advantage of *spillover* effects on workers' skills and the competitiveness of local industry. A multinational may find it advantageous to accept such invitations not only for the benefits it could obtain in terms of tax treatment and labor and environmental regulations, but also because it could take possession of the local firms' innovative skills. Note that this type of advantage differs from that described in type A, in which the main reason for internationalization was the need to defend the company's monopoly power over knowledge already in its possession. The point here is to favor the acquisition of new knowledge.

3. In many cases the big multinationals find it convenient to break up the production process and manufacture certain components requiring specialized labor (computer scientists, engineers, physicians, etc.) in various emerging countries (India, Singapore, Brazil, Eastern European nations). These countries have modern education

systems and produce workforces with the same level of skills as advanced countries, but at much lower costs; multinationals that relocate investments in this manner manage not only to reduce the costs of specialized labor, but also to exploit knowledge and human capital that they did not contribute to producing. This strategy is followed by many German firms that relocate the production of intermediate goods in Eastern Europe.

Type D reasons:

1. Perhaps the most important motive behind contemporary firms' push toward internationalization is their desire to tighten control over *production costs*, and above all *to control labor*. In this perspective multinationals take advantage of globalization in various ways:

   - by locating plants in several countries, to avoid creating the large national industrial concentrations that facilitate the organization and establishment of trade union power, and to break up the workforce geographically so as to impede connections between workers' struggles;
   - by locating plants in developing or emerging countries without strong cultures and traditions of class conflict in order to limit employees' militancy;
   - investing in poor countries allows them to pay lower wages and impose longer working hours and a faster pace of work, while having to respect less rigorous safeguard regulations;
   - the threat of relocating investments abroad can be used to discipline national workers and unions at the parent company: this threat is made credible by the relocations that have already taken place. A typical example of this strategy is offered by FIAT, which while heavily investing in the Americas and Eastern Europe blackmailed Italian workers with the threat of disinvestment, and was successful to the point of obtaining a "democratic" vote of the workers to increase their exploitation and reduce their rights.

2. Multinational companies also accumulate bargaining power over suppliers, especially those producing natural resources in the South.

When the suppliers are numerous and small, multinational firms exploit their competition, exercising monopsony power. When the suppliers are large and operate in imperfectly competitive markets, the multinationals may avoid creating situations of bilateral monopoly by takeovers.

3. Multinationals cultivate bargaining power over national governments. Using the enticement of investments, they seek to gain advantages in terms of lax regulations on labor protection and safety, as well as of low wages and disorganized unions. Hence, besides reducing production costs, the increased bargaining power over governments also contributes to enhancing the power of the multinationals over workers and suppliers. Lastly, multinationals also exploit their political influence to obtain special tax treatment, as well as attempting takeovers of publicly owned companies and commons. Nor should we forget that once factories have been set up in one country multinationals' blackmailing power can be enhanced by the threat of relocating to yet another country.

The urge of multinationals to attain monopolistic positions is incessant because having market control means they can earn monopoly profits. Another reason is that market power usually translates to political power, which companies can use when dealing with unions, suppliers, and states.

In some cases, particularly in the South of the world, multinationals manage to achieve stable positions of power. Governments are often forced[59] to privatize nationalized companies operating in natural monopoly sectors (telecommunications, rail transport, energy networks) or sectors controlling commons (forests, mining resources, water). In other cases, control over patents and trademarks provides multinationals with monopolistic positions. Yet they rarely have absolute economic power. Apart from the case of natural monopolies, positions of power can be contended by other multinationals. If they rely on patents, for example, they can be jeopardized by competitors' technological innovations.

In general, the market form in which multinationals operate globally is that of *oligopolistic competition*. It is not perfect competition, because many sectors are characterized by the presence of big firms holding significant market shares, and prices are therefore fixed by a few producers rather than by the market. Above all, firms seek to avoid triggering price wars, which are detrimental to the interests of all competitors. Groups of rival companies often get together to form more or less tacit collusions, joint ventures, industrial or commercial alliances. This does not imply a complete lack of competition. In fact, the companies operating in an oligopolistic industry produce similar but differentiated goods. Hence, non-price competition prevails, involving innovation and imitation, product differentiation, marketing, advertising, market strategies, struggles for corporate control, investment localization, as well as the lobbying and corruption of national governments.

As the drive for innovation and pseudo-innovation is incessant, if nothing else for survival, and as new multinationals are continuously being born, almost no monopolistic position and no oligopolistic collusion can be considered stable and safe. In other words, reasons intrinsic to the dynamic of capitalist accumulation prevent the formation of a single world trust or monopoly, or even of a "central inner circle" of transnational capital.

This observation serves to raise a crucial theoretical problem. For Karl Kautsky, the formation of a single world trust would have led to the establishment of a sort of *benevolent* supremacy of capital over the nation-states. As capital is concerned with creating a climate of orderly economic exploitation of the world by trustified companies, states would ultimately be forced by capitalist interests to overcome their rivalries and establish a system of international relations based on the principles of peace and collaboration.

World peace has certainly not been achieved in contemporary global imperialism, nor is there even a vague inclination to achieve it. Nonetheless, a certain propensity to collaborate has materialized among the main states. This predisposition has surfaced in the tendency to organize joint military operations with the aim of opening recalcitrant countries to capitalist penetration, and in the more or less ineffectual efforts of the various G2, G7, G10, G20 to frame common economic policies. In many cases, both tendencies are encouraged by the big capital. They may also be favored by the actions of powerful national capitalist lobbies. The interesting thing is that in the global capitalist system these lobbies, be they U.S., European, or Japanese, manipulate the political classes in the interests of all multinational capital. Therefore, in a certain sense, which I will clarify in the next chapter, it is true that *capital's supremacy over nation-states* is materializing, yet the effects are anything but *beneficial*, considering that the fundamental law of regulation is *competition* among capitals for the maximization of exploitation.

THE ROLE OF INTERNATIONAL ORGANIZATIONS

Of the international economic organizations, those that work most effectively to achieve the expansion of "freedom" are the World Trade Organization, the International Monetary Fund, and the World Bank, the three main political institutions charged with preparing the world for capitalist penetration.

The WTO was founded with the primary aim of favoring the expansion of international trade, and was equipped with effective instruments for disciplining opportunist countries. It fulfills the function of issuing international trade rules and rendering them enforceable better than any national empire has ever managed to do. It achieves this through multilateral agreements carrying binding commitments for signatory states.

With the Dispute Settlement Understanding (DSU) these agreements are enforceable. The "judgments" handed down by the WTO's Dispute Settlement Body (DSB) oblige noncompliant countries to conform to the rules, under the threat of economic sanctions ranging from compensating an injured country for damages to the implementation of retaliatory measures.

The rules, especially those known as "nondiscriminatory clauses," are supposed to foster the expansion of free trade. In reality, they effectively force member states to accept penetration by multinational corporations. The *National Treatment* clause, for example, obliges governments to extend the best treatment afforded to national firms, including state-owned companies, to foreign ones. The *Market Access* clause, in turn, prohibits governments from hindering the entrance of multinational firms.[60] Together these rules have contributed to creating a norm that encapsulates the essence of the whole set of regulations, a sort of "most favored firm" clause. If an advantage is granted to a firm, for example, a national company, it must be granted to all firms. This implies, among other things, that once a state-owned company has been privatized there is hardly any going back, even if it results in a market failure.

The TRIPs (Trade-Related Aspects of Intellectual Property Rights) serve to safeguard the ownership of the products of scientific and technological research, trademarks, and the like, and thus to guarantee the profitability of their use. Patents, which are mainly registered in the countries of the imperial Center, cannot be used by developing countries unless they pay the royalties established by the multinational companies to which the patents belong, often even if they apply to vital drugs.[61] In the TRIPs, the World Trade Organization clearly reveals its nature as a political organization with the purpose of safeguarding the interests of multinationals. Not by chance, the big corporations played a key role in drawing up the TRIPs agreements.[62] While all the other agreements formally have the aim of expanding competition and free trade, the TRIPs agreement takes the form of a protectionist regulation. It explicitly seeks to protect monopoly positions and the monopoly profits provided by scientific and technological research, an activity in which the big multinationals of the North excel.

Even more blatant are the agreements known as TRIMs (Trade-Related Investment Measures). Their content is essentially disciplinary, as they prohibit the adoption of the economic policy instruments[63] that the governments of many countries use to protect their economies from certain negative consequences of foreign direct investments. The TRIMs serve to disarm states in their attempts to implement industrial and commercial policies for the benefit of local populations. They mete out discipline in the interests of the multinationals.

But possibly the most brazen of all these agreements is the GATS (General Agreement on Trade in Services), which regulates a highly heterogeneous sector (with 160 sub-sectors) effectively covering the production of all nonmaterial goods, from finance to postal services, from water supply to electricity, from telecommunications to transport, from insurance to banks, from education to health. The sector is so vast that it accounts for two-thirds of global output.

The GATS was expressly proposed, prepared, and armed by certain Anglo-American financial multinational lobbies whose names are well known.[64] According to economic science, a large part of the goods covered generate market failures[65]—because they are produced in conditions of natural monopoly (for example, water supply), because they generate significant externalities (for example, pollution), or because they are commons (for example, woods), public goods (for example, justice), or merit goods (for example, education). This is why their production was traditionally controlled or regulated by the state in the public interest. The GATS instead considers policies that pursue public aims in the production of services as discriminatory. Under the pretense of making markets competitive, it forces signatory states to dismantle public sectors that regulate services and sell off the firms that provide them. In contrast to the other agreements, the GATS is not confined to regulating existing markets but plays a fundamental role as a *creator of markets*. It seeks to commodify public goods, public utilities, and commons, and to privatize natural monopolies.

Joining the WTO implies acceptance of the rules of *national treatment* and *market access*, as well as the principle that public monopolies and public services are unacceptable. Then, when a serious economic crisis arises and leaves a country in need of financial help from the IMF and the WB, the government is forced to sell off state-owned companies and commons to the multinationals.

The WTO has become a partial substitute for gunboats in imperial governance. Through it, the big capital clears and paves the way for expansion and accumulation on a global scale. What is more, it does so with the consent of the exploited countries, which are induced to join the organization to gain access to flows of foreign direct investments from multinationals, assistance from advanced countries, and financial aid from the IMF and WB.

As for the IMF, following the *Washington Consensus* (of "free market" economics) this pawnbroker for desperate states took on the role of liberator. Previously, based on the Keynesian approach of the Bretton Woods system, the IMF imposed restrictions on the *demand side*, while granting credit to check the severity of those restrictions as much as possible. With the success of the monetarist ideology of Milton Friedman and the Chicago School in the late 1970s, the "structural" adjustments imposed were expected to affect the *supply side*, that is, mainly structures of production and ownership, rather than aggregate demand alone. Moreover, a "long-run perspective" was to be preferred, rather than focusing on the "short run." Thus, from 1979 onward, the IMF began to impose structural reforms with the aim of "relaunching development." According to neoliberal ideology, such reforms require the deregulation and liberalization of markets. This meant the cutting of tariffs and other forms of protectionism to boost competition, the liberalization of prices to cure inflation, the deregulation of labor markets to foster flexibility and reduce labor costs, the deregulation of financial markets to encourage capital mobility, and the privatization of public utilities to balance national budgets and expand competition. Thus the IMF acts as a bulldozer, preparing the ground for the arrival of multinational capital in desperate states. It does so to make this arrival as profitable as possible: it cuts wages and the cost of raw goods, makes labor flexible, and gets states to sell off public utilities and natural resources at fire-sale prices.

Lastly, the WB plays a more subtle, but no less effective, role in bringing about the expansion of "freedom." It offers help to developing countries by funding investments in the infrastructure necessary for industrial takeoff, or, in other words, for penetration by multinational capital. Like the IMF, with which it often acts in cooperation, the WB gives nothing for free. In particular, among the conditions for access to its loans, it also demands the demolition of trade barriers, the privatization of services, and the selling off of the commons to private companies.

Could the big multinationals let control over the great international economic organizations slip from their hands? And how could they get those organizations to serve their own interests while maintaining the decision-making autonomy of their managers? A powerful ideological campaign was called for. No sooner said than done. Having unleashed the most imaginative economists and even enlisted the help of the international academic body that decides on the recipients of the Nobel prize for economics, the right doctrines were promptly produced, one more audacious than the other: the right doctrines to replace the dated nineteenth- to twentieth-century free trade theory.[66] Then the markets for allegiance, the mass media, the most prestigious U.S. universities, research institutes, and culture academies, sprang into action to defend the new orthodoxy and put the right people in the right places. This is how the great international economic organizations came to be capable of acting *autonomously* in the interests of multinational capital.

FIRMS, STATES, MARKETS

Having clarified in the previous chapter how discipline is practiced, now it is time to get to the heart of the matter and answer the question: Who disciplines whom?

Multinational capital is the dominant actor in global imperialism. Those who suffer its discipline are the citizens of the world. As employees, they are under the command of the capitalists in the production process. As consumers, they are under the companies' oligopolistic power. Capital practices these forms of discipline *directly*, "in the first person," so to speak.

Yet this is not enough, as the citizens of the world are also the citizens of nation-states. Formally they have rights, not least the right to elect their own representatives in state legislative bodies. However, it is well known that the governments of modern "democratic" countries cannot act "against the opinion of the individuals and groups who contribute to setting the state's economic, administrative, and cultural agenda: the establishment, so to speak, whose resources can be *weighed*, while citizens' votes can only be counted" (Fabbrini, 2012, 1).

The ruling classes of states have the monopoly of power within national boundaries. The challenge for multinational capital is how to ensure that states' power is used to serve its own ends, and how to prevent it from being used against its interests. To put it even more clearly: How can states be disciplined? How can citizens be disciplined through states?

One of the first ways in which capital acts is by pressurizing a state's political class, for example, through lobbying and by controlling and funding political parties. Especially in advanced countries, where the decision-making centers of the multinationals are based, what Lenin defined as the "personal link-up" between government and business has now reached unprecedented levels of sophistication and efficiency. In the United States, this type of "link-up" has progressed so far that many observers (including some whose minds are not clouded by Marxist ideology) have interpreted it as a case of the supremacy of capital over the state.

In contrast, in the countries of the South, where the multinationals are playing away from home, two different kinds of pressure prevail. One is exercised through negotiations in which foreign investments and technology transfers are at stake, and the other uses the threat of withdrawing investments. Many of these countries are undergoing industrial takeoff and are hungry for capital. As they have to compete with each other to attract investments and as they have limited bargaining power, they are easily dominated by the big multinationals, to which they offer various special conditions: policies of low wages, labor legislation favoring super-exploitation, environmental policies allowing for the externalization of pollution costs, and preferential tax treatment.

Here I need to make a brief digression to deal with a theoretical problem and clarify why I have sometimes used quotation marks for the words "efficient," "market," and "natural." First, I need to clear the field of a highly pervasive economic ideology. In contrast to the two neoliberal tenets I mentioned in the previous chapter, markets are not efficient in an *allocative sense*. They are certainly not as allocatively efficient as the utopic markets described by the neoclassical theory of competition, with all its far-fetched hypotheses of no externalities, the completeness and symmetry of information, atomistic economic agents, Olympian rationality, etc., etc. Indeed, neoclassical liberalism can actually be used to demonstrate that markets in the real world are *not* allocatively efficient, as they do not correspond to these hypotheses. On the other hand, neither can non-neoclassical liberal thought, such as the neo-Austrian school, talk of allocative efficiency, as it refuses to use the concepts of general equilibrium theory. Though it can preach with some success of the market's superiority over bureaucratic planning systems in terms of *informative* efficiency, it has no scientific grounds for arguing that oligopolistic firms are more efficient than public management in the production and allocation of public goods, commons, or goods distributed under natural monopoly.

In what sense, then, are capitalist markets efficient? They are efficient from the point of view of *accumulation*, in the sense that they make it possible to maximize the exploitation of workers and consumers to fuel accumulation. In this perspective private capitalist firms are undoubtedly better equipped than state firms, at least to the extent that the latter aim to provide public services for citizens' well-being rather than to maximize profits. As capitalist firms treat consumer well-being as instrumental to their own lucrative ends, they can manage the distribution of water, for example, or the provision of health and education services, in such a way as to obtain the profits and savings necessary to support investments. State firms, especially in a world dominated by a race to the bottom in public spending, have great difficulty in valorizing capital as much as private firms. Thus, even disregarding neoliberal arguments about state failures supposedly caused by the corruptive effects of politics and bureaucracy on firm management, governments wishing to stimulate capital accumulation more than citizen well-being have good reasons for privatizing state-owned companies and favoring the "market."

Having clarified the sense in which the markets of the real world are efficient, we need to ask how "natural" their laws are. Again, we first need to clear the field of a widespread ideology, which places the state and market against each other, seeing the first as the domain of rules produced intentionally and artificially and the second as that of transactions regulated by spontaneous and unintentional processes. Markets cannot function properly if not regulated by *enforceable* rules. They cannot exist without an organization that issues laws and implements them, an organization with a judicial and police apparatus.

Capitalism cannot exist if companies are not capable of entering into relatively simple contracts (regulated, therefore, by institutions) to set themselves up and exchange goods and productive requirements, and especially if they are incapable of enforcing contractual obligations. Capitalism needs the state and its judicial and police apparatus above all to provide the social and political discipline necessary to exploit labor. In other words, big multinational capital not only needs a global sheriff to bring into line the countries resistant to globalization. It also needs a multitude of minor social gendarmes to discipline the workers of individual nations. To play the role of social gendarme, the political actors with the monopoly of power need to be forced to use that power to give capitalist firms control over economic resources and provide the social discipline necessary to conduct economic activities. *The state as a social gendarme has to create the political and judicial conditions for the maximization of exploitation.*

How do multinationals exercise this sort of control over states? In modern global imperialism, forms of direct control are accompanied by others of *indirect control*, which are the most effective. Indirect forms of control are those achieved through the commercial and financial discipline discussed in the previous chapter. This kind of control is exercised by means of market processes. Without one multinational corporation or another needing to make an explicit threat, competition forces states to comply with the interests of capital. And competition takes place on different fronts. On the tax front, the desire to attract foreign investment drives states to reduce taxation on businesses and profits and shift the tax burden to personal income and consumption. Thus one of the objectives of the *Washington Consensus* is achieved "naturally," spontaneously, and by free political choice: less progressive taxation to stimulate investment and a broader tax basis, including less well-off social classes, to compensate for reducing the burden on the richest classes. Equally spontaneous, governments seek to reduce labor costs by keeping wages low, reducing workers' rights, and weakening trade union organizations. If they do not do this, foreign investment will not arrive and national investment will take flight. A similar situation occurs with environmental policies, which tend to be as permissive as possible.[67] Moreover, governments are induced to sell off natural resources and commons to the multinationals, which know how to exploit them "efficiently."

Ultimately, it all boils down to this: by forcing the various states to compete with each other to attract capital, the "markets" let governments know what needs to be done to ensure an efficient use of labor.

In short, the multinationals enjoy both direct and indirect control over mankind. Direct control is exercised within the productive organization of the companies themselves, while indirect control is exercised via state control over citizens and that of capital over states. Indirect control can have the form of the pressure exerted by the big multinationals and their lobbies on the political classes, or that of the discipline imposed by the "markets."

CAN LOCAL POLITICS RESIST GLOBAL "MARKETS"?

The increased exploitation favored by contemporary globalization entails an amplification of economic inequalities and of working-class social unease, thus exacerbating class conflict. The social gendarme role may turn out to be insufficient to deal with this problem in the long run. Even independently of citizen capacity to exert a true power of mandate and control over the political classes (which they don't effectively have anywhere in the world, not even in states with formally democratic institutions), the fact remains that a government should play the role of social peacekeeper. And it should do so above all in the interests of the bourgeoisie, toward which it tends to act as a *national collective capitalist*.

Economic growth is a crucial condition for the successful performance of this role. In a capitalist country negative growth is highly damaging, as it creates unemployment, reduces tax revenues, weakens the welfare state, increases inequalities and poverty, and consequently exacerbates class conflict and political instability.

The economic policy model adopted by all advanced countries after the Second World War provides the classic example of states acting as collective capitalists. In the 1960s, the main capitalist countries equipped themselves with extensive public welfare systems. They also managed to ensure (almost) full employment and create the political conditions that allowed capital to grow at a significant pace and generate substantial profits. What's more, the international payments system established at Bretton Woods allowed the orderly expansion of international trade, which in turn contributed to boosting growth.

There was no need to postulate a "personal link-up" of capital with governments to explain the subordination of political decisions to the interests of capital. Indeed, governments could even go against the immediate interests of one industrial sector or another, by, for example, nationalizing some companies. Their task, in fact, was to work for the long-run interests of the whole *national* bourgeoisie. There was no need for a country's political class to take orders directly from its industrial leaders. The politicians sought to ensure social peace, and therefore the economic growth it depends upon, in their own interest, that is, with the aim of consolidating their own power.

The question is whether this model of capitalist state is still valid in the era of global imperialism. In developing countries accumulation condemns entire populations to poverty, drives farmers who use non-capitalist methods of production toward unemployment or emigration, and employs workers in capitalist factories with starvation wages and inhuman working conditions. In advanced countries it generates economic stagnation and consequently increases unemployment, poverty, and uncertainty, raises workers' tax burdens and shrinks welfare services. All these transformations exacerbate class conflict.

In other words, the global empire generates a *contradiction between nation-states and multinational capital.* On the one hand, the state should act as a social gendarme; on the other, globalization reduces its ability to assuage class conflict. In the long run, the social gendarme can only work well if it is also a national collective capitalist capable of guaranteeing economic growth. But globalization corrodes precisely this condition.

To what extent are the governments of today's nation-states bound by the multinationals and global markets, and to what extent do they manage to implement autonomous growth policies? More precisely, do national governments succeed in using macroeconomic, fiscal, monetary, commercial, industrial, and currency policies to lead their countries toward full employment and maximum national well-being? According to David Harvey (1996, 136): "The thesis of globalization has become a powerful ideological tool against the socialists, the welfare state, and nationalisms. The core of this thesis is that the political autonomy of nation-states has diminished." The prevailing opinion in the left is that this thesis is wrong and only works as an ideological distortion. Are there any grounds for this opinion? The answer is: it depends.

In the Bretton Woods system, small countries had somewhat limited political autonomy, as their domestic demand was strongly affected by the world business cycle and therefore by U.S. economic policy. Keynesian policies in Peripheral countries were effective only because they were also practiced by the U.S. government. This government enjoyed almost absolute economic policy autonomy while its fiscal and monetary policies governed aggregate demand and the money supply for the whole world.

By issuing the key international reserve currency, the United States was not exposed to external constraints. Moreover, it carried significant influence in international trade flows, and was able to take advantage of the international trade multiplier of a large economy. The first condition allowed U.S. citizens to systematically live above their means. The second ensured that, as the growth in U.S. GDP and imports boosted other countries' exports and GDP (and therefore their imports), the upsurge in U.S. imports also generated a (less than proportional) increase in its own exports. Under these conditions an expansive fiscal policy, not strictly bound by the balance of payments, was able to achieve full employment, while favoring expansive policies in other countries at the same time. From the second half of the 1960s onward, when the *gold exchange* standard had already effectively become a *dollar* standard, U.S. monetary policy became even more autonomous. Because the burden of adjustment in the currency market (to keep exchange rates fixed) fell to all the other countries and not to the United States, the American government was able to adopt expansive monetary policies and cut domestic interest rates without the consequent increase in foreign currency demand forcing the Federal Reserve to trim down reserves or reduce the supply of money. But other countries' central banks did have to intervene, by buying dollars to avoid national currency appreciation. Thus expansive U.S. monetary policy was not hindered by short-term capital movements, and was transmitted to other countries.

The post-Bretton Woods era can be divided into two phases: the "stagflation" era toward the end of the last century (roughly from the mid-1970s to the early 1990s) and the wave of expansion of neoliberal globalization that began in the 1990s.

In the first phase, by virtue of a certain breakdown in international economic discipline with the abandonment of fixed exchange rates, the policy autonomy of some big industrialized countries increased. It is known that monetary policy is easier to achieve in a flexible exchange rate regime than in a fixed one. However, the policies of dominant countries in that period were mainly restrictive and served to support a frontal attack on workers' movements. The depressive consequences on the world economy then led to a further reduction in small country political autonomy, because these made their foreign constraints more stringent.

The rejection of Keynesian policies that occurred during the late twentieth-century's stagflation was the result of precise political and ideological choices. Julian Jessop (1994) pointed out that the state did not really withdraw from the economy at that time; instead there was an about-face in the nature of state intervention. The *welfare state* was replaced by a *workfare state*, a new model of political action that openly aimed to subordinate social policies to the goal of making labor more flexible, reducing industrial employment, and redistributing income in favor of profits. The generation and maintenance of a depressionary climate is an integral part of this type of intervention. In other words, some important advanced countries (Great Britain, Germany, Japan) used their increased political autonomy following the demise of the Bretton Woods system to strengthen their role as social gendarmes, to the detriment of their role as social peacekeepers. As if preparing the way for globalization, they mostly gave up their role as national collective capitalists, focusing instead on repression.

The situation changed again in the second post–Bretton Woods phase, especially thanks to the decisive liberalization of international trade and capital movements decided in the Uruguay Round. These processes led to further losses of autonomy for most countries, and this time also for advanced countries. However, the effects differed from one group of nations to another.

Small countries (such as Great Britain, France, and Italy) now have practically no autonomy. Not only states with stagnant economies, but also those that have launched robust growth processes (such as Turkey and South Korea), manage to attain growth only if they are capable of attracting foreign investment and impeding the outflow of national capital. If they seek to resist globalization by implementing full employment policies and favoring national business systems,[68] they are likely to end up with catastrophic economic crises triggered by capital flight and financial speculation. Expansive fiscal and monetary policies aimed at improving social well-being are only possible in the presence of economic growth. Otherwise they generate public budget and balance of payment deficits, which contribute to triggering crises.

Big countries are a different matter. Among them, a further distinction has to be made between emerging and advanced countries, which depends on the effects of globalization on growth.

In the *big emerging countries*, thanks above all to low labor costs, low taxation on businesses, and the weakness of environmental policies, globalization feeds growth because it favors exports of goods and imports of capital. National debt shows limited growth and trade balances exhibit substantial surpluses, which grant national governments significant autonomy on fiscal and monetary policies. This autonomy can be used to counter the contractionary effects of international economic crises. China and other emerging countries have suffered relatively little from the great crisis of 2007–13, seeing just a decline in their GDP growth rate rather than full-blown recession. This has happened because their governments have been able to compensate for decreased exports with expansive fiscal policies, which demonstrates the existence of significant economic policy autonomy.

In other words, in emerging countries, which ride on the crest of the wave of international capital movements, the state still plays the role of national collective capitalist relatively well, as it manages to guide industrial development and ensure social peace by attracting external resources. But note that the state is only a good national collective capitalist as long as it bends to serve multinational capital. These countries' governments enjoy a certain degree of internal policy autonomy because they are in tune with the interests of global capital.

In the *big advanced countries*, on the other hand, globalization has depressionary effects. These countries suffer strong competition from emerging countries in goods markets, and many national firms react by offshoring, outsourcing, and relocating investments abroad. Their public budgets and trade balances tend toward systematic deficit, which drastically constrains their governments' economic policies: if the policies are too expansive they deteriorate the trade balance and increase public debt. Both these events create the conditions for economic crisis. The government of big advanced countries find themselves in an ambivalent relationship with big national capital. On the one hand, they seek to favor it, especially in its projection toward global markets, while on the other, they have to counter the depressionary effects of globalization on the national economy.

To avoid this dilemma the United States and Germany have used various tricks—in fact, full-fledged political stratagems—based on the formation of an organic alliance between the state and the national bourgeoisie. However, as I shall argue in the next two chapters, the "markets" have ultimately brought the chickens home to roost, triggering the great crisis of 2007–13.

In short, global imperialism has radically changed the nature of the relationship between state and capital. It is true that "actually existing globalization ... means the opening of subordinate economies and their vulnerability to imperial capital" (Wood, 2003, 134), but this does not mean that the states of *emerging countries* are impotent, at least not in the biggest countries. Precisely because these countries' economies act in tune with global capitalist accumulation, they have preserved a remarkable level of policy autonomy with which they manage to counter some of the deleterious effects of globalization, and by virtue of which they can continue to play the role of national collective capitalists. Instead, it is no longer true that in the countries of the North "the imperial economy remains sheltered as much as possible" (Wood, 2003, 134) from the adverse effects of globalization. In reality, globalization causes depression in advanced countries and reduces the availability of the public resources needed to maintain social peace. State policy autonomy is consequently reduced. Governments cannot implement highly expansive fiscal policies, ensure full employment, or keep public well-being at socially acceptable levels. What they can do is intervene with *workfare* policies in domestic markets and in industrial relations. In contrast to emerging countries, in advanced countries the function of collective capitalist in the interest of the national bourgeoisie diverges from that of social gendarme at the service of the multinationals.

This is undoubtedly big news. For the first time in at least five centuries, the states of the former great imperial powers are losing their sovereignty and, with it, the ability to govern accumulation (Wallerstein, 1999, 33).

5. The Great Crisis

*If you calculate who gains and who loses in this operation,
you will find that there is nothing casual or inexplicable in what
is happening. It is blatant class struggle waged the world
over by the capitalists against the workers, pensioners,
young persons: against the people.*
—Ferrero, 2012

Several observers have compared the crisis that blew up in 2007 to that of 1929, and pointed out various similarities between them. In reality, if we look back through the history of capitalism, we can see that other great crises have occurred. One, for instance, took place in 1857–61, another in 1836–38.[69]

Four great crises are sufficient to justify the elaboration of a notion and a theory to explain the phenomenon in its typicality and without resorting to the hypothesis of exceptional shocks. The notion might simply be that of a "great crisis," an event not attributable to normal business cycle recessions, and yet hinging upon a definite logic.

Here are some of the salient characteristics of a great crisis:

- *Intensity*, as manifested in the vertical breakdown of production, chain bankruptcies, and a marked increase in unemployment;
- *Pervasiveness*, as the fall in production involves all sectors—industrial, commercial, and financial;
- The *speculative bubble*, which sets the stage for a crisis by swelling and triggers it by bursting;

- The *liquidity trap* and *credit crunch,* which take place during the lowest dips;
- *Long-lasting,* longer than a normal cyclical recession;
- All great crises start in the Center of the imperial system and rapidly spread all over the world, taking on the form of a *global* crisis.[70]

Great crises are *system crises,* involving the breakup of the institutional foundations of national economic policies, international relations, world payment systems, and the apparatuses of ideological hegemony. The crisis of 1929, for instance, blew up during a long transition between the colonial imperial system, founded on British monetary and commercial domination, and the post-colonial one dominated by the United States, and between the gold standard and the gold exchange standard. There is no doubt that inter-imperial rivalries, in addition to the monetary policy constraints imposed on central banks by the gold standard, contributed to extending and deepening the crisis and, more generally, to inflicting a depressionary tendency on the world economy in the 1930s.[71]

My impression is that we are currently experiencing one of these "great crises," and that it exploded during the transition from the post-colonial imperial regime of the late twentieth century to a new regime of global imperialism. This new regime has already unleashed many destructive effects on the world economy and international relations, which will probably only be fully appreciable after the end of the crisis.

In analyzing the conditions that led to the present crisis, we need to distinguish between triggering factors and fundamental causes. The former pertain to the structure, functioning, and dynamics of the international financial system. Financialization, monetary innovations, the growth of universal banking, and the liberalization of capital markets played a decisive role in swelling the speculative bubble and sparking the crisis. Yet this kind of analysis only touches the surface. The fundamental causes have to do with the real economy, the effects of globalization on economic growth and income distribution in advanced countries, and the policies adopted by their governments.

Thus I will explain the crisis in two steps.[72] In this chapter, I will deal with its *modality*, describing the global financial context and the monetary dynamics of U.S. and European economies that marked its evolution. In the next chapter, I will investigate the *real economic conditions* from which the crises emerged, focusing especially on the policy strategies adopted by the governments of some great countries to cope with the depressive effects of globalization on their economies.

FINANCIALIZATION AND DEREGULATION

The U.S. speculative bubble swelled from the late 1990s to 2005. It first rode the wave of the "new economy," and, following the dot-com crisis, went wild in the real estate business. The *low interest rates* prevailing in those years made a significant contribution to preparing the crisis. A decisive input came from Federal Reserve monetary policy, which was quite expansionary. Moreover, portfolio investments in U.S. markets by the sovereign funds of China and other emerging countries, as well as by big international banks, led to an increased money supply.

Another important factor was the *deficit spending* policy adopted by the U.S. government, especially to sustain military expenses (Bellofiore, 2009; Perelstein, 2009).[73] This deficit fed the growth of aggregate demand and then contributed to expanding production; the consequent increase in credit demand boosted the supply of bank money. By causing a rise in imports, it also produced a heavy current account deficit and a consistent money outflow. Then the emerging countries with trade surpluses used their dollar reserves to buy shares, bonds, derivatives, and government securities in the United States, so that the money created by American banks flowed back into the United States.

A third important factor has to do with the emergence of *universal banking*. In 1999, the Glass-Steagall Act was repealed, completing a process of financial deregulation that had begun in the 1980s. This law, passed in 1933 following that earlier crisis, separated investment banks from commercial banks and the functions of banking from brokerage and insurance. The aim was to prevent banks from taking risky and speculative positions. Once this law was out of the way, a new kind of banking intermediary materialized, which was capable of short-term borrowing and long-term lending, thus giving rise to very risky balance sheets. Moreover, financial globalization induced the great banks to cross the borders of national states and expand their businesses to a global scale (Barth et al. 2000). Banking laws similar to the Glass-Steagall Act were in force in other countries too, and most were abolished in the 1990s. In the same period, central control over banking activities slackened. Nowadays, the difference between commercial and investment banks is not particularly clear. Yet some diversity remains, with small local banks tending to behave more as commercial banks, while investment and speculative business prevails in the big international banks.

The deregulation process was ideologically justified by neoliberal thought (Wade, 2008) and involved all the markets and countries in the world to varying extents. In the United States, it was achieved through specific political measures starting on June 2, 1987, when Ronald Reagan appointed as the Federal Reserve chairman Alan Greenspan, who was much more favorable to deregulation than former chairman Paul Volcker.

Here are some of the most recent and significant deregulation measures:

- In 1997, Greenspan rejected the stricter derivatives accounting proposal put forward by the Financial Accounting Standards Board;
- In 1999, Bill Clinton signed the Gramm-Leach-Bliley Act, which repealed the Banking Act of 1933 and limited controls on investment banks;
- In 2000, by initiative of Senator Phil Gramm,[74] a 262-page amendment was included in the Commodity Futures Modernization Act, deregulating the derivatives market;
- In 2002, George W. Bush launched a housing plan to enable most citizens to buy real estate, with the aim of realizing Mrs. Thatcher's utopia of an ownership society; to this end he permitted banks to grant loans without checks even to low-income borrowers;

- In May 18, 2004, for the first time in the history of the Federal Reserve, Greenspan was nominated (by President George W. Bush) to serve as the chairman for a fifth term; in the same year the SEC drastically reduced controls on stock exchanges, and enacted a voluntary self-regulation program for banks that made it possible to raise leverage ratios from 10:1 to 30:1;
- In 2004–5 multistate banks were gradually exempted from the "predatory credit" rules: no-doc and low-doc loans proliferated.

Deregulation favored the emergence of a fourth bubble factor. A broad sector of non-bank and quasi-bank financial intermediaries developed: loan originators, pension funds, financial insurers, monetary and bond funds, mortgage brokers, hedge funds, broker-dealers. Particularly important were various kinds of conduits, known as Special Purpose Entities (SPE), Special Purpose Vehicles (SPV), and Structured Investment Vehicles (SIV). These intermediaries trade in financial and inter-bank markets without being subject to the safety requirements typical of banks. They are capable of expanding their assets with highly risky investments, self-financing without resorting to deposit collection, and are exempt from central bank supervision. Thus an enormous *shadow banking system* has developed, whose asset value amounts to roughly half that of the regular banking system, and this process involved all the principal advanced countries.[75] Interacting with banks, these intermediaries played a decisive role in the expansion of securitization and other complex financial innovations and made a considerable contribution to the spreading out of derivatives traded over-the-counter in badly regulated, thin markets with limited transparency.

A fifth factor contributing to the bubble and subsequent crisis came from international regulation. In 1988, the ten most important countries in the financial markets signed the Basel I Accord. This was considered necessary to regulate international banking, as the controls implemented by national authorities were deemed inadequate. Its main target was to establish safety requirements to be adopted by all national authorities. The most important requirement was an

8 percent capital-to-risk weighted assets ratio. However, the accord functioned in an adverse way, as banks reacted by trying to elude regulations (Chick, 2009) and by developing financial innovations that helped feed speculation, debt accumulation, and risk proneness. Moreover, the accord left the task of risk evaluation to the rating agencies, which are private corporations not subject to public supervision. In a period of market euphoria and asset inflation, these agencies tend to endorse investor buoyancy, whereas when a crisis breaks out they tend to exacerbate pessimism.

I have focused on instability factors in the United States because it is there that the crisis began and deregulation was most advanced. In reality, deregulation and financialization have been global processes, involving all the countries of the imperial Center and most of the Periphery. They have been particularly marked in Europe and certainly contributed to the euro crisis. All the above-mentioned instability factors were present to some extent in several European countries. Here, rather than applying the same analysis to Europe, I will limit myself to pinpointing some peculiarities of the old continent.

Deregulation of the financial markets was launched in Europe before the United States. To be precise, it began with the Single European Act of 1987 and the Second Council Directive 89/646/EEC of 1989, and was officially completed with the 1999 Financial Services Action Plan, a five-year financial harmonization plan. Based on these rules, and with the objective of creating the single market, other European directives continually pushed member states to adopt measures in favor of financial market liberalization, as well as to relinquish any form of control over capital movements.

Among other things, the burgeoning of neoliberal thought in both right- and left-wing politics led to the privatization of big banks in some countries, like Italy, where they were previously publicly owned. Not surprisingly, this did not favor competition, but caused the concentration of firms and the development of universal banking.

In Europe, more than in any other region of the world, neoliberal ideology contributed to diffusing the conviction that central banks must be autonomous from governments. Such a theoretical idiocy was justified by the idea that the monetary funding of public debt would favor lax fiscal policies and feed inflation. In some countries this conviction led to the declaration of "divorces" separating the central bank and the Treasury.[76] In reality, the idea happily espoused a German political tenet according to which the central bank should have the function of a whip for the trade union movement, punishing any attempt to negotiate "excessive" wage rises with deflation. With the birth of the EU, the idiocy was included in the Constitutive Treaties, so the European Central Bank (ECB) was assigned the duty of ensuring price stability, while being forbidden to fund public debts. (In the next chapter, I will argue that preventing it from functioning as a lender of last resort for EU states created the conditions for mounting speculative expectations on the risk of sovereign debt defaults and contributed to the explosion of the euro crisis.)

An extensive shadow banking system also formed in Europe. Prior to the subprime crisis, it was almost as big as the U.S. system, and afterward it grew even more.[77] European banks and non-bank intermediaries played with derivatives that, following the subprime crisis, heavily impacted bankruptcies. Besides this some countries, like Spain and Ireland, attempted to imitate the American speculation-led growth model, thus helping to trigger real estate bubbles that caused disasters in Europe too.

Following the first act of the crisis (2007–9), European banks invested heavily in government securities, which seemed less risky than derivatives. However, to correct a defect of the Basel I Accord, which had left the task of evaluating risks to rating agencies, the Basel II Accord obliged the banks to record balance sheet entries using the mark-to-market criterion.[78] Fair value accountancy, in which values must be recorded at market prices, or at realistic prices reflecting market quotations, produces pro-cyclical movements of balance sheet assets. Therefore, its application worsened the banks' balance sheets during the crisis, when asset values decreased while their risk weights increased (Wallison, 2008; Fratianni and Marchionne, 2009). Thus after 2011 the default risk of some European sovereign debt was transferred to banks, in the form of increased losses and bankruptcy risks.

Finally, with the aim of strengthening the resilience of the banking sector, the Basel III Accord established an increase in liquidity and capital requirements. Even before the accords were enacted, the European Banking Authority recommended a drastic rise in Core Tier I capital ratios, thus compelling European banks to reduce lending and sell securities just when the southern European debt crisis was exploding. This further impacted the euro crisis.

As in the United States, public debts and deficits were exhibiting an upward trend in many European countries as early as the 1980s. The aggregate debt/GDP ratio of the G7 countries was 42 percent in 1980 and soared to 72 percent in 1998. The usual explanation is that in the United States this trend was mainly determined by escalating military spending, while in Europe it was mainly ascribable to funding the welfare state, attained by the workers' struggles of the late 1960s and early 1970s. But this explanation does not fully grasp the complexity of the phenomenon. To start with, military spending significantly increased in Europe when the United States, applying the sheriff-and-posse model, involved many of its Atlantic allies in disciplinary intervention in the Middle East. Moreover, public debt soared in the 1980s, partly due to the worldwide interest rate hike caused by Reagan's military and monetary policies. It continued to mount in the early 1990s, due to an upsurge caused by the financial policies with which Germany tried to make the rest of the Europe pay for its unification. Besides, in some countries, such as Italy, the "divorce" of government from the central bank also contributed to swelling public debt, since the bank could no longer act as a stabilizer of government bond yields. Finally, beginning in the 1980s, the advanced countries, especially in Europe, saw a slowdown in GDP growth, that is, the denominator of the debt/GDP ratio, and therefore a rise in the ratio itself, even independently of their mounting budget difficulties.

THE MILLENNIUM BUBBLE

If we consider all the factors of instability described above, we can see how the financial markets influenced the swelling of the speculative bubble. As observed, universal banking played a particularly prominent role. This sort of intermediary carries out short-term borrowing by accepting customers' deposits and selling deposit certificates and other liabilities, then makes long-term investments by buying shares, bonds, and derivatives and granting loans.

Most bank liabilities are money. An apparently strange process takes place with banks: the more they invest in loans to companies and households, the more their deposits rise, as the liquidity created in this way is normally held in current accounts. Thus when the banks increase lending they simultaneously expand the money supply.[79] *Bank money* covers 90 to 95 percent of the means of payment in circulation in a modern economic system.

When banks speculate for a rise in asset prices by expanding their assets more than their liquid reserves, they contribute to feeding the bubble, not only because they raise the demand for long-term assets, but also because they increase the credit and money used by other speculators. At the same time, they cause a surge in overall indebtedness.

In the American housing bubble, banks and loan originators expanded lending especially because of the profits they made through fees and commissions. They were not particularly motivated by the interest paid on loans, because most of these assets were not kept in their portfolios. They created new firms, like the conduits, which were formally independent and had autonomous balance sheets. In this way they were able to limit leverage and, at the same time, unload their balance sheets of many risky assets.

The conduits were the main vehicles of securitization. They got hold of loans and securities of varying riskiness, then "packaged" them up as collateral on the derivatives they produced.[80] These mostly consisted of mortgage-backed securities. The rating agencies who graded them tended to hold the same belief as the conduits themselves, that the prices of mortgaged houses in different states, and therefore the risks of sundry loans packaged in a security, were not correlated, which is tantamount to assuming the impossibility of a general crisis of the housing market, a crisis involving the entire nation.

Who invested in the derivatives markets? Other banks and other conduits, like SIVs, created by the banks themselves. SIVs bought the derivatives produced by first-stage conduits and then recycled them, producing other derivatives of the commercial paper kind. Thus the assets returned to the banking system in the form of short- to medium-term paper (such as short-term asset-backed commercial paper and medium-term investment notes), which appeared less risky than the original loans. The system is known as "originate-to-distribute," and gives the impression of reducing banking sector risks by spreading them over a large number of intermediaries.

Traditional commercial banks granted loans after monitoring borrowers' ability to pay. They carried out a useful action in controlling households' and firms' riskiness. This practice has been abandoned by the big international banks, who can free themselves of their credit and pass their risks on to others.

After deregulation, risk was evaluated by rating agencies, which used mathematical models to measure risk in terms of default probability. These were calculated by observing the frequency of defaults in recent years. Moreover, the models were based on log-normal distributions, which assign low frequencies to extreme events. Since failures to pay are infrequent during the growth stage of a bubble, the riskiness of many assets is assessed as low. So rating agencies, quite independently of any subjective interest in favoring their clients, tended to sustain and help realize the speculators' extrapolative expectations (Kregel, 2008; Nesvetailova, 2008).

Overall indebtedness tended to rise during the growth phase of the bubble. *Household debt* increased to fund real estate purchases and the consumption of luxury goods; *firm debt* grew to fund investment by borrowing from banks and issuing bonds and commercial paper; *bank debt* grew as bank deposit liabilities expanded hand-in-hand with credit.

This escalating debt was encouraged by asset inflation, as people are more prone to borrow when their wealth is growing. Asset demand was fed by self-realizing optimistic expectations. Speculators bought increasing quantities of shares, bonds, and derivatives, anticipating a rise in their prices, and thus making them rise. The demand for houses escalated as their prices were expected to rise, thus making them rise. House prices doubled in the United States between 1999 and 2005. The banks granted a growing quantity of loans, expecting markets to easily absorb the derivatives resulting from loan securitizations. In this way they created the money required to buy an increasing quantity of derivatives and goods.

In general, it can be said that all speculators are more prone to increase their debt during a bubble (Kregel, 2008) because they believe they will be able to service it with part of the capital gains they expect to earn from trading. Moreover, almost all of them tend to reduce their liquid assets just when the quantity of money in circulation is rising, and accumulate illiquid assets just when their prices are swelling. It is a sort of "gold rush," resulting in a situation of *illiquidity preference*, or a reduced liquidity preference. When this sentiment deepens, the market pays an illiquidity premium. In other words, the liquidity premium decreases, which is reflected in a flattening of the yield curve. This phenomenon, called "bull flattening," will then occur repeatedly during the crisis and immediately after the bubble crash as a reaction of financial markets to expansionary monetary policies.

A speculative bubble also has repercussions on the markets for consumption and investment goods. Asset inflation produces a *positive wealth effect* by which, since everyone feels richer, everyone tends to spend more on buying all kinds of goods: not only shares, bonds, derivatives, and houses, but also cars, clothing, and holidays. In this way, the bubble boosts aggregate demand and industrial production and sustains prosperity. Firms tend to produce more and increase investments to face an increasing demand for goods.[81] Employment rises, too. A bubble helps prop up economic growth, both because it produces a wealth effect that stimulates consumption and investment, and because it favors the monetary expansion needed to nourish the growing volume of transactions. At the same time, however, it causes household and business debts to swell. This is precisely what happened in the U.S. economy in the ten years preceding the crisis.

Obviously, the process cannot continue indefinitely. Everybody knows that sooner or later the bubble will burst, and that the risk of a crash rises with: 1) the passing of time, since there has never been a bubble that did not burst; 2) the level of indebtedness, since debts ultimately have to be repaid, or defaulted on; 3) the value of assets, since the more they differ from fundamentals, the higher the probability they will go back to them; 4) the financial leverage, since its increase implies a reduction in safety margins.

ACT I: THE SUBPRIME CRISIS

The downturn occurred when smart speculators (the best-informed ones) anticipated the crisis and tried to beat the market. They had bought when prices were increasing. Now they began to sell to buy back at lower prices.[82] Bear speculation set off. As this sentiment spread, the swelling of the bubble slowed down. When the news reached the herd, the bubble burst. This happened abruptly when, realizing the danger, almost everybody tried at the same time to get rid of assets whose value was still fairly high but decreasing.

Destabilizing speculation prevails while a bubble is swelling; when it bursts, speculation becomes stabilizing.[83] It might seem paradoxical, but a bubble burst is a stabilizing event, as it takes place after a period of marked destabilization in which prices drift away from the fundamentals. However, this change of course may soon give way to destabilizing bearish expectations if the contraction is marked.

In the U.S. financial markets there was a transition phase, with a slowdown lasting from 2004 to 2007. In that period the Fed raised interest rates, boosting the federal funds rate from 1 percent to 6.25 percent. In late 2004, the revaluation rate of house prices began to decline, becoming negative toward the end of 2006. However, a securitization boom took place in the same year. Banks reacted to the interest rate hike by offering "low-doc" and "no-doc" loans, for which borrowers were required to present limited or no documentation. Besides this, teaser rates were proposed, easy credit terms with none or very low interest rates for the first two to three years but high and floating rates in subsequent years. Most borrowers took the bait, as they thought house prices would rise in those first years, allowing them to resell with a net capital gain or obtain a new mortgage loan with easy terms. In the same period, the number of NINJA borrowers (No Income, No Job or Assets) increased. However, some hedge funds, which are smart money par excellence, started to bear, selling their riskiest derivatives. And the bubble began to deflate. Nonetheless, the situation was still not entirely clear in 2006.

Between 2007 and 2008, there was a significant increase in *distraints* (property seizures). Since many loan agreements were not honored, banks tried to sell the mortgaged houses. But prices were diminishing, and some banks found themselves faced with liquidity problems and bank runs. Various hedge funds that had not been quick to sell short suffered heavy losses. The rating agencies started to downgrade many derivatives, as their evaluation models suggested default risks were increasing. This impacted the crisis, since downgraded securities lose their value. The conduits that had issued the derivatives found it increasingly difficult to refinance their investments. For instance, Collateralized Debt Obligation (CDO) issues, which had reached $178 billion in the second quarter of 2007, sank to $0.57 billion in the third quarter of 2009. Similar falls affected all the different kinds of derivatives.

Now, let's go back to Basel. I already observed that the 8 percent safety margin recommended by the Basel I Accord had induced the banks to create conduits. Basel I thus helped feed the bubble by encouraging financial innovations and securitization. To correct some defects of the first Accord, the Basel II Accord was signed in 2004 and subsequently revised several times until 2008. It aimed, among other things, to impose more detailed and more cogent capital requirements by taking into account various kinds of risk. Basel I had focused on credit risk, the risk of debtor default. Basel II also contemplated market risks (the risk of losses due to changes in asset prices), interest risks (the risk of fixed-income assets losing value due to changes in interest rates), and operational risks (the risk incurred by an organization's internal activities). Banks were obliged to set aside capital and reserves to hedge against all kinds of risks. Moreover, the accord required market risks to be assessed by the banks themselves rather than by the rating agencies, and assets to be valued by observing the effective prices of securities.

Unfortunately, the accord entered into force in the United States and EU in 2008, the worst year of the crisis. At that time the precautionary requirements imposed by the Accord added to those prompted by the crisis itself. Banks had to drastically increase their reserves and reduce leverage. Moreover, by valuing assets in a time of crisis, they had to attribute them increasing risk and weights. For these reasons, they were compelled to substantially restrict their credit supply. In other words, the Basel I and Basel II accords had adverse effects (Balin, 2009): the former fed the bubble, the latter exacerbated the crisis.

Some dates and data can help illustrate the evolution and intensity of the collapse. On September 15, 2008, the Lehman Brothers bank went bankrupt. This event was highly symbolic, as it involved in one the five biggest U.S. banks. It was followed by the first "black Monday" on Wall Street, on September 29, which saw the Dow Jones plunge by 8.7 percent. The following week saw the second black Monday, with a 3.86 percent fall. The entire week from the 6th to the 10th of October was a black week, in which the Dow Jones tumbled by 22.8 percent. Between October 9, 2007, and October 10, 2008, it lost 42.55 percent. Similar collapses occurred in the stock exchanges of all advanced countries.

During the crash that follows a bubble the prices of long-term assets sink, as all investors try to raise safety margins, reduce leverage, and augment liquid balances. Banks do the same, and strive to reduce the riskiness of their balance assets by cutting their credit supply. As a consequence, the quantity of money shrinks just when the public most needs it to expand to help them cope with debts. It becomes difficult to repay loans, but many people are obliged to do so. Thus a debt deflation process is set in motion.[84] Everybody tries to repay their debts at a time when it is difficult to obtain new credit. The financial markets are consequently shattered by a credit crunch, or what Marx called a "money famine." Debtors are compelled to sell their assets while their prices are plummeting. This reduces them even further. Since many industrial and financial firms are indebted to one another, painful processes of chain bankruptcy are set in motion.

Monetary authorities can help to slow the fall. They can bail out banks from bankruptcy by expanding the supply of base money, furnishing them with last-resort credit at low interest rates. A method widely used by the U.S. Federal Reserve was "quantitative easing," through which it bought bonds and securities with new money. Another was "credit easing," by which it bought or underwrote asset-backed securities. The ECB used the "securities markets program" to buy securities on secondary markets and "long-term refinancing operations" to lend money to banks.

At any rate, both U.S. and EU governments made an important contribution to rescuing many financial and industrial concerns, with "a giant transfer of private debt into public, that is to say, a simple socialization of losses" (Giacché, 2012a, 43). In the United States, an Emergency Economic Stabilization Act was passed in 2008. This enabled the treasury secretary to provide firms with liquidity and recapitalize some of them, even by purchasing derivatives. The Troubled Asset Relief Program then bailed out several industrial corporations by purchasing their bonds and shares. Similar interventions took place in Europe, where, for instance, the British, Belgian, and Dutch governments partially nationalized various banks. Overall 2.8 trillion dollars were used in the United States to bail out 1,366 banks, and 2.4 trillion euros to bail out 174 European banks (Onado, 2012, 8).

Nonetheless, the economies entered a liquidity trap, a situation in which the central banks' expansionary policies have little effect. Since most investors increase their liquid balances, and many others desperately demand credit, the quantitative and credit easing policies of central banks bring down short-term interest rates but fail to reduce the costs of mortgage loans and credit for firms. In effect, the Fed's monetary expansion helped immediately lower short-term interest rates, but not long-term ones. In the most acute phase of the crisis, the spread between assets of different maturity and riskiness increased (Fratianni and Marchionne, 2009), a clear sign that liquidity preference had risen among all investors. The spread between the Federal Funds Rate and the LIBOR (London Interbank Offered Rate) also increased, revealing reciprocal distrust among financial intermediaries.[85]

Moreover, since banks tended to reduce loans and investments, the increase in base money did not result in a sufficient increase in the over-all money supply. Finally, as expectations were gloomy and interest rates low, the liquidity available was accumulated by speculators and did not accrue to the industrial sector. Although the expansionary monetary policies immediately helped break the fall of the financial sector and the collapse of banks, it did not succeed in triggering industrial recovery.

The consequences of the crisis on the real economy were even more dramatic, as strong negative wealth effects were set in motion. Everybody felt poorer due to the fall in asset values. Then everyone reduced spending. The firms that did not go under still produced less. Unemployment rose, and the wage bill and consumption shrank even further. Exports diminished as the crisis became international. Due to the intensity of the crisis, its effects lasted a long time, as all stimuli to effective demand had waned. Moreover, the crisis of the real economy had a negative effect on the financial crisis, as the bankruptcies and defaults of bank borrowers weighed heavily on bank balance sheets.

Under these conditions, only massive intervention on the part of governments, particularly with expansive *fiscal* policies to relaunch public and private spending, can help trigger real recovery. However, in the present crisis the governments of the advanced countries have been somewhat cautious with expansive fiscal policies. True, their budget deficits swelled significantly due to the bank bailout measures. Yet the increase in public spending mostly consisted of a transfer of losses to taxpayers, rather than a rise in their disposable incomes and then in effective demand.

A few words remain to be said on the international diffusion of the crisis, which took place through two channels: financial and commercial. Financial capital moves freely in international markets. The giant speculative bubble swelled and then burst in the advanced countries, which were endowed with large and sophisticated financial markets.

However, the speculators of all countries invested there. Hence, the explosion of the bubble dragged all capitalists downward, including those of the Peripheral countries, and the chain bankruptcy and debt deflation processes rapidly spread all over the world. The contagion of the industrial crisis, meanwhile, spread through international trade. When the slump began in advanced economies, reductions in consumption and investments brought about a drop in their imports, and consequently in the exports of developing and emerging countries. Aggregate demand contracted there too and, as a result, production and employment. In this way, the production crisis was transmitted to the whole world economy.

Summing up, the subprime crash triggered the typical events of debt deflation: a fall in asset prices, flight to liquidity, leverage reduction, bank credit contraction, and chain bankruptcies. Borrowers had serious difficulty honoring their obligations. Many of them were compelled to sell their real and financial assets at fire-sale prices. The monetary authorities tried to slow this fall by expanding the supply of base money, but the economy entered a *liquidity trap*. Moreover, the increased availability of base money did not lead to a rise in the overall money supply, as bank lending contracted. Then the crisis impacted the real economy through a strong negative wealth effect, which caused a drop in consumption and investment. Unemployment rocketed and the wage bill sank, causing consumption to fall further. Finally, the industrial crisis had a negative effect on the financial sector, as the bankruptcies and defaults of the banks' customers heavily affected their balance assets, bolstered reciprocal mistrust, and compelled them to contract credit even more.[86]

ACT II: THE EURO CRISIS

In the aftermath of the subprime bubble burst, several economists predicted that the crisis would be W-shaped: dip-recovery-dip-recovery. Some expected the second dip in the near future, and even predicted that it would take the form of a fiscal crisis of the states triggered by speculative attacks on sovereign debts (for instance Giacché, 2009, 49–50). This is precisely what happened.

As mentioned above, central banks attempted to deal with the crisis in 2008 and 2009 by implementing expansionary monetary policies. The Fed did so when the bubble burst to prevent the banking system from collapsing, and carried on throughout 2010–13 to encourage recovery.[87] Following the interest rate cuts, the dollar depreciated, so that the dollar cost of short-term borrowing became decidedly negative (up to –20 percent). This was an excellent remedy from the speculators' viewpoint, as they found it highly profitable to borrow dollars. But what could they do with the liquidity? They invested in speculative trading by buying shares, bonds, derivatives, raw materials, oil, gold, etc. From January 2009 to January 2010, the MSCI index of world stock exchanges jumped from 700 to 1195, and the London gold price from about $800 to $1,050. The real economy, also dragged by speculation, recovered in 2010. All problems seemed to be resolved.

Quite the contrary. Since this mini-boom was pulled by a new bubble, and since indebtedness was still distinctly high, speculators knew the recovery was precarious. So they turned their attention to fathoming the new weak point of the world economy. In 2011, they identified it: the sovereign debts of some Euroland states. "Why them?" we may ask.

The subprime crisis had caused many European banks serious problems: because they had portfolios full of derivatives, like the German banks; because they had grown too much with the complicity of supervision authorities, like the British ones; or because they had propped up a housing bubble, like the Spanish and Irish banks. To cope with the 2009 crash, not only did the European Central Bank expand the money supply, but the governments used public funds to bail out banks from bankruptcy. They effectively succeeded in rescuing the banking system, allowing only a limited number of banks to go under, but as a consequence budget deficits and public debts grew massively. Moreover, the GDP drop in 2009 reduced fiscal revenues and raised the debt/GDP ratios, nurturing mistrust in the public debt sustainability. In 2010 the U.S. debt/GDP percentage ratio was 94.3, Germany's 80, Japan's 220.3,

Italy's 119, and Greece's 142. The deficit/GDP percentage ratios were 10.6, –3.3, –9.5 , –4.6, and –9.6, respectively.

Speculators started betting on default, and in 2011 the second dip occurred. The attack was directed against the weakest links of the German imperial chain: the southern European countries, those with not only a high debt/GDP ratio, but also a stagnant economy and a current account deficit. When GDP does not grow and the public budget is in deficit, the debt/GDP ratio and the default risk rise. Moreover, a current account deficit implies that the country tends to step up its public and/or private debt, which bolsters the default risk.

The credit default swaps on public debt securities started to grow, the prices of government securities to fall, and their yields to rise. The bear rally rapidly spread out to all markets and stock exchanges, bringing them close to collapsing in the summer of 2011. After that, an alarming deflationary spiral was triggered. The governments of attacked countries implemented restrictive fiscal policies, thus reducing aggregate demand and generating recession. Then the debt/GDP ratios rose instead of falling, both because their denominator had dropped and because the speculative attack had swelled debt service costs. Next, the crisis impacted financial intermediaries, which had large quantities of European government securities in their portfolios.

The bankruptcy risks of banks grew, and these reacted by trying to rebuild reserves and reduce leverage. By doing so, they cut the credit supply and swelled interest rates. The banking system's troubles were then magnified by the European Banking Authority, which, in compliance with a policy instruction by the European Council and Ecofin (the Economic and Financial Affairs Council of the European Union, composed of all the finance ministers of the twenty-seven member-states), and anticipating a reform provided for by the Basel III Accord, issued a key recommendation (EBA/REC/2001/1). This required the seventy-one largest European banks to build an exceptional and temporary capital buffer against exposure on government securities and to double Core Tier 1, the most solid part of capital, bringing the safety margin to 9 percent. All was supposed to be accomplished before June 30, 2012! "This was the coup de grâce."[88]

An EBA recommendation is not law, and should therefore not be binding. But in a regime of "market obligation," in which speculators and the rating agencies[89] lay down the law, such recommendations cannot be ignored. The banks had to further reduce leverage, while their assets were depreciating and the weight of their riskiest assets increasing. They further reduced the credit supply and set up asset/ credit disposal programs. Still, the credit contraction was also determined by a reduced demand for loans to finance investments and an increased demand to cope with losses and pay circulating capital—the riskiest form of bank lending.

Industrial companies, observing a contraction in aggregate demand and the credit supply and an increase in the cost of finance, reduced production and dismissed workers. As a consequence, fiscal revenues diminished just when the cost of debt servicing was rising. Governments enacted new restrictive fiscal policies.

Obviously, the crisis did not remain confined to Southern Europe. As most banks in northern Euroland had invested in Greek, Italian, and Spanish securities, they also experienced balance sheet troubles, and thus restricted credit. Furthermore, since a large portion of European countries' exports are to other European countries, the decline in consumption in Southern countries induced a decline in exports in the Northern ones. Thus the crisis spread throughout Europe.[90] As Europe is a rich market for emerging, developing, and advanced countries' exports, these too had to deal with a contraction in exports and production. Thus the second dip of the crisis has triggered a worldwide slowdown.

As in 2009, the monetary authorities quickly reacted to avoid panic, by flooding the markets with liquidity. The Fed started off, the ECB and the Bank of England followed suit. Speculation had some respite and stock exchanges went back bullish. Between January and February 2012 the gold price jumped over 11 percent and the oil price about 14 percent. The Dow Jones went back to precrisis levels and by February 22, 2012 it had recovered 21.7 percent from its minimum of 2011. The S&P 500 regained 23.9 percent. Even the European stock exchanges exhibited a strong upturn: the Stoxx600 grew by 23.1 percent, the Dax30 by 34.8 percent, and the FTSE MIB by 22.9 percent.

In 2012, and more so in 2013, the U.S. and European economies followed divergent paths. Obama's expansionary fiscal policies helped spread optimistic sentiments in financial markets, and the Federal Reserve's expansionary monetary policies sustained them. While GDP began to grow again, a new speculative bubble was swelling in the stock exchanges that inflated especially the prices of shares, and that lasted throughout 2013. In that year the S&P soared by 29.10 percent, the Nasdaq by 37.5 percent, while corporate profits rose by only 5.7 percent, half of what was expected at the beginning of the year—a clear sign of misalliance between financial and fundamental values. Speculative expectations were fed by the dollar's tendency to depreciate and by the anticipation of a continuation of GDP growth, and these tended to help the expectations become reality. In this way they generated a special kind of positive wealth effect, a windfall effect linked to a rise in the firms' financial assets, which in turn added to the anticipation of a growth in aggregate demand, inducing companies to invest and thus to make aggregate demand grow. The process was reinforced by a shrinking of household and firm debt. All of these processes were sustained by monetary expansion. It is a virtuous circle that brought the U.S. economy out of the crisis, but one that could swiftly transform into a vicious one when the bubble bursts.

In Europe, instead, the new mini-bubble triggered by monetary policies rapidly deflated. In April 2012 all the financial markets, dragged down by the European ones, went back to being bear markets. Investors understood that even if the Fed was capable of reinforcing the tentative expansive fiscal policies of the U.S. government, the ECB was unable to contrast the negative effects of European governments' restrictive fiscal policies, and was therefore incapable of stopping the crisis of the real economy. However, in July 2012, when the ECB president declared he was determined to implement a program of outright monetary transactions to salvage the euro at any cost, a new mini-bubble began to grow, and stock exchanges recovered throughout 2013, when the Euro Stoxx rose by 17.7 percent. It seems that financial markets were having quite a roller-coaster ride. At any rate, the real economy remained trapped in a recession, which worsened throughout 2012 and gave no sign of a true recovery in 2013. We cannot exclude the possibility that the global bubble will burst in Europe before the United States.

I will address the basic causes of the crisis in the next chapter, and deal with the political conditions surrounding the crisis. Meanwhile, I cannot conclude this chapter without indulging in a philosophical reflection. The governments of advanced countries, especially the European, currently *seem* incapable of understanding and tackling the problem at its roots, and ultimately of resolving it. The only thing they have done well is activate the monetary pump, blowing up financial bubbles when they are deflating. In this way they have succeeded in temporarily avoiding financial crashes, but they have not saved production from recession, industrial firms from bankruptcy, nor workers from unemployment and impoverishment. We are witnessing the triumph of the "casino economy," which is now a rigged triumph: "It is as if mountains of chips were being donated or sold at a great discount at the casino entrance" (Longo, 2012, 11).

I said they *seem* incapable of understanding. In reality, the sharpest minds of the European ruling classes (among others) know very well what is happening, since it is precisely what they wanted to happen, as I am about to explain.

6. The Basic Causes of the Crisis

> The intention of this federation is to create a new
> type of ... European population, one prepared to accept
> suffering and poverty, to accept even lower wages than the
> Chinese. And the correlation of such a federation with
> the federal union of humankind goes hand in hand
> with the current conception of "globalization."
> —APOSTOLOU, 2012

Opinions that ascribe ultimate responsibility for the crisis to financial market inefficiency and monetary policy errors are hardly convincing.[91] In reality, "an assessment of the fundamental causes of the crisis must go beyond the regulatory problems of the financial system" (Fornasari, 2009, 89). Since the measures responsible for the great crisis adhere to certain specific political schemes, we cannot hope to understand the nature of the crisis unless we grasp the sense of these schemes.

The form of imperialism emerging from the liberalization of global markets is based on an implicit pact between the big capital of advanced countries and that of emerging economies. The latter have obtained access to the goods markets in the North of the world and a flood of foreign direct investments from the big multinationals. The former have obtained the TRIPs, GATS, and TRIMs agreements: the first to protect patent and trademark ownership rights; the second to create markets for services; the third to open the markets for corporate control.[92]

Emerging countries have been able to exploit their competitive advantage in labor costs. They produce low-tech consumer goods with imported technologies and then export them to advanced economies, thus fighting the latter's less dynamic firms with ruthless competition. They have also increasingly invested in technological research, based mainly on creative imitation, adaptation, and improvement innovations, which has partially helped to reduce the technological gap with advanced countries.[93] Above all, what they have done has served to raise labor productivity and hence keep labor costs low.

Advanced country multinationals gain triple benefits from globalization: having ensured a legal monopoly over the resource for which they enjoy a competitive advantage—high-tech research—they can exploit it to redistribute income from the Periphery to the Center of the empire; moreover they take advantage of competition in the goods markets to redistribute income from wages to profits; finally, they use financial globalization to relocate investments abroad and buy companies and natural resources in the Peripheral countries.

As a consequence, labor conditions and the wage share deteriorate in advanced economies, and mass consumption languishes. Thus, as both investments and consumption slow down, these countries tend to stagnate.

Moreover, these economies are hit by chronic foreign account unbalances caused by globalization. Emerging countries, especially China and those in East Asia, as well as oil producers, including Russia, enjoy significant structural surpluses in their current accounts. Conversely, most advanced economies have to endure big deficits, the greatest of which is that of the United States. Yet there are exceptions. Germany and Japan, in particular, have sizable surpluses (World Bank, 2013b, 11). We will soon see why.

In the present chapter, I put forward an argument that derives directly from the vision of globalization as a process of formation of a global imperial system. This process generates a fairly novel political contradiction in the economies of the imperial Center: although the states of advanced countries promote globalization to satisfy the demands of multinational capital, they try to counter its depressionary effects on their economies. The United States, in particular, has excelled in this policy of resistance. Other countries, like Germany, have sought to exploit globalization to build an outdated mercantilist kind of imperial

TABLE 2: The Wage Share as a Percentage of National Income[95]

	1960	1970	1980	1990	2000	2010
U.S.	71.20	71.98	69.89	67.82	67.70	63.69
Japan	76.80	66.81	75.36	67.39	67.88	62.01
Germany	66.91	68.36	70.75	64.96	65.69	66.29
France	73.28	72.40	76.37	68.18	66.39	67.35
Italy	74.07	71.42	70.44	67.73	61.56	63.33
UK	70.42	74.85	74.87	74.31	71.97	73.10

Source: European Commission (2012)

power. Ultimately, the great crisis has exploded. It would appear to be a reaction of the "markets" to the political devices through which some advanced-country governments have striven to oppose or exploit the depressionary tendencies. Its virulence seems to prove that the "markets" have ultimately managed to discipline the national governments that had been attempting to mete out discipline themselves.

THE EVOLUTION OF THE WAGE SHARE IN ADVANCED COUNTRIES

It is well known that the wage share in national income has shrunk in most of the world during the era of contemporary globalization. I already dealt with this issue in the first chapter. Now I wish to focus on the countries of the imperial Center, where, after having peaked in the 1970s, the share has systematically declined.[94] Table 2 shows some basic data to illustrate this trend.

The peak years were: 1970 in the United States (71.98); 1974 in Germany (71.43); 1975 in Italy (73.38) and Great Britain (78.32); and 1977 in Japan (78.06). France saw a peak in 1976 (76.17), then a drop, to reach a second peak in 1981 (76.70). The lowest value was reached in most countries in 2007. From 2008 to 2012 there was a recovery of the wage share, especially in the European countries, due to the GDP fall in the crisis years.

The decreasing trend over the last thirty-five to forty years has been caused by several factors:

- Competitive pressures determined by globalization,[96] which have brought about a slowdown in production and a contraction in industrial employment;
- Then, as a consequence, reduced workers' bargaining power;
- Deregulation of labor markets, reduced legal protection for workers, and the diffusion of "flexible" employment contracts;
- Labor-saving and skill-intensive technological changes that mainly account for increasing inequality between blue and white collars and among the latter.

In any case, a distinction needs to be made between two different periods: the end-of-century stagflation era (mid-1970s to early 1990s) and the globalization era (the 1990s onward). One of the major causes of the end-of-century stagflation was the deflationary policies adopted in almost all the advanced countries. Instead, the effects of market liberalizations became more tangible in the second period.

The wave of anticapitalist struggles in the late 1960s to the early 1970s had various destabilizing effects. They forced a redistribution of income from profits to wages; impacted the Fordist-Keynesian system of industrial relations,[97] which undermined social peace, the control of labor in the production process, as well as power relations in society; and created or reinforced certain institutional arrangements for the protection of the working class (welfare state, labor laws, civil rights), making it difficult for capitalists to recover profits through simple factory restructuring.

Capital reacted first with an "investment strike," and then by launching a political and ideological counterattack, which brought to power a new ultra-liberal and conservative political class in the main countries of the imperial Center and in the most important international organizations. Keynesian economic policies were declared ruinous, and the new prophets replaced the call to "accumulate, accumulate!" with an exhortation to "deflate, deflate!"

The restrictive policies adopted in the 1980s in almost all advanced countries were justified by the need to block the spiraling inflation triggered by the oil shocks. Yet there was no need to drive these economies toward stagnation, unless the goal was really to restore profit margins at the expense of wages. The justification of curing inflation was specious. A political motive lurked behind the neoliberal and monetarist theories, as they aimed at achieving two basic objectives: 1) to reconstruct the conditions for complete capitalist control over production processes; 2) to redistribute income from labor to capital, and from the Periphery to the imperial Center. The main weapon wielded in this attack was the *reduction of industrial employment* through restrictive monetary and fiscal policies.

The Phillips curve, refashioned into a monetarist shape in the 1970s, postulates a negative correlation between wage inflation and the unemployment rate, at least in the short run. But this is more ideology than theory. Nominal wage changes do not trivially depend on labor market conditions, on the demand and supply of labor. They depend on workers' bargaining power, which is affected above all by *changes* in industrial employment. The reason is simple. Whereas companies can boldly resist a strike when aggregate demand shrinks, warehouses are overloaded, and labor is redundant, workers, in contrast, become more cautious in periods of mass dismissals and fear of losing their jobs plays a decisive role in curbing militancy. Thus wage escalation depends on the degree of workers' militancy and on variations in industrial employment, besides inflation. The empirical data are clear: in France, Germany, and Italy, for instance, a 1 percent reduction in industrial employment determines a 1 percent cut in the growth rate of nominal wages (Screpanti, 1996; 2000). In the most important capitalist countries, inflation peaked around 1980 and then began to slow down. Industrial employment started to decline at that time. The restrictive policies enacted since the end of the 1970s were effective in curbing inflation and triggering a redistributive trend in favor of profits. In fact, they served to crush workers' militancy. One of the clearest objectives of the conservative governments of the 1980s was to bring the workers' movement into line. Margaret Thatcher and

Ronald Reagan started the ball rolling, and the main European governments followed suit.

In short, the high unemployment levels experienced in the 1980s were caused by the deflationary obsessions that dominated the main capitalist countries' economic policies during the end-of-century stagflation era. *At that time mass unemployment was an essentially political phenomenon,* as it was determined by mindful policy choices.

The situation changed in the mid-1990s, when the effects of globalization began to be felt in the labor markets of Northern countries. The liberalization of international trade made a decisive contribution to bringing workers' movements to their knees. In fact, the workers were those who suffered most from emerging countries' ruthless competition. Imported low-price goods crowded out local firms and compelled them to reduce production. Employment in advanced countries was reduced by simple commercial competition. Moreover, many companies reacted to competition by offshoring, outsourcing, and relocating investments in countries with lower labor costs and tax pressure. This shrank domestic investment in advanced countries and further reduced employment.

Competitive pressures also come from migrant workers, who are pushed to leave Peripheral countries by demographic growth and the destruction of traditional economies and cultures caused by capitalist penetration. Therefore the workforce expands in advanced countries just when employment is declining. Not only does the size of the workforce change, but so does its political attitude. Given the level of poverty they leave behind them, migrant workers are usually willing to accept any kind of job, wage, working hours, and conditions. Moreover, they are scarcely unionized and are easily blackmailed. Consequently, they also weaken local workers' bargaining power by favoring de-unionization, disorganization, and hindering mobilization.[98]

The effects of technological progress are no less devastating. R&D investments are greater in advanced countries, where innovations tend to save on unskilled labor. Yet the intensified use of highly skilled workers is confined to rather narrow sectors and social strata, and does not provide a significant boost to overall employment. These processes of labor substitution further weaken working-class bargaining power.

In the same period, not only did neoliberal monetary and fiscal policy theories become fashionable, but so did theories of production that blamed unemployment on labor rigidity and the proposed remedy of labor flexibility. The idea is that flexibility enhances productivity and then bolsters recovery by raising competitiveness. Still, labor flexibility has little effect on productivity if investments and aggregate demand are stagnant. If anything, it has depressionary effects on wages and workers' expectations, thus reducing consumption and effective demand.

The dynamics of productivity depend not only on R&D investments, but also on the expansion of production. Improvements in productivity are largely associated with endogenous technical progress, and are an increasing function of production levels (and hence of GDP). This is what the Kaldor-Verdoorn Law predicts.[99] When accumulation is vigorous, capacity utilization rises and increasing returns to scale are set in train, as well as learning by doing and the innovations embodied in machines. The latter process causes productivity to grow with investments, which, in turn, are pulled by aggregate demand. Advanced countries enjoyed high productivity growth in the 1950s to the 1970s because production was growing rapidly. Most of them did not make significant investments in R&D; they simply took advantage of technology transfers and imports of machines from the United States. Over the last twenty years, the opposite has occurred. Productivity has slackened[100] because aggregate demand and GDP have stagnated. International competitiveness has been impaired and aggregate demand has been insufficiently driven by exports. Then, in an inexorable vicious circle, the slowdown in output has depressed productivity growth. In short, globalization produces the following effects in advanced economies:

- *Consumption slackens* due to a decline in employment and the wage share;
- *Investment slackens* due to the commercial competition of emerging countries and the consequent offshoring and outsourcing reactions of national companies, which thus become multinational;
- *Public spending is contained* due to fiscal competition among states and the deflationary vocation of governments;[101]

- *Productivity slows down* because output slackens;
- *Exports do not grow enough* due to a loss of international competitiveness;
- *Industrial profits shrink* because of all the above.

It should now be clear why globalization causes a long-lasting depressive tendency in the economies of the North.

POLICY MODELS: CHINA AND THE UNITED STATES

The governments of some advanced countries have sought to contrast this tendency or to exploit it in the interests of national capital. The variety of policy choices is wide, but some models, adopted by various governments, can be identified. The "U.S. policy model" and the "German policy model" have the appearance of political tricks,[102] and can be interpreted as reactions to the policies enacted by emerging countries. For this reason, it might be helpful to briefly illustrate a "Chinese policy model," a paradigm followed by many developing countries.

I will deal with the German model in the next section. Here I present the Chinese and American models, which seem to be in a relationship of complementarity, the former aiming to produce a trade surplus, the latter a deficit.

China, like many other emerging countries, used globalization to promote industrial takeoff, but did not trust too much in "free trade" and comparative advantages. By exploiting the rules of the WTO, it used an aggressive commercial competition, mainly based on low wages and weak environmental policies, to export in the North the same goods that were produced by advanced countries. At the same time, in defiance of WTO rules, it used its state-owned multinationals to create exclusive barter relationships in the South. It engaged in bilateral agreements with many emerging and developing countries, offering investments in infrastructures in exchange for raw materials and energy supply, besides political alliance.

The government adopted shrewd industrial policies, by which it created more than 250 great industrial concerns under the supervision of SASAC (State-owned Assets Supervision and Administration Commission), founded in 2003. Then it encouraged the formation of small and medium-size private firms in strategic industries, while it favored the Northern multinationals' foreign direct investments, from which it obtained transfers of technology and organizational capacity. Moreover, China invested massively in scientific and technological research, to the point of overcoming Japan in R&D expenditures.

Industrial policy was backed by a banking system that is almost entirely public-owned. In 2003 80 percent of balance assets in the sector were covered by public firms. The banks, under the supervision of the People's Bank of China, worked to stimulate the birth of new companies and to bail out firms in financial trouble. The four major state-owned banks funded massive investments in infrastructures, agriculture, and export-oriented industries, and a myriad of local commercial and mutual savings banks backed the growth of small firms.

The emerging countries need to maintain low wage regimes to remain competitive and bolster accumulation. If wages are low, aggregate demand cannot be adequately propped up by mass domestic consumption. After all, industrial takeoff requires a high propensity to save. The Chinese savings rate has increased conspicuously over the last twenty years, and especially in the last ten, reaching 53 percent in 2007 (Yang, Zhang, and Zhou, 2011). This extremely high rate was partly determined by cautious fiscal policies, partly by the tendency to redistribute income from wages to profits, and partly by an underdeveloped social welfare system and the resulting worker uncertainty. The liberalization of international trade enabled China and other emerging countries to benefit from export-led growth.[103] Yet the current account surpluses determined by increased exports and sluggish consumption might excessively raise exchange rates, thus impairing competitiveness. To avoid this, the governments implemented smart exchange rate control policies. The desire to prevent currency appreciation, or a too strong appreciation, is a good reason for accumulating dollar reserves

(Costabile, 2009). In any case, the Chinese yuan has been gradually appreciating since 2005.

The model aiming at propping up export-led growth, as enacted by most developing and emerging countries, follows a scheme adopted by China until the full-flowering of the crisis. In the final chapter, I show how it is changing in the present.

Chinese policy model
- Restrictive fiscal policies
- Centrally administered monetary and banking strategies
- Protectionist commercial and industrial policies
- Mercantilist currency policies

Undervaluation of the yuan enabled China to trigger a virtuous circle of accumulation that caused its GDP to grow at double-digit rates. This works as follows. A favorable exchange rate promotes exports, while restraining consumption limits imports. Exports and investments drive aggregate demand, whose high growth brings about continuous productivity improvements.[104] From 1997 to 2010, nominal wages rose rapidly, but so did prices; hence real wages did not increase much. In any case, they rose less than productivity, and labor costs were kept low. This attracted massive flows of foreign direct investments from the multinationals, which brought capital, machinery, organization, and technological know-how that further promoted productivity growth. Finally, capital movements and the banking system were kept under strict state control, so that monetary policy could be used to support industrial policy.

Advanced countries experience the increasing penetration of goods from emerging and developing countries, and would have to endure a permanent current account deficit if they tried to achieve high GDP growth through expansive fiscal policies. Moreover, sustained output growth would raise employment, strengthen trade unions, and inflate wages. This would further feed consumption and output, but also imports. Besides, the higher labor costs would impair profits and competitiveness. The current account deficit would grow, which would cause currency depreciation and inflation.

The United States made a clear political choice in an attempt to contain the depressionary effects of globalization. Governments of either party could not afford stagnation. They sought to prop up growth at any cost in order to perpetuate U.S. imperial domination. They desperately wanted to go on playing the three functions of global central governance: world sheriff, global banker, and driver of growth.

I will address the U.S. loss of economic and political hegemony in the next chapter. Meanwhile, let me just point out that the United States achieved its highest level of economic supremacy in the Bretton Woods system, when the country was the biggest economic power in the world in both production and trade. Afterward, from the last decade of the twentieth century, things changed rapidly. The value of the U.S. GDP is still the greatest in the world, when measured in dollars. It is no longer so when measured in Purchasing Power Parity. In this case its weight in global GDP, which was 27.3 percent in 1950, dropped to 18.6 percent in 2008. In 2010, despite returning to 19.1 percent, it was overtaken by the Chinese (21.8 percent). The U.S. GDP share decreased, especially in comparison to emerging and developing countries. Even stronger is the fall in the international trade share, so much so that in 2013 China overtook the United States as global trader in *goods* (valued in dollars).

This demotion means that the United States will increasingly be unable to perform the role of growth driver. Moreover, because it can no longer use the international trade multiplier of a large economy to lower the external constraint, the United States will find it increasingly difficult to implement expansive fiscal policies autonomously. In the dollar standard era, the external constraint was slackened by the proneness of other countries, especially China, to use their current account surpluses to fund both public and private debt in the United States. This enabled the American government to preserve a certain monetary hegemony and to secure substantial seignorage, but at the cost of losing some of its policy autonomy and hegemony. In fact, the U.S. capacity to perform the function of global banker increasingly depends on the will of the Chinese government. In other words, the longer the United States insists on playing that role, the more it boosts the blackmailing power of China and other emerging countries.

The U.S. ability to perform the two functions of global economic governance was impaired by globalization and its depressionary effects on advanced economies. To tackle this difficulty, U.S. governments tried to force growth by means of a speculative bubble driven by monetary expansion. In this way, American accumulation was still able to drive expansion in China, India, Russia, Brazil, etc. The United States stimulated exports and growth in emerging countries with its current account deficit.[105] At the same time, it provided the money flow needed to sustain the expansion of trade and the accumulation of reserves in the rest of the world. The U.S. interest in this process is evident: as long as the dollar remains the key international currency, the United States maintains seignorage and the ability to consume more than it produces; and as long as U.S. GDP grows, it will be able to expand military expenditure.

Part of U.S. public expenditure was financed with debt, but the budget deficits were insufficient to maintain sustained GDP growth. What was to be done? How could the U.S. governments prop up growth while domestic investments were stagnating due to the multinationals' tendency to offshore? It had to rely on consumption. And how could it encourage an increase in mass consumption while the wage share was tending to shrink? The solution adopted was *debt-led growth*. This was the policy trick with which the United States tried to counteract the depressionary effects of globalization. A strong stimulus to aggregate demand was created through a process of substituting debt accumulation for wage progression.[106]

U.S. debt is composed firstly of the *private debt* of households and firms, especially the debts taken on by the middle class and part of the working class to buy houses, SUVs, and other consumer goods. Secondly, it comprises *public debt*, caused by the massive budget deficit. Thirdly, a significant part of it consists of *foreign debt*, due to the tendency of many emerging countries to reinvest the dollar flows gained through their net exports in American financial assets. Foreign debt also includes debt created by the tendency of international speculators to invest in securities and derivatives issued by U.S. firms and institutions. Expansive monetary policy served to feed all three processes of increasing indebtedness: private debt, by easing bank credit expansion;

public debt, by facilitating debt servicing; foreign debt, by nourishing speculation through reducing the cost of short-term borrowing by speculators. Furthermore, the processes of financial deregulation I described in the preceding chapter helped the expansion of bank business and the financial investment of profits.

Finally, a more or less tacit collusion with China played an important role in ensuring that the mechanism functioned well: besides serving to prevent a dramatic dollar crisis, Chinese portfolio investments also served to prevent domestic monetary expansion in the United States from being fully drained abroad.

In short, the debt-led growth process was governed following the

U.S. policy model
- Expansive fiscal policies
- Expansive monetary policies
- Financial deregulation
- Currency policies in collusion with China

This whole ruse works fairly well, as long as the bubble continues to swell. But it has two weak points. The first is that, sooner or later, all bubbles burst. We have seen and felt the disastrous effects of a maxi-bubble explosion in the center of the global financial system. The second is that the entire trick works as long as the other countries accept dollar seignorage. The present crisis may therefore lead to a breakdown of international political equilibria, as I will argue in the next chapter.

The German Policy Model

The German trick was quite different.[107] To begin with, this country took advantage of the process of the regionalization of European economies, which began with the Common Market. The national governments created, first, a free trade area and, then, a customs union. Subsequently, with the Currency Snake (a system of adjustable fixed exchange rates) (1972) and the European Monetary System's Exchange

Rate Mechanism (1979), they created a fixed exchange rate area that eventually resulted in monetary union. All the EU countries benefited from regionalization, until the creation of the euro.[108]

Continental regionalization seeks to maximize the advantages of free trade by creating an economic zone that is relatively protected from foreign competition, against which member states maintain higher trade barriers. In this way, firms can exploit economies of scale by taking advantage of the expanded market, the relative cultural homogeneity of populations, the common level of education of workforces, integrated continental infrastructures, and convergent legal reforms. Most foreign trade is intra-industry, as countries are endowed with similar industrial structures, and can also increase by virtue of the reduced uncertainty brought about by exchange rate stability. The process should have gone ahead in the common interest of all the countries' capital, giving birth to a true federation endowed with a government capable of using the necessary policy instruments, especially fiscal and monetary, to sustain continental growth. But, following German unification, this country's governments made a different choice, favoring the interests of national capital to the detriment of the European people.

Euroland countries can be divided into two groups: virtuous and non-virtuous.[109] Take, for example, Germany and Italy. The former (virtuous) enjoys high productivity growth because firms invest heavily in R&D. The latter (non-virtuous) could maintain some international competitiveness by resorting to devaluation when necessary, if there were no single currency. If Germany implemented a fiscal policy aimed at full employment and/or permitted the appreciation of the German mark, its current account would tend to balance. The German economy would drive the growth of non-virtuous countries, where, as a consequence, production and productivity would rise. But profits would decrease in Germany, since real wages would be swelled by both currency appreciations and enhanced trade union bargaining power due to increasing industrial employment. This scenario is obviously not relished by German capital.

Nor is it attractive to the ruling classes if they have imperial ambitions. Germany does not want currency depreciation because it is trying to play alongside the United States in its role as global banker. It wants a strong and stable currency, so that an increasing number of emerging and developing countries will be induced to use it as a reserve instrument in the place of the dollar. Yet it does not want too strong a currency, because that would be detrimental to its exports and encourage imports.

Thus a strict alliance emerged between the national bourgeoisie and the ruling class, leading to the adoption of beggar-my-neighbor policies. From this perspective German fiscal policies are aimed at avoiding an excessive rise in employment, to hamper the workers' movement and prevent excessive wage increases. This is a necessary condition for both preserving industrial competition and stabilizing the exchange rate. Wage growth was put under control, while flexibility and the impoverishment of workers increased, so labor costs rose less than in non-virtuous Euroland countries.

As observed by Lapavitsas et al. (2012, 21–27), German beggar-my-neighbor policies are based on a beggar-my-worker strategy. This was implemented between 2002 and 2005 with the "Hartz reforms" (named for Volkswagen's director of personnel who chaired the Kommission für moderne Dienstleistungen am Arbeitsmarkt—the Committee for Modern Services in the Labor Market—founded by the Schröder government in February 2002). The reforms, among other things, compelled unemployed workers to accept "mini-jobs" and "midi-jobs" that paid less than 450 euros a month, and even jobs that paid 1 euro an hour, with the threat of cutting unemployment benefits. Firms do not pay payroll taxes on these wages, with the result that labor costs shrink considerably while labor flexibility rises. So, unwilling to bring about a nominal devaluation of the euro, Germany implemented real depreciation, through which it impoverished her neighbors by impoverishing her workers. "The German 'miracle' rests on a gigantic social dumping" (Blondet, 2012). I will return to this issue below.

One form of real depreciation is based on *wage devaluation*. Restrictive fiscal policies reduce industrial employment and increase workers' fear of losing their jobs. Trade unions are forced to accept wage cuts, worsening labor conditions, and sweeping industrial relations "reforms." The cost of labor falls and domestic inflation drops relative to that of the main international competitors. Exports grow and imports shrink. Another form of real depreciation is based on *fiscal devaluation*.[110] Payroll and business taxes are reduced, and the Value Added Tax and other indirect taxes are raised. Consequently labor costs and real wages fall. The higher VAT is not applied to exported goods, so the relative prices of exports fall. However, it *is* applied to imported goods, so the relative prices of imports increase. In principle, fiscal devaluation does not require domestic deflation, but if workers practice resistance to lower real wages, jobs will need to be cut to prevent the higher prices caused by the raised VAT from being followed by increases in nominal wages, thus defeating fiscal devaluation. In Germany this problem was handled with the Trade Unions' collaboration, and thus real depreciation generated less unemployment and labor hours than in other European countries.

Insofar as they help economic recovery through exports, wage devaluation results in social dumping and fiscal devaluation in fiscal dumping. These two types of policy can be used together in varying proportions, yet both tend to reduce domestic demand. In principle they could work in the long run, but only if practiced by a few governments, while the others sit and watch.

Weak GDP growth in Germany serves to slow down imports on the one hand, and to favor income redistribution from wages to profits on the other. The German governments have chosen to strengthen national capital at home and national currency abroad, through a process of modest export-led growth and an exchange rate that appreciates in international markets but not in Europe.

German trade surpluses have forced the trade balances of southern European countries into deficit. Moreover, Germany has pushed the other European governments toward deflation and a wage and productivity slowdown with its fiscal policy constraints. It seems that a new division of labor is being established, in which the southern (and eastern) countries specialize in low-cost and low-tech production, while Germany takes on the role of lead innovator and its firms seize half of Europe's capital.

Particularly interesting is the role reserved for eastern European countries, which are outside the Monetary Union and enjoy skilled workforces and very low wages. German firms move the production of most intermediate goods to these countries, thus reducing labor costs, then import them to Germany and export the final products at high profits. What's more, this form of decentralized production means that euro appreciation reduces the cost of those intermediate goods and hence does not much impair the international competitiveness of German firms.[111]

In other words, Germany is reducing the other European economies to a domestic imperial market it can dominate with its industrial production. Euroland countries cannot react defensively with devaluation, while eastern countries lose increasing surplus value when the euro appreciates. Some, apparently not without reason, fear a permanent structural dualism, with a shrinkage of industrial production in Southern countries and the acquisition of their capital by German firms, while their workers are forced to migrate to northern Europe (Brancaccio and Passerella, 2012, 89–92). A long time ago, Wynne Godley (1992) had already predicted that the weak nations in the monetary union would enter a "cumulative and terminal decline" until reaching the condition of colonial states.

It is not by chance that the German state is considered a champion of neo-mercantilist imperialism.[112] In the last half-century all German governments, both left and right wing, even those more committed to neoliberalism, have worked to bend the needs of European citizens to the interests of German *national* capital. In this system the imperial state defends *domestic* industry as such, and not as a part of multinational capital.[113] Furthermore, it encourages collaboration between trade unions and capital, especially through the practice of *Mitbestimmung* (codetermination, by which union representatives have some voice in the firms' boards of directors). This is how German governments perform the function of collective national capitalist. Finally, it tries to project itself into the international arena as a global central banker in competition with the United States. The expedient used to reconcile these two objectives is a combination of restrictive fiscal policies and exchange rate stabilization policies.

German governments have always liked fixed exchange rates. They already tried to bind the other European currencies to the German mark in the decades between the fall of the Bretton Woods system and the rise of the European Monetary Union. The problem was that the other countries still had the ability to devalue their own currencies. This obstacle was finally overcome with the single currency. Euro exchange rates depend not only on the German balance of payments, but on the sum of all Euroland countries' balances of payments. Since some of them have current account deficits, the euro does not appreciate as the mark would. In other words, *the euro is a structurally undervalued mark*. This gives Germany a systematic competitive advantage in global and European markets, which allows it to maintain a chronic current account surplus and let its growth be driven by exports. However, GDP growth is limited, as Germany's fiscal policies, aimed at containing wage increases and imports, are generally deflationary. In fact, its GDP grew by 1.07 percent per year in 2001–6 and 1.03 percent per year in 2007–13 (see Table 3). But profits have risen at the expense of wages. From 2000 to 2007, Germany's wage share fell from 65.69 percent to 61.21 percent, much more than in the other main European countries.[114]

Conversely, *the euro is a structurally overvalued lira*. A deficit in the Italian current account is not balanced by markets because the euro does not only depend on the Italian balance of payments. The same situation occurs in other European economies. Italy, France, Spain, and the other non-virtuous countries suffer from a systematic competitive disadvantage in global markets. Worse still, since a large portion of Euroland countries' foreign trade is intra-European, Germany's trade surpluses *cause* the southern European countries' deficits.

During the single currency era the German current account balance has always shown a surplus, and has grown from 2 percent of GDP in 2002 to 5.7 percent in 2010. The same occurred in other virtuous countries. Italy, in contrast, showed an increasing deficit, from –0.1 percent in 2001 to –3.5 percent in 2010. Greece, Spain, Portugal, and Ireland saw the same debacle. France, which is sliding toward the group of non-virtuous countries, had a surplus until 2004 and a deficit in subsequent years (Vernengo and Pérez-Caldentay, 2012, 103).

TABLE 3: Annual Growth Rates of Real GDP (in percent)

	1991–2000	2001	2002	2003	2004	2005	2006
U.S.	3.4	1.1	1.8	2.5	3.5	3.1	2.7
Germany	2.1	1.2	0.0	−0.2	0.7	0.8	3.9
Japan	1.2	0.2	0.3	1.4	2.4	1.3	1.7
China	10.4	8.3	9.1	10.0	10.1	11.3	12.7

	2007	2008	2009	2010	2011	2012	2013
U.S.	1.9	−0.3	−3.5	3.0	1.8	2.8	1.9
Germany	3.4	0.8	−5.1	3.6	3.1	0.9	0.5
Japan	2.2	−1.0	−5.5	4.4	−0.6	1.4	1.7
China	14.2	9.6	9.2	10.4	9.3	7.7	7.7

Source: IMF (2012a; 2014).

It must also be pointed out that German trade surpluses produce money inflows that are then rechanneled by banks into the non-virtuous countries as loans, contributing to financing their trade deficits. In other words, Germany lends money to Italy, Spain, and Greece, with which they buy German goods. In some countries, such as Spain and Ireland, this situation helped to trigger real estate bubbles, which propped up GDP growth, but also a worrying increase in bank leverage and private debt. In others, like Italy, where public debt is fairly high and its yields rather good, banks preferred to invest in public securities rather than in private debt. There were no relevant housing bubbles, but, as a consequence, GDP was not adequately driven by consumption, exports, investment, and public expenditure, and thus experienced limited growth. Productivity was not fed by R&D investments nor pulled by production, so increased very slowly. Industry systematically lost competitiveness, thus worsening the balance of trade.

There is no hope of substantially depreciating the euro with a courageously expansive monetary policy. Until the explosion of the great crisis the ECB, under the Bundesbank's hegemony, demonstrated a clear deflationary vocation, always maintaining higher interest rates than the Fed. As I already observed, in the German policy strategy the euro has to be weaker than a German mark would be, but generally stronger and more stable than the dollar. From this perspective "the euro project" must be seen as "the greatest challenge to the dollar's world hegemony launched to date" (Giacché, 2012a, 23).

Basically, Germany's policy strategy to counter the depressionary effects of globalization *on profits* boils down to the creation of a mercantilist imperial dominion, which, while trying to challenge the United States in the role of global banker, subordinates the whole European economy to German industrial and commercial interests. The result is evident: in the period 2001–13 German GDP grew less than that of the US (1.05 percent yearly, against 1.71 percent) and dragged Europe toward depression. Increasing intra-European divergence in GDP and productivity growth ensued. But, *until the explosion of the euro crisis* Germany's objectives had been achieved: growth in German industrial and banking profits and an appreciation of the euro against the dollar.

In short, the German pattern of (modest) export-led growth was achieved through the simple

German policy model
- Restrictive fiscal policies
- Real depreciation policies
- Restrictive monetary policies
- Euro stabilization policies

THE "MARKETS" THWART POLITICAL SCHEMING

The great crisis of 2007–13 has to be seen as the markets' revenge over politics. The United States' and Germany's outdated imperialist policies produced some economic sins that international speculation eventually brought back to haunt them. It is no coincidence that the crisis has been W-shaped: dip-recovery-dip-recovery. Or that the second dip was triggered in Euroland. In fact, the tragedy has evolved in two acts: the first in the United States, the second in Europe.

The subprime crisis. Speculation gorges on bubbles, but also on the financial crashes that follow them. A downturn can be triggered by any kind of shock at all. Significantly, the subprime crisis was sparked by a monetary policy change in 2007, when the Fed raised the federal funds rate to 6.25 percent. Whatever the motivation—to hold back inflationary impulses, to deflate the speculative bubble, to stop the dollar weakening against the euro—the policy change revealed the difficulty of continuing to use political scheming to counter the effects of globalization on the real economy. With monetary expansion and financial deregulation, all asset prices had become bloated and a monstrous castle of derivatives had been built. These were backed by very risky guarantees, and could only be considered highly profitable so long as the bubble was swelling. Bank profits also grew, but so did leverage and bankruptcy risks.

When the "markets" realized that the roof of the house of cards had been reached, they plunged into bear speculation and made it collapse. They unmasked the policy tricks and brought asset prices back to their fundamentals, thus forcing the authorities to admit their impotence. If no bubble had been blown up, the yearly GDP growth rate in 2001–11 would have been fairly low. Monetary policies and speculation caused it to rise in the boom period, but the crisis turned it negative, so that the average yearly rate for the entire period was low anyway: 1.66 percent. In 1991–2000, in contrast, it had been 3.4 percent.

Ultimately, looking at the long-run effects, the political scheming turned out to be futile and failed to produce the desired growth. Still, the global instability created when the bubble burst decreed the defeat of the U.S. super-imperialist project. Multinational capital was the undisputed winner, as the crisis reduced industrial employment and accelerated the global process of labor cost leveling. The U.S. wage share shrank from 67.70 percent in 2000 to 63.69 percent in 2010.

The euro crisis. The second dip started when, following the 2007–9 crunch, some countries experienced an alarming rise in their debt/ GDP ratio. Speculators began to suspect that these countries would find it difficult to continuously refinance their public debt when GDP was not growing and their current account deficit had become structural. Why did the sovereign debt crisis break out in Euroland, which had an average debt/GDP ratio of 85 percent and a budget deficit/GDP ratio of 6.1 percent, rather than in the United States or Japan, which had higher ratios? For two reasons: one minor and one irreparable.

The first reason was that part of the German political trick consisted of forbidding the ECB to finance European states. Remember that the aim of this rule was to impose a deflationary policy on the monetary authorities to hinder expansive fiscal policies and excessive wage increases on the one hand, and to strengthen the euro against the dollar on the other hand. In contrast, U.S. and Japanese central banks are authorized to act as lenders of last resort to their respective states. This implies that their states cannot default, as they can always monetize their debts. Speculators avoided betting on Japan's default risk despite the fact that its debt/GDP ratio was much higher than the Italian and Greek ratios. Speculating on the depreciation of securities and public debt default in the knowledge that the central bank is always ready to undertake massive purchases implies a very high risk.

This cause of the crisis, however, was not irreparable. The ECB dealt with it by enacting unconventional monetary policies. Between the end of 2011 and the beginning of 2012, it implemented the Securities Markets Program, through which it intervened in secondary markets to block upsurges in security yield spreads (BTP-Bund, Bonos-Bund, etc.). Then, with its long-term refinancing operations, the ECB tried to intervene *indirectly* in primary markets. It lent liquidity to the banks at a low discount rate. The banks used this liquidity partly to rebuild their base money reserves and partly to buy securities at Treasury auctions. In other words, the ECB tried to bypass the prohibition against financing states by conceding finance with the mediation of banks. At the same time, it tried to unburden the banks' positions by preventing further depreciation of their assets. This maneuver was immediately effective, as it temporarily modified the speculators' expectations. When the markets realized that the ECB had the means to prevent a worsening of the *financial* crisis, and that it would not permit a further spread increase, they started to bull. If yield spreads are not allowed to rise, the prices of securities cannot fall. At this point speculation seemed to help overcome the financial crisis. But in March 2012, when the markets realized the depressionary effects of the Italian government's austerity policies and observed the worsening of the Spanish banks' balance sheets, they went back to betting on defaults, and the spreads rose again. In July 2012, the ECB intervened again, this time only with a warning, and declared that it was ready to enact outright monetary transactions, that is, to buy securities without limits. Then bull sentiment returned. Subsequently the spreads continued to fluctuate under a great variety of influences: the Italian general election of February 2013, the discovery of some banks' escapades, the depreciation of the yen, the Fed's monetary policies, and the like.

It remains to be seen whether the ECB will be able to keep intervening in financial markets with policies that Germany deems inflationary and fiscally permissive. What is more, it is unclear whether it will be able to expand the *money* supply. In three years' time the banks will have to return to the ECB the liquidity borrowed through the long-term refinancing operations, even by selling securities, which will inevitably depress the markets. As a matter of fact, by the first quarter of 2013 they had already returned the 60 percent of the borrowed liquidity. In this situation any new base money creation by the ECB will tend to be ineffective in stimulating the real economy. Although the crisis of production has brought about a reduction in investments and firms' credit demand, it has raised their bankruptcy risk. In deep recession firms demand credit almost exclusively to pay circulating capital and cover losses. Therefore banks do not expand lending and tend to return liquidity to the ECB. This results in a combination of a credit crunch and a liquidity trap. Base money creation does not result in bank money expansion, or help to bring down long-term interest rates. We might eventually discover that the ECB's unconventional monetary policies have only served to prolong the agony.

The Central Bank is incapable of tackling the EU's economic malaise at its roots. The basic cause of the crisis has to do with the other German imperialist trick: the euro. Remember that the aim of this ploy was to secure a systematic competitive advantage in global and European markets. Unfortunately, it also gave a systematic disadvantage to southern European countries, which have been condemned to economic stagnation.

When GDP languishes, it is not easy to bring down the debt/GDP ratio, even with an accommodating monetary policy. The governments of Southern Euroland are being driven to continuously enact austerity policies, entangling their economies in three recessive vicious circles:

- An increasing debt/GDP ratio prompts restrictive fiscal policies to reduce the budget deficit, which, however, cause the GDP to decline and hence raise the debt/GDP ratio further.[115]
- Since the euro is an overvalued lira (and franc, peseta, etc.), the international competitiveness of southern Euroland is impaired and exports do not grow enough to raise aggregate demand and output; since domestic demand is also stagnant, GDP does not grow and productivity does not rise to keep down labor costs, resulting in a further loss of competitiveness.
- Current account deficits swell foreign debts; if governments adopt restrictive fiscal policies to reduce imports, they may raise, besides public debt, private debts too (as they trim incomes and savings),[116] and thus raise the default risks of households, banks, and firms, besides public finances. This is the situation in Italy. If, instead, as in Spain, governments try to bail out the banks by socializing losses, they transform part of the private debt into public debt, thus raising the risk of state default; in both cases interest rates rise, discouraging investments; this reduces GDP growth on the one hand, and on the other boosts the cost of debt servicing; ultimately, the debt/GDP ratio increases.

These three vicious circles feed each other. Clearly, to interpret the recession as a mere debt crisis is to touch only the surface of the phenomenon. This is a euro crisis; the single currency is the basic cause of southern Euroland's difficulties. The speculative attack on banks and sovereign debts was only a triggering factor. In the end the crisis will reveal its true nature. When this happens, Germany, too, enters a recession.

The process of transmitting the crisis to the virtuous countries began in mid-2012. In the fourth quarter of 2011, Germany had a slightly negative (quarter-over-quarter) GDP growth (−0.2 percent). In the first three quarters of 2012, taking advantage of a temporary euro depreciation, Germany increased extra-European exports and returned to positive growth rates (0.5 percent, 0.3 percent, 0.2 percent). In the fourth quarter of 2012, dragged down by the Southern European recession, the German GDP plummeted to −0.7 percent (Trading Economics, 2013). Exports pulled less than expected, since the non-virtuous countries' crisis had reduced intra-European trade, and appreciation of the euro[117] had reduced extra-European trade. Moreover, fiscal policy was restrictive (with a 0.1 percent German budget surplus/GDP ratio). Finally, firms' expectations worsened and investments decreased, despite the low cost of money.

In short, 2012 was a year of recession for almost the whole of Europe. The GDP growth rate was negative in all non-virtuous countries, including the UK. In the second half of the year, it also became negative in many virtuous countries. The average growth rate of seventeen Euroland economies was −0.6 percent in 2012. As Europe is an important market for the emerging countries and the United States, the rest of the world underwent a slowdown.

The big advanced economies saw a contraction.[118] The crisis was prolonged in most of 2013, especially in Europe.[119] According to many observers, 2014 will be the year of recovery. Recent data seem to back the *moderate* optimists.

The emerging countries strongly felt the crisis triggered in the economies of the North. All experienced a slowdown in 2012 and 2013, and are unlikely to return to their stunning precrisis growth rates in 2014.[120]

The moral of the story is clear: the "markets" have ultimately thwarted the political tricks with which the German ruling classes sought to bend the effects of globalization to serve the interests of their national industry. The euro crisis marks the defeat of Germany's outdated imperial strategy. And peoples all over of the world are paying for this defeat. In Europe the winner is multinational capital; the crisis will eventually result in an acceleration of the process of labor costs reduction.

7. A Crisis of Transition

The basic political contradiction of capitalism
throughout its history has been that all capitalists have
a common political interest insofar as there's a world class
struggle going on. At the same time, all capitalists are rivals of
all other capitalists.... We have entered a chaotic world.... This
chaotic world situation will now go on for the next twenty or
thirty years. No one controls it, least of all the United States
government. The United States government is adrift
in a situation that it is trying to manage all over the
place and that it will be incapable of managing.
—WALLERSTEIN, 2003

In this chapter I deal with various outdated forms of imperialism
produced by the great states, showing the way in which these made
resistance to the effects of globalization. The United States tried to
perpetuate the post-colonial hegemonic system its leaders built in the
second half of the twentieth century. Meanwhile China, Germany, and
Japan have resorted to a neo-mercantilist type of imperialism, although
the former country seems to be converting to a more advanced form
rather similar to the American. The United States, on the other hand,
is sliding toward mercantilism. I will interpret the present crisis as a
process of overcoming the old forms of imperialism and thus as a crisis
of transition to the fully-fledged global imperialism.

In the process of transition, the contradiction between capital
and state manifests itself on two levels. The first is that of domestic

economic policies. I dealt with these in chapter 4, where I showed that the contradiction takes the form of a contrast between the ambitions of the states' political classes and the interests of multinational capital. To consolidate their own power, the politicians aim to play the role of *national collective capitalist*, and therefore to favor the economic growth needed to build social cohesion. Global capital, on the other hand, by fostering the processes of liberalization and international competition, generates a tendency toward economic depression and the impoverishment of the working classes in advanced countries. In this way it contributes to exacerbating social conflict, thus pushing states to act above all as *social gendarmes*.

However, global capital also needs the great powers to operate in the international arena and fulfill the three functions of central governance: *global sheriff, driver of accumulation*, and *global banker*. In this context the contradiction takes on the form of a contrast between the geopolitical ambitions of the various states' ruling classes and the economic interests of multinational capital. These geopolitical ambitions continually generate inter-state rivalries between the great powers. The economic interests of capital, on the other hand, require the orderly performance of the three functions of governance, the attenuation of interstate rivalries, and the economic and military power of the imperial Center's states to open up markets and discipline the recalcitrant countries of the Periphery. I deal with this second type of contradiction in this chapter.

The United States fulfilled the three functions of central governance quite effectively until the mid-1990s. Then the acceleration in the process of globalization exposed advanced countries to the competition of emerging economies, reducing their capacity to govern the world. Above all, this process eroded the economic bases of U.S. hegemony, slowing its growth, impairing its balance of trade, and reducing the weight and stability of the dollar as an international means of payment.

U.S. governments tried to continue exercising imperial hegemony, compensating for the weaknesses of the real economy by making unrestrained use of the monetary pump. At the same time, the revival of German imperial ambitions and the emergence of Chinese imperial ambitions led to an intensification of interstate rivalries. Both processes contributed to the explosion of the current great crisis. The crisis itself has also exacerbated rivalries among the great powers, as each of them is trying to get out of it by adopting typically mercantilist beggar-my-neighbor policies. Thus in 2012–13, a currency world war broke out that is making its own contribution to deepening the crisis.

It seems difficult to escape from the vicious circle of rivalry-crisis-rivalry without sweeping away the current system of political relations among great powers and creating a new system with differently distributed roles and weights. At the end of this chapter, I will seek to outline the emerging form of the new geopolitical equilibrium and the new system of international payments. For now, it may be useful to take a look at Table 4, which shows the evolution of the weight of the main economies in global production. One can see that in 2010, China for the first time overcame the United States in the share of global GDP. True, these data are contestable, since they are measured in Purchasing Power Parity. If GDP is measured in dollars, quite different results come out, as U. S. output was twice as big as the Chinese in 2011: 15 trillion against 7.3 trillion (Bloomberg, 2013).

In any case, what really counts is the trend. The United States started from a position of absolute predominance, but saw its share systematically shrink until the mid-1970s. It then stabilized, before falling again at the start of the great crisis. Europe's share grew until 1960, when it overtook the United States, then began to shrink and, from the 1980s onward, diminished more rapidly than that of the United States. Japan's share grew steadily until the early 1990s, then shrank abruptly following China's leap ahead. In the era of stormy globalization, all advanced countries have seen their shares decline drastically, while China's has grown spectacularly. Lastly, the crisis that began in 2008 hit advanced countries particularly hard, while boosting China. In the year of recovery (2010) after the first dip of the crisis, the EU and United States regained some of their weight, while China bounded ahead even further.

Even more impressive are the foreign trade data, from which we observe that in 2012 China overcame the United States: the summation of its imports and exports of *goods* reached the figure of $3.87

trillion, whereas that of the United States stood at $3.82 trillion. Of course, these data too are contestable, especially because there may be problems with the measurement methods. Moreover, if one adds the values of trade in services, the United States is still ahead (Bloomberg, 2013). Yet again, what really counts is the trend.

There is no doubt that China is rapidly progressing and that the moment when it will overcome all the advanced countries both in production and trade is not far away. Clearly, the balance of powers in international relations will have to change.

THE UPS AND DOWNS OF U.S. HEGEMONY

U.S. imperialism reached its apex in the Bretton Woods era after the United States had destroyed Europe and Japan as colonial powers. Encouraging the processes of decolonization, U.S. governments established relationships of alliance and dependence with former European and Japanese colonies, as well as with the former colonialists, and imposed upon two-thirds of the world a Pax Americana based on a post-colonial type of imperial power.

This hegemony was built on a series of *supremacy* factors:

- *Production.* U.S. industry emerged from the war strengthened, and producing almost a third of global GDP;
- *Technology.* The United States was the unrivaled leader of innovation and its industry was consequently highly competitive, despite the high wages;
- *Organization.* U.S. firms adopted advanced organizational and management models that allowed them to take advantage of significant economies of scale; as they grew, they expanded into international markets through foreign direct investments; in the 1950s and 1960s most multinationals were American;
- *Trade.* The competitiveness of U.S. firms also allowed them to expand through exports; in 1948 the United States enjoyed a 25 percent share of world trade;

TABLE 4: Percentage of Global GDP*

	1950	1955	1960	1965	1970	1975	1980
U.S.	27.3	26.5	24.3	24.2	22.4	21.1	21.1
EU12[†]	24.1	24.4	24.7	24.4	23.6	22.3	21.4
Japan	3.0	3.6	4.4	5.4	7.4	7.6	7.8
China	4.5	5.1	5.2	4.7	4.6	4.8	5.2

	1985	1990	1995	2000	2005	2008	2010
U.S.	21.5	21.4	21.2	21.9	20.0	18.6	19.1
EU12	20.2	19.4	18.5	17.8	15.5	14.5	14.8
Japan	8.1	8.5	8.1	7.2	6.2	5.7	5.7
China	6.9	7.8	11.1	11.8	16.2	17.5	21.8

* GDP values in purchasing power parity.
† EU12=Austria, Belgium, Denmark, Finland, France, Germany, Italy, The Netherlands, Norway, Sweden, Switzerland, and the United Kingdom.
Source: Maddison (2010) and Maddison Project (2013).

- *Finance.* U.S. financial markets were the most developed in the world, the top ten banks were American, and the dollar was the key international currency;
- *Energy.* The United States boasted its own enormous oil reserves, while the "Seven Sisters" controlled 96 percent of world production
- *Culture.* U.S. universities and the U.S. culture industry were the best in the world and contributed to propagating the "American way of life" worldwide;
- *Ideology.* Partly due to its constitutional imperial hubris, the United States set itself up as the champion of liberalism and induced all the nations of the empire to adopt free trade policies, through democracy, where possible, or by other means;
- *Military.* Needless to say.

Trade supremacy allowed the United States to exploit the international trade multiplier of a large economy. In chapters 4 and 6 I explained how this advantage afforded U.S. governments a high degree of economic policy autonomy. In a big economy the international trade multiplier weakens external constraints on fiscal policies, because increased imports due to expansive policies generate greater exports and higher GDP in other industrialized countries. The resulting increase in those countries' imports boosts U.S. exports. This advantage is what allowed the country to fulfill the function of *driver of global accumulation* effectively: its ability to grow without significant external constraints enabled the main European and Asian countries to launch export-led growth processes.

The Bretton Woods agreements, with the gold exchange standard, made the dollar the key reserve currency and awarded the United States the role of *global banker*. Substantial government aid and the flourishing foreign investments of U.S. firms ensured that the international currency expanded to sustain an increasing volume of global transactions. The United States enjoyed monetary seignorage, which allowed for still weaker external constraints, even beyond the limits of the international trade multiplier of a large economy. It also allowed U.S. citizens to live beyond their means, maintaining a long-lasting balance of payments deficit.

Finally, economic growth brought rising tax revenues and, with them, the possibility of funding the enormous military expenditure necessary to maintain imperial order. This helped the United States to fulfill the role of *global sheriff* effectively, and provided capitalists the world over with a fundamental public good in the form of military security.

In short, U.S. hegemony in the golden age of capitalism (1950–70) was based on an economic supremacy that allowed U.S. governments to pursue expansive policies on military, industrial, and currency fronts, so that each sustained the other in a virtuous circle of escalating power without precedent in human history.

However, this hegemony was not destined to last. It began to show signs of weakness in the 1970s, when several of the supremacy factors began to crumble. Economic growth in the golden age had enabled the main countries of the North of the world to reduce their economic gap with the United States. The productivity gap was initially reduced thanks to technology transfers from U.S. firms, and subsequently through growing investments in R&D by the big European and Japanese firms, many of which became multinationals during the 1970s. These firms generated a significant flow of direct investments toward the United States, but they also managed to gain sizable shares of international trade by competing aggressively with U.S. exports. By 1970, the U.S. share of international trade had shrunk to 10 percent (it was 25 percent in 1948). What is more, due to the high growth rates of industrialized countries, which had exceeded that of the United States for two decades, the U.S. share of global GDP (measured in PPP) shrank to 22.4 percent in 1970 and 21.4 percent in 1990. It was 27.3 percent in 1950.

In the 1970s the Bretton Woods system collapsed. The cost of the Vietnam War had increased public expenditure and the money supply in the United States. The balance of payments and current account showed significant deficits, which were accompanied by a substantial outflow of financial assets. Moreover, the expansion of European financial markets in the previous decade had led to the formation of the eurodollar market. The growing supply of eurodollars and the Federal Reserve's expansive monetary policies generated such a severe *dollar glut* that the gold coverage of the U.S. currency fell from 55 percent to 22 percent. The dollar was subjected to downward pressures. In May 1971 Germany refused to revalue its currency, but the dollar dropped 7.5 percent anyway. Nonetheless, it remained overvalued against the market price of gold. Faced with the risk of a drastic devaluation of dollar reserves, and in view of an opportunity for speculative gains (by selling on the market gold obtained from the Federal Reserve), several countries demanded redemption of their dollars for gold. By July 1971 France had claimed the redemption of $191 million and Switzerland $50 million. The situation had become unsustainable. On August 15, President Nixon issued Executive Order 11615, with which he declared (besides a 10 percent increase in tariffs, and a wage and price freeze) the inconvertibility of the dollar: the gold exchange standard ceased to exist. By March 1973 most industrialized countries had given up fixed exchange rates.

This was an unprecedented slap in the face for U.S. prestige. Yet it did not definitively reduce its monetary supremacy. In fact, after the initial shock, it led to the establishment of the dollar standard and, with it, the fully-fledged hegemony of the dollar. I will come back to this later.

But the United States endured even greater humiliation with the Vietnam War, and for two reasons. One, because it suffered the first great military defeat in its history, and two, because the war provoked global resentment toward the United States and prompted a protest movement with strong anticapitalist implications. U.S. military and ideological supremacy were both damaged, and its hegemonic powers diminished (Wallerstein, 2003; Hoffman, 2009).

It should also be recalled that the formation of OPEC resulted in a loss of energy supremacy, as the 1970s oil shocks demonstrated to the whole world. Add to this that European and Japanese multinational capital emerged in the 1970s and 1980s and the U.S. share of international trade shrank considerably, and it is easy to understand why many observers began to glimpse the beginning of the end of U.S. imperialism. Many Marxist-Leninists were already celebrating the return of irreconcilable inter-imperial contradictions and dreaming of their violent explosion.

However, an unexpected turn of events occurred toward the end of the 1980s and in the early 1990s, when ultra-conservative U.S. governments began to fight back. With the Plaza Accord, they forced Japan and Germany to accept a sizable dollar depreciation, under the threat of raising trade barriers. The U.S. economy recovered, while European economies, and especially the Japanese, entered a long phase of depression. Japan's subsequent "lost decade" was only the start of this.

Moreover, with the triumph of the Washington Consensus toward the end of the 1980s, the free trade ideology was taken to extremes and the United States became its uncontested champion. A first significant effect was the liberalization of capital movements and acceleration of the financialization of global markets. The U.S. currency, which was already the denominator of crude oil prices and the most used means of financial transactions, gained strength as an international reserve currency, bringing about a new dollar hegemony (Gabriel, 2000; Liu, 2002).

Then the Soviet empire collapsed. The system of international relations suddenly became unipolar and the United States appeared to have
gained absolute control of the world. For a moment U.S. hegemony
seemed to have reached its apex. By the way, this is when the theories of
super-imperialism emerged. But it turned out to be short-lived.

Toward the mid-1990s globalization exploded with its maximum
intensity and emerging countries broke onto the world economic stage
with unprecedented trade aggressiveness. The advanced countries felt
the blow and entered a depressionary phase from which they have not
yet escaped. The U.S. economy was also hit by competition from emerging countries, and all its factors of economic supremacy crumbled.

At the same time, U.S. control over energy resources weakened significantly. Nowadays Russia is the biggest producer of crude oil and
natural gas, the United States having been relegated to third place.
Worse still, the United States has lost political control over the majority of hydrocarbon producing countries: not only Russia, but also Iran,
China, Venezuela, and other OPEC countries.[121]

American cultural and ideological hegemony has also been questioned by both the left and right wings the world over: from the
anti-globalization movement to religious fundamentalists. The United
States still leads the world in technological innovation, especially in
frontier research, such as biotechnology and nanotechnology, but nowadays knowledge spreads very fast and various emerging countries, led
by China, as well as Japan and Germany, have been investing heavily in
research, so that this factor of U.S. supremacy is also being gradually
eroded (Pape, 2009; Zakaria, 2009).

The U.S. share of global GDP and trade then shrank even further.
The balance of payments settled with a large deficit, which became
structural, and what was formerly the world's biggest lender became the
biggest borrower nation (Pietroburgo, 2009). The channels through
which the Federal Reserve provides the world with international currency have changed over the decades. Between 1958 and 1971, with
the exception of two years (1968–69), the United States ran a balance
of payments deficit, but from 1950 to 1970 it also maintained a current account surplus. This means that it produced international money

through capital movement. Today the situation has turned around.
A structural current account deficit, accompanied by a net inflow of
short-term capital, mean that the Federal Reserve supplies the world
with money by virtue of the American tendency to consume more than
is produced.

The United States has reacted to this state of affairs with revived
military activism, which has served to reaffirm a certain degree of hard
hegemony, but has also led to excessive growth in its public and private
foreign debt. Similarly, the unrestrained use of the monetary pump may
have served to back growth for a few years, but has ultimately exacerbated the difficulties. As I argued in chapters 5 and 6, this type of policy
contributed to blowing up the speculative bubble that burst at the start
of the current crisis. I doubt that the United States will be capable of
emerging from this crisis with a strong and long-lasting revival of accumulation and a full return to economic hegemony.

THE UNITED STATES AND CHINA: AN ARMED FRIENDSHIP

I mentioned above that the dollar's hegemony over currency markets
is not justified by a real predominance of U.S. trade. Instead it is based
on a collusion between the United States and China, the continuation
of which now depends more on the will of Chinese leaders than on
the strength of the U.S. economy. This collusion is not the result of an
international treaty or policies agreed between governments; instead it
has the form of a symbiotic exchange that lasts as long as it is advantageous to both parties.[122] This is how it works. China, benefiting from an
undervalued yuan, has obtained a current account surplus and a glut
of savings and foreign reserves. It has used these reserves for portfolio
investments in U.S. assets, thus contributing to funding consumption,
public expenditure, and the U.S. current account deficit, and to inflat-
ing the speculative bubble. On their part, U.S. multinationals have used
some of the profits produced by the bubble to make significant direct
investments in China, which has helped boost Chinese production,
productivity growth, and exports.

This symbiotic exchange is not without frictions, especially concerning currency policies. It is a "complex relationship of economic interdependence" (Callinicos, 2006, 128), a sort of conflicting collusion, but it has undoubtedly worked well in sustaining the speculative bubble. It is also part of the implicit pact I talked about at the beginning of chapter 5: the collusion upon which global imperialism is based, between the big capital of the North and the capital of Peripheral countries. China and the United States appear as the protagonists on the political front, but in reality various other emerging countries are involved. These nations see China as the forerunner of a development process that could change the balance of powers between continental political blocs. As such, the collusion is intrinsically unstable.

Before the great crisis broke out the hegemony of the U.S. currency was threatened by the euro. The dollar's share of global reserves had shrunk by 1 percent per year from 2000. At that time it was 71 percent, dipping to 62 percent in 2010. In contrast, the euro's share, which was 18 percent in 2000, rose to 28 percent in 2009. Until April 2008 the value of the euro was gaining against the dollar, reaching a peak rate of 1.591 dollars. But then the crisis caused a fluctuation in the euro, reducing its attractiveness. What's more, a substantial increase in the quantity of international euro reserves is held back by Germany's deflationist vocation, the low growth rates of European economies, and the not particularly audacious policies of the ECB. Following the crisis, the percentage of world reserves in euros has been gradually shrinking, passing to 25.1 percent in 2012 and 24.2 in the third quarter of 2013 (IMF, 2013). In any case, the euro is no longer a dangerous competitor for the dollar, as its stability is not certain, given the European economies' dire performance during the second dip of the crisis.

The most serious threats may come from elsewhere because a more alarming dollar competitor is emerging: the yuan. According to SWIFT (2013), in January 2012 the dollar weighted 85 percent in global trade finance, the euro 7.86 percent, and the yuan 1.89. In October 2013 things changed remarkably: the dollar was at 81 percent, the yuan at 8.66 percent, and the euro at 6.64 percent.

U.S. economic leadership is starting to be contested by emerging countries, which have accumulated massive quantities of dollar assets. Bear in mind that for a long time the U.S. balance of payments has had a structural deficit in the current account, partly balanced by portfolio capital inflows, a situation that would make the dollar rather vulnerable to speculation. If the value of the dollar depended on market forces alone, it would probably have already experienced a dramatic crisis when the subprime bubble burst. The exacerbating effect on the crash is easily imaginable. This did not happen because the system of payments based on the dollar standard withstood the blow thanks to the symbiotic exchange along the Washington-Beijing axis.

After the American government began a gradual dollar devaluation in 2009, some observers conjectured that the United States and China were working on stabilizing their currencies. Depreciation is good for U.S. capital, as domestic growth can be relaunched at least partially through an export revival. Stabilization is more advantageous for the Chinese, for various reasons. Firstly, because a catastrophic fall of the dollar, apart from drastically reducing the competitiveness of Chinese exports, would devalue the enormous mass of dollar assets held by China.[123] A slow and moderate decline, followed by stabilization, would allow China to restructure its reserves and portfolio investments gradually and without high costs. In fact a tendency to sell dollar assets and substitute them with gold and other financial assets, especially in euros, emerged in recent years. This tendency would also help China in its plan to complement or substitute the dollar with a global currency in the form of special drawing rights issued by an IMF in which China would occupy a stronger position. Chinese leaders put forward such a proposal during the G20 meeting held in London in March 2009.

Meanwhile the real economies of both countries are undergoing profound changes. Following the U.S. production crisis its imports declined in 2008 and with them the U.S. role as growth driver in emerging countries. The dollar depreciation that began in the same year also made U.S. goods more competitive. Imports began to grow again in 2010, but exports grew more. Obama's expansive policies have sought to relaunch the U.S. economy and reaffirm its role as the driver of world growth, but the European crisis has reduced their effectiveness and threatens to condemn this attempt at hegemonic reassertion to failure.

On its part, China cannot afford to be caught up in the crisis for reasons of internal political stability. The opposition of democratic groups and unrest among farmers will only remain manageable as long as the government can count on the consensus of the middle classes and the patience of the working class, which are ensured by economic growth. A significant increase in unemployment would have catastrophic political effects. The People's Bank of China has calculated that a GDP growth rate of at least 8 percent is needed in order to create twenty million new jobs each year for people migrating from the countryside to cities.[124] The government has consequently reacted to the first signs of crisis with $600 billion of public expenditure on investments and social services, and with a $2.5 trillion stimulus package between 2008 and 2009. The People's Bank of China, on its own part, enacted an expansive monetary policy that fed investment growth. In contrast to the collapsing advanced economies, in 2008, 2009, and 2011 Chinese GDP grew by 9 percent, 8.5 percent, and 9.2 percent, respectively. China's growth model would appear to have undergone an impressive conversion from export-led to self-sustained.[125] Imports have also increased, to the extent that in 2008 the emerging countries' exports toward China exceeded those toward the United States. In short, China could potentially replace or flank the United States as driver of global accumulation. But much has yet to be done before it can fulfill this function well (Yongnian, 2010). Due to its low wages, China is not yet capable of driving global demand with an increase in its domestic consumption. Neither is its trade share sufficient to allow it to benefit from the international trade multiplier of a large economy to alleviate external constraints on fiscal policies. Least of all can it turn the yuan into a reserve currency capable of keeping up with the dollar and euro.

The second dip of the crisis has also aggravated China's problems, as Europe is its greatest export market. In 2012 and 2013 China's GDP growth rate was 7.7 percent, below the threshold for political and social stability. In reality, the whole world has seen a slowdown in growth.

Global trade grew by 2.7 percent in both years (compared to 5.9 percent in 2011) and global GDP by 3.1 and 3 percent in 2012 and 2013 (against 3.9 percent in 2011)); emerging and developing countries' GDP grew by 4.9 and 4.7 percent (compared to 6.3 percent in 2011); and that of advanced countries by 1.4 and 1.3 percent (against 1.6 percent in 2011) (IMF, 2014).

At any rate, China has persisted in a policy of slow and orderly revaluation of the yuan against the dollar.[126] As a matter of fact, expansive monetary policies helped prevent an excessive revaluation caused by current account surpluses. Within a policy of domestic demand expansion, aimed at contrasting the effects of the slowdown in world trade, currency revaluation serves various purposes: to control inflationary pressures by cutting the cost of imported raw materials and intermediate goods, especially energy and food; to favor a rebalancing of production from tradable to nontradable goods; to bolster the prestige of the yuan in view of a future reshuffling of the international payment system. In this way China meets U.S. wishes and reinforces the symbiotic exchange between the two countries while taking a more authoritative and less opportunistic position than in the past.

The strengthening of the yuan's prestige aims at favoring its circulation in offshore markets, which had been hampered by the currency control policies of the People's Bank of China. In 2009, a process of liberalization of the foreign exchange market was launched, which, although still imposing some control, enabled companies to freely exchange foreign currencies with the yuan, beginning in 2012. Furthermore, the monetary authorities, to promote the use of the yuan as a means of international payment, signed a series of currency swap agreements with the central banks of various commercial partners, like the United Kingdom, the European Union, Hong Kong, South Korea, Brazil, Turkey, and others. Then they made an agreement with the BRICS to establish an international development bank different from the World Bank. This agreement establishes that 50 percent of the exchanges are not paid in dollars. Finally, China has recently bought oil from Iran and Russia, paying for it in yuan, and it seems to intend to carry on with this policy. One can understand why, as noted previously, the share of the

Chinese currency in global trade finance has grown rapidly. In 2013, it jumped to second place, overcoming the euro share (8.66 percent against 6.64 percent).

However, it is possible that the Chinese economy will fail to react to the present economic slowdown in the advanced countries and to their depreciation policies. Worse still, it might precipitate into a crisis, thus triggering a third global dip, possibly together with Japan. Several signals are worth noticing, starting with the worsening of the Chinese entrepreneurs' expectations, which helped trigger the "black Thursday" on the Tokyo stock exchange on May 23, 2013. Exports are decreasing and excess capacity rising—a clear sign that industrial demand is not pulling the economy forward. The government has fixed a target of 7.5 percent GDP growth for 2014. If this were achieved, it would be the lowest since 1990 anyway, but many observers surmise that 7 percent is more realistic, an alarmingly low rate for political stability.

Moreover, the production and prices of real estate are rising more than the demand. In Beijing alone, 3.81 million homes were vacant in 2012 (one million more than in the whole United States). This unprecedented housing bubble could burst at any moment. And banks, with their balance sheets overloaded by bad loans, are already bearing the consequences. Firms and local authorities are pressing them for loan extension, while corporate delinquencies are rising.

Besides, monetary policy is becoming restrictive. In June 2013 the People's Bank of China invited banks to reduce financial leverage and cut credit to firms with excess capacity, and declared that it had no intention to provide new liquidity. One aim was to discourage speculative uses of money, which state-controlled firms are especially fond of. Another was to curb a financial bubble propped up by a shadow banking system whose value had reached 55 percent of GDP. Still another was to put the brakes on inflationary pressures. A negative effect immediately surfaced in the interbank market. In late June the overnight interest rate jumped to 28 percent. This hazardous policy may well result in an onerous goal: if true monetary restriction comes about, the financial and housing bubble, rather than slowing down, could burst. Banks are full of bad debt. Industrial companies and local administrations are heavily indebted. New credit is demanded just to serve outstanding debt. And some alarming cases of bankruptcies and defaults have already occurred. This is why the People's Bank of China, in December 2013, seemed to be reconsidering its intentions to restrict credit, and returning to a policy of injecting abundant liquidity, after the interbank rate of interest had again jumped (10 percent).

There are important novelties in foreign policy too. The Communist Party's new general secretary, Xi Jinping, seems intent on changing China's strategy. Immediately after his election, he visited Russia, where he signed important trade agreements for the purchase of natural gas, Su-35 fighter jets, and Lada-class submarines. He is evidently strengthening diplomatic ties with Russia, while resuming the increase in military expenditure. His second visit was to Africa, not only to participate in a BRICS (Brazil, Russia, India, China, South Africa) summit. Subsequently he visited India and Pakistan. Now that advanced countries can no longer provide adequate stimulation for Chinese exports, it is easy to see that Xi Jinping wants to redirect trade toward emerging and developing countries, with which both exports and imports have expanded. In short, it seems that China is compelled by the crisis to stand for the economic and political leadership of a bloc of formerly Peripheral countries, which now want to adjust the balance of powers with the former imperial Center. But it is doubtful it can succeed if a third crisis dip bursts and social and political instability mounts.

THE DIFFICULTIES OF EUROPE AND JAPAN

Germany's policy in the current euro crisis seems to exacerbate the difficulties of the world economy rather than help to resolve them. Not only has Germany opposed the ECB's expansive monetary policies, doled out its contributions to the European Stability Mechanism (ESM) and the European budget grudgingly, and applauded the restrictive maneuvers of the other European governments. It has also imposed upon EU countries a "crazy" fiscal compact that could condemn Euroland to stagnation for the next twenty-five years at least. I have put "crazy" in quotation marks because there is a possibility that behind Germany's apparent stupidity[127] lies a well-defined political strategy, if not a "trap shrewdly created after a long preparation" (Amoroso and Jespersen, 2012, 52). I will return to this issue.

Nobody can make reliable predictions in a situation as chaotic as this. But it is easy to foresee that Euroland will not emerge from the current crisis with an appreciable economic recovery that will relaunch growth. Unless a radical political change takes place, the European economy will probably enter either a protracted depression or a profound crisis.

The first possibility, involving a long period with very low growth rates, may occur if the ECB, the ESM, and the Banking Union are capable of avoiding the precipitation of a default emergency in Italy and Spain and preventing a continental banking crisis. If the debt/GDP ratios stabilize and bank bankruptcies are avoided, the fiscal maneuvers may not be too restrictive. But neither will they be expansionary. The deflationary commitments imposed by the fiscal compact will be suspended in times of recession but activated in times of recovery, so that phases of prosperity will be short and stifled. As the fiscal compact provides for the reduction of the debt/GDP ratio to 60 percent over twenty years from 2014, it is easy to imagine how long the depression will last.

If this happens, the German dream of gaining political power as a consequence of its economic strength is condemned to failure. Perhaps *Europe is destined to become increasingly relegated to a corner of the world chessboard.*

The second possibility, of a profound and devastating crisis, would seem to correspond to very specific class interests. We can glimpse the sense of these interests from Mario Monti's uncontainable rise. As soon as he became the president of the Italian government, the banks' man of the moment enacted a restrictive fiscal maneuver that exacerbated the recession in Italy, to the delight of the whole global neoliberal circus. The excuse was to prevent a debt default, but in reality his plan was to trigger a deep crisis so as to justify a shock therapy and introduce the "structural reforms" needed to cure European economies of the problems created by globalization.[128] These problems are caused by competition from emerging countries in goods and capital markets, which is fueled by low wages and high levels of exploitation, as well as by low tax burdens and weak regulations for multinational firms. As I explained in chapters 2 and 3, in the long run global markets will tend to level out conditions of exploitation, meaning lower labor costs in the North, shrunken welfare states, and weakened civil rights and legal safeguards for workers.

If it were to take place in the smoothest and least painful way possible, this process of leveling out would be a very long one, possibly taking decades. As demonstrated by Naomi Klein (2007), a catastrophic crisis can serve to administer the shock therapy needed to accelerate the process. This has happened with almost all the crises of globalization. The "markets" trigger a recession, after which (and sometimes even before) the Chicago boys come on the scene and implement the necessary "structural reforms." When direct, indirect, and deferred wages have been cut, when the trade unions are on their knees, when poverty and unemployment are rife, when all this has been achieved to such an extent that workers are forced to accept capital's autocracy without a word of complaint, European goods might be able to compete with Chinese goods.

Economists call this *real depreciation*. Not being able to recover international competitiveness by devaluing the lira, franc, or peseta, attempts are made to achieve the same effect through policies aimed at cutting the prices of exports and raising those of imports. These policies have been and are being implemented by various countries in Europe. Germany started with the "Hartz reforms" in 2002–2005, extended once in 2007, and again in 2013.[129] Italy, France, and Spain did it heavily in 2012 and 2013. As I will argue later on, real depreciation policies are ineffective in relaunching growth precisely because they are practiced by several countries in competition with each other, and consequently result in deeper and more widespread crises. However, they are very effective in redistributing income from wages to profits and in reducing labor costs.

If the crisis continues to deepen and spread, it might lead to the demise of the euro and the formation of two distinct eurozones (northern and southern) with two separate currencies. This would allow the southern countries to reinforce the effects of real depreciation through nominal devaluation, which, by further impoverishing workers, would serve to relaunch international competitiveness. Thus advanced countries could accelerate the process of leveling out labor costs.

A profound crisis can achieve this leveling effect in three to four years, rather than thirty to forty. From this viewpoint Mario Monti's maneuvers and "reforms" in Italy, and the attempts at imitation promptly introduced in other European countries, acquire some sense. Besides enacting various budget maneuvers to reduce public expenditure and taxation on firms while increasing workers' and consumers' taxes, Monti's government sought to pass a labor reform. This was done following an explicit suggestion from the European Commission, the ECB, and the OECD, and an implicit mandate from the markets. The "bank's man" would appear to be the leader of the Italian Chicago boys.[130]

From this viewpoint it becomes clear that the governments of the various European states are effectively no longer working for "national interests," and not even for German interests, but for those of big multinational capital. Real depreciation would be good news not only for European multinationals, but also U.S., Japanese and Chinese multinationals investing in Europe. There is no need to suppose that the Hydra is acting as if she had a single head, or a single lobby pursuing her aims. She works through the hundreds of thousands of independent heads writhing about in the "markets." Through the crisis, these heads let governments know what needs to be done to bring the economic system and social relations into equilibrium and reignite accumulation.

Ultimately, we will find that *the political ploys with which Germany has sought to promote the imperial interests of its national bourgeoisie have been twisted by the markets to serve the interests of big multinational capital.*

If Europe managed to emerge from a catastrophic crisis with renewed growth and launch a process of real convergence of its national economies, it may not be condemned to marginalization in the international political arena. I am talking of Europe as such, not as a periphery of Germany. The current crisis, with its neutralizing effects on Germany's old-fashioned imperial policies, is demonstrating that no single European country can counter the discipline imposed by multinational capital through its markets.

A strong recovery in Europe is improbable. Prolonged depression is more likely. However, if growth were to begin anew, it may follow a shock therapy and a euro breakup: two changes that would help create the conditions for a revival of growth based on a drastic increase in labor exploitation.

Finally, a few words on Japan. Its decline began in the late 1980s following the Plaza Accord which, by imposing a marked revaluation of the yen, reduced the competitiveness of Japanese goods, weakened its exports and dragged its economy toward stagnation. In the early 1990s a Japanese speculative bubble burst and triggered a recession. The situation then worsened due to the consolidation of neoliberal ideology in Japan too, and the adoption of a policy scheme similar to the "German policy model." Consumption taxes rose dramatically in 1997, resulting in a deep recession, with four years of negative GDP growth. This period is looked back upon as a "lost decade" (1991–2000), but globalization and the competitive aggressiveness of China and the Asian tigers have prolonged that decade to 2012.

A nationalist reaction came in late 2012, with the election of Prime Minister Shinzō Abe, who launched "Abenomics." This strategy rejects monetarist dogmas and relies on a strongly neo-Keynesian program to reinvigorate aggregate demand: expansive monetary and fiscal policies, and desperate currency devaluation without fearing inflation. Public expenditure is supposed to rise by 2 percent a year, while the deficit/GDP ratio will grow to over 11 percent (it was 3 percent in 2008). The Bank of Japan will buy public securities without restraints. The discount rate will be negative. Real wages will be heavily downsized, not only through the yen devaluation, but also with consumption tax hikes of 8 percent in 2014 and 10 percent in 2015.

It seems that some expansive effects materialized immediately. From July 24, 2012, and December 30, 2013, the yen devalued against the dollar by 34.2 percent. The GDP growth rate jumped by 1.7 percent in 2013. Were all Japan's problems solved? I think not.

The strong yen devaluation irritated all the competitor governments and unleashed a currency world war, the effetcs of which nobody can predict. The real wage cuts will slow down imports and might have a global recessionary effect. If wages, consumption, and imports are also reduced in other countries, Japanese exports will not grow much and will not produce all the desired expansive effects. Moreover, if the Bank of Japan continuously intervenes to finance the public budget and keep interest rates down, capital flight might ensue. If instead capital outflow is to be prevented, nominal interest rates will have to be raised. The value of securities will shrink and the banks will be faced with mark-to-market losses. A crisis could be triggered in the financial markets.

A first sign of possible negative backlashes materialized on May 22, 2013, when Ben Bernanke announced that the Federal Reserve is contemplating a policy of tapering. Then came the news that expectations for Chinese industrial production were rather gloomy. Thus on May 23 the Tokyo stock exchange tumbled by –7.32 percent. Other advanced countries immediately reacted with stock exchange drops of –2 to –3 percent. On May 27 and 30, there were two more plunges of the Nikkei 225 index: –3.73 percent and –4.23 percent. Between May 23 and June 13, it had fallen by –20.36 percent. Then there was a rise until June 23, and a new fall in July 25. In any case, as a consequence of strongly expansive monetary policy, the Nikkei index grew in 2013 by 56.7 percent, though the strong oscillations signal a remarkable instability, so much so that some are fearing a third dip of the crisis. Could the world crisis be not W-shaped, but VVV?

I doubt that Abenomics will succeed in reviving the fortunes of Japanese mercantilist imperialism. The yen is losing value and prestige as an international reserve instrument. And Japan, like Europe, may be doomed to be sidestepped in the system of international relations.

Be that as it may, one effect is certain: the redistribution of income from wages to profits. The crisis and its national policy "solution" will accelerate the process of leveling out labor costs in Japan too. Ultimately, the markets will succeed in bending even Keynesian national policies (when they are not supported by fixed exchange rates and the control of capital movements) to serve the interests of multinational capital.

A Currency World War

In 2012, a world war of competitive devaluations and deflations broke out, in which the principal advanced countries have been particularly bellicose. The United States, the UK, and Japan have adopted highly expansive monetary policies, thus trying to devalue their own currencies. These monetary policies brought about inflows of portfolio investments to Europe, which have helped to sustain financial speculation, but have also eased a revaluation of the euro against the yen (by 53.25 percent between July 24, 2012 and December 30, 2013) and the dollar (8.55 percent).

Euroland has pursued a policy of real depreciation. As a large portion of all European countries' exports remain within Europe, and as none of these countries can devalue their own nominal exchange rate, they have all adopted policies of competitive deflation. Unfortunately, the reduction in labor costs they all achieve in this way does not contribute to relaunching significant exports, as everyone's imports have declined. It is true that current account balances have improved. This is thanks to the reduction in imports, especially in countries such as Italy, which have more restrictive fiscal policies. But another consequence is that the euro is not being devalued, thus facilitating dollar, pound, and yen devaluation policies. The ECB's "quasi-German" monetary policy has exacerbated the difficulty. It is a moderately but not markedly expansive policy and keeps EU interest rates low yet systematically higher than U.S. and Japanese rates. Thus the extra-European competitive advantages obtained by Euroland countries through real depreciation are cancelled out by the nominal appreciation of the euro. As a consequence, extra-European exports do not provide sufficient drive. This has contributed to deepening the crisis, to the point that in the last quarter of 2012 Germany too entered a recession, and the entire Euroland contracted its GDP by −0.7 percent in 2012 and −0.4 percent in 2013.

The currency world war raged with full virulence in the fourth quarter of 2012, had a turning point in May 2013, and perhaps will cease in 2014, if the Fed monetary policy becomes less expansive. To understand what happened, let's observe the exchange rate movements between September 2012 and the end of 2013. The most important countries involved in this war can be divided into two groups.

To the first group belong the United States, Euroland, Japan, and the United Kingdom. The United States has been gradually devaluing the dollar against the yuan since 2005, and more markedly since the subprime crisis. Devaluation stopped on May 22, 2013, when Ben Bernanke declared his intention to give up quantitative easing and start a long period of tapering. There was another devaluation jump in October, after Ben Bernanke declared he was planning to postpone tapering to better times. Then the dollar-yuan exchange rate seemed to settle in December 2013, when Bernanke announced the launching of a moderate tapering in the new year. The euro went on revaluating against the dollar up to January 2013, when devalued for three months subsequently it recovered a revaluation trend to finally stabilize in December. The British pound devalued from December 2012 to March 2013, then it suffered the dollar devaluation until October. Finally, the yen strongly devalued in mid-2012 and throughout 2013.

Summing up, these four economies went on waging war against each other on currency markets. Yet their industrial growth remains weak. Unemployment is still rather high, GDP growth rates are low (the U.S. rate is a little higher). The point is that (nominal or real) depreciation has not produced significant effects on growth, as it was implemented by all big advanced countries.

Perhaps some hoped that the currency beggar-my-neighbor policies in advanced countries could help unload the burden of reflating the world economy on the emerging and developing countries. But they have remained disillusioned.

In fact, most of these countries reacted with competitive devaluation themselves. The Russian ruble began a strong devaluation trend against the dollar in February 2013. The South African rand began devaluing in January 2013 and accelerated in May. The Indian rupee, Indonesian rupiah, Brazilian real, and Thai baht began a trend of strong devaluation in May 2013. In some cases these devaluations were set in motion as policy reactions to the advanced countries' attacks but, after the Federal Reserve's shock announcement of May 22, much capital and liquidity flew from emergent countries to return home in Northern countries, and devaluations became real breakdowns, which the monetary authorities tried in vain to resist.

It seemed that this currency war might trigger crises in various emerging and developing countries. India is a typical case. The world demand slowdown reduced Indian exports and caused a big trade deficit that rose to 4.8 percent of GDP. As a consequence, the GDP growth rate has fallen from 11.2 percent (in 2010) to 5 percent (in 2012) and 4.6 percent (in 2013). Speculation started to bet on a strong rupee devaluation, and capital began to fly. The Sensex index sparked off a decreasing trend. The rates of interest rose. Then devaluation fed strong inflation pressures, which further weakened the country's export capacity. Monetary authorities reacted and tried to put a brake on devaluation, but the consequences were disastrous: the country risk increased, interest rates rose further, bear speculation on the exchange rate and financial assets raged, and depreciation was not stopped. Eventually, faced with a continual and useless currency reserves shrinkage, the Central Bank surrendered: on August 21 it decided to give up defending the rupee. Between the end of August and the beginning of September, the rupee resumed a revaluation trend.

With the exception of China, whose yuan went on revaluing against the currency of all principal countries, exchange rates crises have taken place in other emerging and developing countries, especially the "fragile five"—Brazil, Indonesia, Turkey, South Africa, and India. They have been particularly serious in those that count on raw materials exports, whose prices are decreasing due to the world trade slowdown. In these countries devaluation does not appreciably raise export volumes, since world demand is not strong enough. On the other hand, it reduces the value of exports in dollars and euros. A vicious circle is triggered—devaluation, inflation, capital flight, balance of payment deficit and devaluation again—that might cause various crises. At any rate, the currencies of many other emerging countries, like the rupee, resumed revaluation between the end of August and the beginning of September.

Perhaps this global currency instability is one of the reasons why on September 18 Ben Bernanke declared that the Fed was not ready to start tapering. The declaration of May 22, which had announced the coming tapering, had stopped dollar devaluation and seemed to have stabilized the advanced countries' exchange rates, but had weakened the bear sentiments in global financial markets while triggering various currency crises in emerging and developing countries. Moreover, the U.S. Congress's resistance to expansive fiscal policies had induced Bernanke to cut his estimates of GDP growth in 2013 and 2014.

After the declaration of September 18, financial markets recovered confidence and stock exchanges started rallying again. The euro sharply and steadily appreciated. The dollar exhibited a daily peak of devaluation against the yuan, the yen, the pound, the rupee, the real, the ruble, and many other currencies.

The Fed, which conducts the global finance orchestra, seems to be cruising between Scylla and Charybdis. If it sets off tapering, it dampens U.S. GDP growth, breeds pessimistic sentiments in financial markets, and sparks off currency crises in the South of the world. If it endures with quantitative easing, it feeds the world speculative bubble and thus the risk of a catastrophic burst. With considerable trepidation, Ben Bernanke chose a middle path, and declared a plan to launch a moderate tapering in January 2014, but still keep interest rates low. The markets reacted well, perhaps because investors thought they could avoid the worst. Thus the exchange rates between the dollar and the euro, the yen, and the pound seem to be stabilizing.

It is difficult to forecast the final upshot. One thing is certain: the currency war was both a slowdown factor for the global economy and a sign of weakness for the countries that declared it. It is also the most evident consequence of the reduced economic hegemony of the United States. This country is no longer the rooster in the henhouse, and is trying to get along by playing *beggar my neighbor*. Neither the eurozone nor the yen or the pound areas seem to be enjoying better health. The advanced countries' attempt to unload the burden of recovery policy on emerging and developing countries has instead pushed them into a growth slowdown and many currency crises.

The trade and financial disorder of the interwar period marked the loss of supremacy of the British pound and the demise of the gold standard, while heralding a transition toward a new international economic order. In a similar way, we are now witnessing a series of major economic and financial disorders caused by the loss of U.S. hegemony, which are heralding the end of the dollar standard. This is the transition to fully fledged global imperialism.

The present great crisis will probably lead to a reshuffling of the international political roles (sheriff, banker and driver) necessary to run the global empire. The era in which the United States filled all these positions has come to an end. There are now four players in the game: the United States, China, Germany, and Japan.

INTER-IMPERIAL CONTRADICTIONS?

The adjustment of global imbalances will not be gradual and painless. To start with, China's leaders could adopt a more aggressive approach in their use of the currency threat, in view of a shift in the balance of powers. They would have no trouble doing so, considering the enormous quantity of dollar reserves held in China. On the other hand, there are the markets. It cannot be ruled out that one day, in the not too distant future, the speculators as well as certain countries with large dollar reserves will all attempt together to bring about a significant depreciation of the U.S. currency, immediately discounting its future adjustment toward a realistic fundamental value: the value of the currency of a country that no longer drives global growth and will no longer be the sole creator of international money.

In 2010, the speculators bet on the effects that the expansive fiscal and monetary policies of China and the United States would have on the revival of world industrial production. Unfortunately, the positive effects on the real economy only lasted a year. The expansive monetary policy adopted by the ECB starting in 2011 to deal with the sovereign debt crisis immediately fueled the revival of bullish sentiment. But the effects were confined to the financial sector, not having been accompanied by expansive fiscal policies. Unemployment has been growing in the North of the world. If the speculators realize that advanced economies will continue to stagnate in 2014, dragged downwards by Euroland or Japan, or even by China, a new wave of financial crashes may occur soon. Then all the chickens of the global economic conflicts will quickly come home to roost, but the rooster will no longer be present, and the readjustment of the balance of powers between continental political blocs could be abrupt.

I am not talking about irremediable inter-imperial rivalries of the type that leads to the outbreak of hostilities, as in the First and Second World Wars. Today's system of global imperialism has brought to light a basic interest common to big multinational capital, which has downgraded inter-imperial conflicts to the role of "contradictions among the people." Above all, these conflicts are caused by the resistance of the governments of certain big states to the effects of globalization on their national economies or by the power ambitions of their ruling classes. Thus some political and economic friction between certain continental geopolitical areas unquestionably continues to exist, but it is not generated by the basic interests of capital.

Nowadays, *big global capital*, in the form of multinational firms, has the whole world as its field of action. These firms, be they American, European, Japanese, or Chinese, all have a common interest in breaking down national economic boundaries, in the liberalization of markets. They also share an interest in leveling out and reducing labor costs. The great crisis of 2007–13 has worked hard to achieve these aims, and competitive devaluations and deflations have resulted in lower wages and greater exploitation. The multinationals are in oligopolistic competition against one another and often seek to induce the government of one country or another to support them in their battles to grab resources and control markets, but they will never push governments to block the processes of liberalization that open up channels for their goods, investments, and profits to flow through. If anything, they press them to open the channels wider and encourage them to implement monetary and fiscal policies aimed at redistributing income from wages to profits. In this way they pursue the interests of all big global capital.

Nowadays, the real world wars are fought directly by manufacturing and financial multinationals. They take the form of oligopolistic competition in goods and corporate control markets, and of speculative attacks on financial markets. The greatest political catastrophe that could be expected from this type of war would be a dollar crisis that marks the end of the Federal Reserve as the main issuer of international money. Then China will feel ready to impose upon the world a G2 governance (China and the United States), as proposed by Bergsten (2009) and by senior World Bank managers Robert Zoellick and Justin Yifu Lin. If the European governments then manage to use a deep crisis as shock therapy (possibly doing away with the euro) and begin a new process of sustained growth, perhaps a G3 could be formed (China, United States, and the EU). More unlikely is a G4 governance, unless Abenomics is fully successful. Even more, a G5 with Russia.

In the international equilibrium that could emerge from such a change, the three crucial functions of *global governance* will no longer be fulfilled by a single country, but by three distinct decision-making organisms. China is not yet capable of filling the position of driver of world accumulation, as it cannot take advantage of the international trade multiplier of a large economy and the currency seignorage. But it did already produce 21.8 percent of the world GDP in 2010. And it is growing rapidly, so rapidly that by 2030 it could well make up 30 percent of world investments (World Bank, 2013a). If it does not precipitate into a deep crisis in the next few years, it might well manage to take on the role of driver of growth in the not too distant future.

A new International Monetary Fund, with a stronger China and reduced influence of the United States, Europe, and Japan, will become the global banker. Some big financial institutions have already outlined projects for the creation of a new world currency. For instance, one by the IMF (2011a; 2011b) focuses on special drawing rights. Another one, by the governor of the People's Bank of China (Zhou, 2009), also refers to special drawing rights but imagines an evolution toward a *super-sovereign reserve currency*. One defect of abstract theories is that they rarely take into account the real processes of historical transformation and the changes in the balance of power between states, as Keynes realized during the Bretton Woods negotiations.[131] Nonetheless, it seems that the balance of power is currently changing, to the extent that some such proposals could become reality, although perhaps not exactly as envisaged in the theories, and certainly not as a hegemonic initiative of the former triad (United States, EU, and Japan). China, and perhaps other emerging countries, will play a key role.

The United States will only keep the function of global sheriff, in which it could be assisted by Europe. Europe could also support China in the role of driver, although this is less likely, and could only happen if Europe is capable of restarting its own growth. The true leading actor of the world government will nonetheless remain big multinational capital, and with an ever stronger role.

The United States will obviously resist such change, but China and other emerging countries have a powerful weapon in convincing it to renounce dollar seignorage: their enormous reserves of U.S. assets. They would not even need to bring about a dramatic dollar crisis to force the United States to hand the role of global banker over to the IMF. It would be sufficient to threaten such a crisis at a crucial moment.

When this changeover has happened, U.S. supremacy will have hit rock bottom, and the global power system will have shifted to effective multilateralism. Once the international system of payments has evolved from the dollar standard to a super-sovereign currency standard, the United States will have lost even the last residues of economic policy autonomy. Its reduced share of international trade has already cost it the privilege of the international trade multiplier of a large economy. Renouncing dollar seignorage will cost the nation its ability to live beyond its productive capacity. External constraints will become hard, and fiscal policy autonomy will be limited, especially if a fixed exchange rate system arises. Moreover, the increased military expenditure necessary to maintain the role of global sheriff may raise the debt/GDP ratio, if global GDP does not grow vigorously. In which case, fiscal policies will have to be restrictive. Thus the U.S. ability to continue playing this role will depend upon the fiscal and monetary policies of China and other big emerging countries. If, on the other hand, exchange rates remain flexible, U.S. economic policies could be more autonomous, but only at the cost of a continual dollar depreciation.

This may be welcomed by big multinational capital. Either via restrictive economic policies or via continual depreciation of the dollar, real wages and labor costs will tend to fall in the United States. In other words, if the end of the current crisis of transition leads to the establishment of a multilateral system of international relations and a system of payments based on a super-sovereign currency standard, the United States will be forced to accept the discipline of the markets, to the extent that it will have to accelerate the process of downward adjustment of the cost of labor. In this way escaping from the crisis would result in the complete triumph of multinationals' global imperialism.

Conclusion: Whither Global Imperialism?

> To sum up, what is free trade, what is free trade
> under the present condition of society? It is freedom of
> capital. When you have overthrown the few national barriers
> which still restrict the progress of capital, you will merely have
> given it complete freedom of action.... The only result will
> be that the antagonism [between capitalists and wage
> workers] will stand out still more clearly.
> —MARX, 1848

The global empire is a system, globalization a process. The theory of imperialism I have developed in this book describes a framework of international relations in which the dominant actors are the big multinational firms, and the laws that regulate the "social balance" are those of the market. State policies are bent to serve the fundamental interests of multinational capital.

The global empire is still far from being fully realized in the pure form described by the theory. This is due, above all, to the fact that some big advanced countries have sought either to counter certain economic effects of globalization or to twist them to boost their political power. The U.S. government in particular has tried to continue fulfilling the three functions of *global central governance*. However, while it is well equipped to play the role of global sheriff, the U.S. economy is proving increasingly inadequate to play the roles of driver of accumulation and global banker. The German government has attempted some weak competition, seeking to launch the euro as an international reserve currency and to build a European mercantile empire under its own domination.

Globalization has depressionary effects on growth in advanced countries and weakens their ability to govern the world. The U.S. economy is no longer the unrivaled leader of global production and trade. To continue to play the role of growth driver, the U.S. government would need to adopt such expansive fiscal policies that its public and foreign debts would reach stratospheric levels. In addition, the higher wages that would follow a move toward full employment would make a serious dent in profits. The decision not to make excessive use of fiscal stimulus measures is also explained by the need to prevent such a redistribution process. Thus the unrestrained use of monetary stimulus becomes an inevitable solution to combat depression. The speculative mega-bubble allowed the United States to continue playing the role of global banker and driver of accumulation, but at the cost of creating financial instability, which ultimately produced one of the greatest crises in the history of capitalism. It will be difficult to escape from this crisis by using speculative bubbles again. And it will be difficult for the United States to continue playing the two roles of economic governance unless it manages to launch a robust growth process. The current administration's policies seem intent on launching a modest recovery of domestic demand using fiscal policies, and accompanying them with currency policies aimed at improving the U.S. balance of payments. This implies that the United States is giving up the role of growth driver. Its insistence on expansive monetary policies, on the other hand, suggests a desire to continue playing the role of global banker, even at the risk of generating a new wave of financial instability.

Germany has sought to compete with the United States in its role as global banker. It could have succeeded and, what's more, would have placed the whole of Euroland in a position to take on the role of driver of growth if the German government had only adopted expansive fiscal policies. By running a current account deficit, Germany could have provided the world with an abundant supply of international currency while driving global production with its imports. Instead, the German leaders were induced by an outdated imperialist strategy to favor the interests of national industry over those of multinational capital, and adopted restrictive fiscal and monetary policies to curb wage increases. By doing so, they created the conditions for the explosion of the euro crisis and thwarted the timid signs of global economic recovery shown in 2010. Germany, and the Europe it dominates, are evidently not capable of taking over the role of driver of accumulation that the United States will be forced to give up.

At the root of this crisis lies a social contradiction that the economic policies of the advanced countries are incapable of resolving. Globalization, through the social, fiscal, and environmental dumping enacted by emerging countries, reduces the income and consumption of workers in advanced countries in a way that no fiscal policy can counter without drawing heavily on profits. Income distribution and balances of power increasingly tend to change to the detriment of the working class. It is difficult to believe that social peace can be maintained for long under these conditions.

The last two decades in the history of capitalism can be seen as a phase of transition toward the full achievement of global imperialism: a historical phase characterized by growing social conflicts and financial instability. The 2007–13 crisis can be expected to accelerate the process of globalization. It has revealed the limits and contradictions of two models of economic policy and global governance followed since the mid-1990s, and reestablished the supremacy of the "markets" and multinational capital over nationalist policies. Moreover, the crisis has highlighted the fact that big capital does not need the political governance of old-fashioned imperial states in order to expand its empire. Instead it aspires to *sovereignless global governance*, in which national political governments submit to the needs of accumulation in the global market.

There is no doubt that globalization is working to realize the capitalist utopia of the minimal state (Beck, 2000, 3). This does not mean a complete absence of the state. It means that individual states are compelled to give up the role of national collective capitalist and subordinate their domestic policies to the interests of big multinational capital, especially by playing the role of local social gendarme. If and when this policy model is achieved, the *fundamental contradictions* of the global empire may well explode with all their destructive force.

I am not talking about inter-imperial contradictions. Interstate rivalries continue to exist, but they are not disruptive as long as national policies are conditioned by multinational capital and its "markets." This kind of conditioning is becoming ever more effective with the growth in number and size of big firms, and especially the growth of multinationals based in emerging countries. On the other hand, with the rise of such multinationals the very distinction between Center and Periphery tends to be blurred. At least one trend seems clear: *in the near future China and other big emerging countries will have joined the imperial Center*. As a consequence, interstate rivalries might be heightened, but, at the same time, multinational capital will become more powerful and its ability to condition state policies will grow.

The *fundamental contradictions* are two, but tend to merge into one.[132] The first is the opposition between the (enlarged) Center and the Periphery of the empire: between the countries where the dominant capitalist class lives and the South of the world, where the vast mass of human and natural resources pillaged by global capital are located. The disciplinary processes through which surplus value and wealth are extracted from the South and transferred to the North are well known. I dealt with these in chapter 3 and will not go back to them now. Here I only want to reiterate that these processes are not based solely on the traditional mechanisms of post-colonial economic exploitation, such as unequal exchange. Instead, they work through processes of destruction of traditional cultures and institutions. These processes aim to create the conditions for the penetration of exploited countries by the modern capitalist system. Global capitalism not only exports goods and money, but also tends to export firms and ideologies, and indeed to export itself as an exclusive mode of production. Thus the masses of the "wretched of the earth" in Asia, South America, and Africa tend to become masses of modern proletarians. This process of economic and social transformation is already very advanced in much of Asia and Latin America, slightly less so in Africa, and will undoubtedly continue to progress.

The other fundamental contradiction is the usual opposition between capital and the proletariat. Globalization exacerbates this opposition. It has a strong tendency to redistribute income from wages to profits and thus to create a growing mass of proletarians (employees, the under-employed, the unemployed, and migrants) who see their working and living conditions continually worsen. The current crisis has accelerated this process by producing a sharp rise in unemployment.

Contemporary neoliberal capitalism seems to be reactivating the conditions of increasing relative impoverishment observed by Marx in nineteenth-century laissez-faire capitalism. On the one side is a narrow class of capitalists and speculators getting progressively richer, while on the other side is a growing mass of proletarians whose income tends to approach subsistence levels, often falling below them. This tendency condemns the reformist practices of labor and social democratic parties to ineffectiveness and generates a process of cultural and political dis-integration of traditional national workers' movements, a sort of "clean sweep" of the old organizational and ideological defenses that aimed to support the working class by integrating it into national power systems.

Such a complex process of economic, social, and political change ultimately results in the *fusion of the two fundamental contradictions of capitalism*. Capital propagates beyond national borders, proposing itself as the engine of global growth. In this way it creates a global proletariat that tends to be increasingly homogeneous in terms of economic pov-erty and political destitution: an ever more "rude pagan race" that will grow in size and exasperation. Herein lies *the* fundamental contradic-tion of global capitalism. As neither the free trade nor the mercantilist policies implemented by the current ruling classes are capable of resolv-ing or attenuating it, this contradiction is likely to get progressively worse, until it culminates in a great international social outburst. The great crisis is bringing that moment closer.

The triumph of global imperialism entails radical changes in the political prospects of class struggle. Theories of neo-imperialism and dependence in the second half of the twentieth century predicted that the exploitative relationship between the Center and the Periphery would lead the conflict between imperialist nations and dependent nations to prevail over class conflict. This is not happening. In the South, and especially in "emerging" countries, the process of accumulation has been propped up by a systematic reduction of labor costs and a marked increase in workers' exploitation in the capitalist factory. By causing the rapid penetration of capitalist relations throughout the whole economy, this process multiplies the numbers of the working class, while increasing relative poverty and social rage. The other side of the coin is that multinational capital's global domination brings ever greater transfers of surplus value from the South to the capitalists of the North. Instead of implying improved well-being for workers in advanced countries, this leads to the increased concentration of income and wealth in the hands of the capitalist class and the impoverishment of the proletariat. Labor aristocracies tend to disappear and labor exploitation grows.

The main political consequences are three. First, the reformist policies of traditional workers' movements become ineffective, due to a lack of economic resources in both the South and North of the world. The amount of surplus value that states can dedicate to social well-being progressively shrinks. Opportunities for reformism disappear, and labor and social democratic parties meet with one defeat after another if they seek to implement advanced social policies. Instead they are compelled to turn neoliberal and work at the service of big capital if they want to stay in power. Second, greater poverty and exploitation force workers to develop increasingly antagonistic attitudes toward capitalism and the political classes that serve it. While the collapse of organized workers' movements deprives workers of their arms of political and ideological defense, it also urges them to adopt increasingly radical and potentially revolutionary stances. The third important political consequence is that the opposition between the immediate interests of the Northern and the Southern proletariat ceases to exist. This may bring to light an awareness of a fundamental interest, common to all the workers of the world: an interest in overturning capitalism.

BIBLIOGRAPHY

Adda, M. 1998. *La mondialisation de l'économie.* Paris: La Découverte.

Acocella, N., ed. 2004. *Rapporto sulla povertà e le disuguaglianze nel mondo globale.* Naples: Fondazione Premio Naples.

Acocella, N. 2005. *La politica economica nell'era della globalizzazione.* Rome: Carocci.

Alessandrini P. and M. Fratianni. 2007. "Resurrecting Keynes to Revamp the International Monetary System", Indiana University, Kelley School of Business, Department of Business Economics and Public Policy, Working Paper N. 19.

Alessandrini P. and M. Fratianni. 2009. "International Monies, Special Drawing Rights, and Supernational Money", Indiana University, Kelley School of Business, Department of Business Economics and Public Policy, Working Paper N. 3.

Alessandrini P., M. Fratianni, A. Hughes Hallett, and A. F. Presbitero. 2012. "External Imbalances and Financial Fragility in the Euro Area." *Mofir Working Paper* no. 66.

Amin, S. 2002. *Oltre il capitalismo senile: Per un XXI secolo non americano.* Milan: Punto Rosso.

Amin, S. 2004. *The Liberal Virus: Permanent War and the Americanization of the World.* London: Pluto Press.

Amin, S. 2008. "'Market Economy' or Oligopoly-Finance Capitalism?" *Monthly Review* 59 (April). http://monthlyreview.org/2008/04/01/market-economy-or-oligopoly-finance-capitalism.

Amin, S. 2012. "Implosion of the European System." *Monthly Review* 64 (September). http://monthlyreview.org/2012/09/01/implosion-of-the-european-system.

Amoroso, B., and J. Jespersen. 2012. *L'Europa oltre l'euro: Le ragioni del disastro economico e la ricotruzione del progetto comunitario.* Rome: Castelvecchi.

Anand, S., and P. Segal. 2007. "What Do We Know about World Income Inequality?" *Journal of Economic Literature,* 46, 57–94.

Anonymous Authors. 2002. *Non è vero: I dogmi del neoliberismo alla prova dei fatti.* Milan: Movimenti Cambiamenti.

Apostolou, A. 2012. "Il nuovo Dachau: L'Unione Europea deve evolversi in federazione di stati." *Il Ponte* 68/11, 44–46.

Archibugi, D., and S. Iamarino. 2002. "The Globalization of Technological Innovation: Definition and Evidence." *Review of International Political Economy,* 9, 98–122.

Archibugi, D., and J. Michie. 1993. "The Globalization of Technology: Myths and Realities." *Judge Institute of Management Studies.* N. 18. Cambridge: Cambridge University Press.

Archibugi, D., and C. Pietrobelli. 2003. "The Globalization of Technology and Its Implications for Developing Countries: Windows or Opportunities of Further Burden?" *Technological Forecasting and Social Change,* 70, 861–83.

Arpaia, A., and K. Pichelmann. 2008. "Falling Wage Share: a Common Trend?"
    Workshops N. 16. (September) Oesterreichische Nationalbank.
Arrighi, G. 1994. *The Long Twentieth Century*. London: Verso.
Arrighi, G. 2005. "Hegemony Unraveling." I, *New Left Review* 32, 23–80; II, *New
    Left Review* 33, 83–116.
Ashman, S., and A. Callinicos. 2006. "Capital Accumulation and the State System:
    Assessing David Harvey's *The New Imperialism*." *Historical Materialism*,
    14/4, 107–31.
Atkinson A. B. 2009. "Factor Shares: The Principal Problem of Political
    Economy?" Oxford Review of Economic Policy, 25, 3-16.
Atkinson, A. B., and A. Brandolini. 2009. "Analysing the World Income
    Distribution." Temi di discussione N. 701, Banca d'Italia.
Bacon, D. 2008. *Illegal People: How Globalization Creates Migration and
    Criminalizes Immigrants*. Boston: Beacon Press.
Bacon, D. 2013. "Growing Clash between Immigrant Rights Activists and
    Washington Power Brokers. " Truthout.org, October. http://www.
    truth-out.org/news/item/19564-growing-clash-between-immigrant-
    rights-activists-and-washington-power-brokers.
Bagnai, A. 2012. *Il tramonto dell'euro: Come e perché la fine della moneta unica
    salverebbe democrazia e benessere in Europa*. Reggio Emilia: Imprimatur
    Editore.
Baldwin, R. 2006. *In or Out: Does It Matter? An Evidence-Based Analysis of the
    Euro's Trade Effect*. London: Centre for Economic Policy Research.
Balin, B. J. 2008. "Basel I, Basel II, and Emerging Markets: A Nontechnical
    Analysis." Washington, DC: Johns Hopkins University School of
    Advanced International Studies.
Barba, A., and M. Pivetti. 2009. "Rising Household Debt: Its Causes and
    Macroeconomic Implications: A long Period Analysis." *Cambridge
    Journal of Economics*, 33, 113–37.
Barba, A. 2011. "Changes in Income Distribution, Financial Disorder and Crisis."
    In Brancaccio and Fontana, 81–98.
Barba Navaretti, G., and A. J. Venables. 2004. *Multinational Firms in the World
    Economy*. Princeton: Princeton University Press.
Barth et al. 2000. "Policy Watch: The Repeal of Glass-Steagall and the Advent of
    the Broad Bank." *Journal of Economic Perspectives*, 14, 191–204.
Bartlett, C. A., and S. Ghoshal. 1991. *The Transnational Solution*. Cambridge MA:
    Harvard Business School.
Beaud, M. 1999. *Mondialisation, les mots et les choses*. Paris: Karthala.
Beck, U. 2000. *What Is Globalization?* Cambridge: Polity Press.
Bello, W. 2005. *Dilemmas of Domination*. New York: Metropolitan Books.
Bellofiore, R. 2009. "L'ipotesi della instabilità finanziaria e il 'nuovo' capitalismo."
    Paper presented at workshop on "The Complexity of Financial Crisis in a
    Long-Period Perspective: Facts, Theory and Models." University of Siena.
Bellofiore, R. 2012. *La crisi globale, l'Europa, l'euro, la sinistra*. Trieste: Asterios.

Berg, A. G., and T. Nilsson. 2010. "Do Liberalization and Globalization Increase World Inequality?" *European Journal of Political Economy*, 26, 488–505.

Berg, A. G., and J. D. Ostroy. 2011. "Inequality and Unsustainable Growth: Two Sides of the Same Coin?" IMF Staff Discussion Note N. 11.

Berger, A., and G. Udell. 2004. "The Institutional Memory Hypothesis and the Procyclicality of Bank Lending Behavior." *Journal of Financial Intermediation*, 12, 458–95.

Bergsten, C. F. 2009. "Two's Company." *Foreign Affairs*. September/October, http://www.foreignaffairs.com/articles/65232/c-fred-bergsten/twos-company.

Bernanke, B., and H. James. 1991. "The Gold Standard, Deflation, and Financial Crisis in the Great Depression: An International Comparison." In R. G. Hubbard, ed., *Financial Markets and Financial Crises*. Chicago: University of Chicago Press, 33–68.

Betti, G., B. Cheli, A. Lemmi, and V. Verma. 2006. "On the Construction of Fuzzy Measures for the Analysis of Poverty and Social Exclusion." *Statistica & Applicazioni*, 4, 77–97.

Betti, G., A. Dabalen, C. Ferré, and L. Neri. 2013. "Updating Poverty Maps between Censuses: A Case Study of Albania." In C. R. Laderchi and S. Savastano, eds., *Poverty and Exclusion in the Western Balkans*, Economic Studies in Inequality, Social Exclusion and Well-Being, vol. 8. New York: Springer, chap. 5.

Bhalla, S. 2002. *Imagine There's No Country: Poverty, Inequality and Growth in the Era of Globalization*. Washington, DC: Institute for International Economics.

Bibow, J. 2012. "The Euro Debt Crisis and Germany's Euro Trilemma." Working Paper N. 721, Levy Economics Institute.

Blanchard, O., and F. Giavazzi. 2002. "Current Account Deficits in the Euro Area: The End of the Feldstein-Horioka Puzzle?" *Brookings Papers on Economic Activity*, N. 2, 147–86.

Blanchard, O., and F. Giavazzi. 2003. "Macroeconomic Effects of Regulation and Deregulation in Goods and Labor Markets." *The Quarterly Journal of Economics*, 118, 879–907.

Blondet, M. 2012. "Il 'miracolo' tedesco: nascondere i senza-lavoro." *Rischio calcolato*, February 9, http://www.rischiocalcolato.it/2012/02/il-miracolo-tedesco-nascondere-i-senza-lavoro-maurizio-blondet.html.

Bloomberg. 2013. "China Eclipses U.S. as Biggest Trading Nation." *Bloomberg News*, February 10, http://www.bloomberg.com/news/2013-02-09/china-passes-u-s-to-become-the-world-s-biggest-trading-nation.html.

Bonaglia, F., and A. Goldstein. 2008. *Globalizzazione e sviluppo*. Bologna: Il Mulino.

Borghesi, S., and A. Vercelli. 2005. *La sostenibilità dello sviluppo Globale*. Rome: Carocci.

Boròn, A. 2001. "El nuevo orden mundial y cómo desmontarlo." In J. Seoane and E. Taddei (eds.), *Resistencias mundiales. De Seattle a Porto Alegre*. Buenos Aires: CLACSO.

Boròn, A. 2002. *Imperio y imperialismo: Una lectura critica de Michael Hardt y Antonio Negri*. Buenos Aires: Paydòs.

Bourguignon, F., and C. Morrisson. 2002. "Inequality among World Citizens: 1820–1992," *American Economic Review*, 92, 727–44.

Brakman, S., H. Garretsen, and C. van Marrewijk. 2006. "Cross-Border Mergers & Acquisitions: The Facts as a Guide for International Economics." Cesifo Working Paper N. 1823.

Brancaccio, E., and G. Fontana (eds.). 2011. *The Global Economic Crisis: New Perspectives on the Critique of Economic Theory and Policy*. London: Routledge.

Brancaccio, E., and M. Passerella. 2012. *L'austerità è di destra: E sta distruggendo l'Europa*. Milan: Il Saggiatore.

Brander, J., and B. Spencer. 1981. "Tariffs and the Extraction of Foreign Monopoly Rents under Potential Entry." *Canadian Journal of Economics*, 14, 371–89.

Brander, J., and B. Spencer. 1985. "Export Subsidies and International Market Share Rivalry." *Journal of International Economics*, 16, 83–100.

Brenner, R. 1986. "The Social Basis of Economic Development." In J. Roemer (ed.), *Analytical Marxism*. Cambridge: Cambridge University Press.

Brewer, A. 1985. "Trade with Fixed Real Wages and Mobile Capital." *Journal of International Economics*, 18, 177–86.

Britto G., 2008. "Productivity Growth and Space: A Multilevel Verdoorn Model." Cambridge Centre for Economic and Public Policy, Working Paper N. 03-08, University of Cambridge.

Broda, C., and C. Tille. 2003. "Coping with Terms-of-Trade Shocks in Developing Countries." *Current Issues in Economics and Finance*, 9, 1–7.

Buckley, P. J., and M. C. Casson. 1976. "A Long-Run Theory of the Multinational Enterprise." In P. J. Buckley and M. C. Casson (eds.), *The Future of the Multinational Enterprise*. London: Macmillan, 32–65.

Bush, O., Farrant K., and M. Wright. 2011. "Reform of the International Monetary and Financial System." Financial Stability Paper 13, Bank of England.

Caldarelli, G. 2012. *La tutela dei diritti di proprietà intellettuale secondo gli accordi TRIPS*. Degree Dissertation, University of Siena.

Callinicos, A. 1991a. "Marxism and Imperialism Today." *International Socialism*, 50, 3–48.

Callinicos, A. 1991b. *The Revenge of History, Marxism and the East European Revolutions*. University Park: The Pennsylvania State University Press.

Callinicos, A. 2005. "Imperialism and Global Political Economy." *International Socialism*, 108, 109–27.

Callinicos, A. 2007. "Does Capitalism Need the State System?" *Cambridge Review of International Affairs*, 20, 533–49.

Callinicos, A. 2009. *Imperialism and Global Political Economy*. Cambridge: Polity Press.

Calvo, G., and C. Reinhart. 1999. "Capital Flow Reversals, the Exchange Rate Debate, and Dollarization." *Finance and Development*, 36, 13–15.

Calvo, G., and C. Reinhart. 2000. "When Capital Inflows Come to a Sudden Stop: Consequences and Policy Options." In P. Kenen and A. Swoboda (eds.), *Reforming the International Monetary System*. Washington, D.C.: International Monetary Fund, 175–201.

Cantwell, J. 1989. *Technological Innovation and Multinational Corporations*. Oxford: Blackwell.

Cantwell, J. 1992. "Innovation and Technological Competitiveness." *In* P. J. Buckley and M. C. Casson (eds.), *Multinational Enterprises in the World Economy: Essays in Honour of John Funning*. Aldershot: Elgar, 20–40.

Carrel, P., and G. Heller. 2012. "US Raises Pressure for Euro Zone Crisis Action." *Reuters*, August 1, http://www.reuters.com/article/2012/08/01/us-eurozone-idUSBRE8700AZ20120801

Casadio, M., J. Petras, and L. Vasapollo. 2004. *Clash! Scontro tra potenze*. Milan: Jaca Book.

Cecchetti, S., M.S. Mohanty, and F. Zampolli. 2010. "The Future of Public Debt: Prospects and Implications." BIS Working Paper N. 300.

Celik, S., and U. Basdas. 2010. "How Does Globalization Affect Income Inequality? A Panel Data Analysis." *International Advances in Economics*, 16, 358–70.

Cesaratto, S. 2011. "Notes on Europe, German Mercantilism and the Current Crisis." In Brancaccio and Fontana, 246–260.

Cesaratto, S. 2012. "Il vecchio e il nuovo della crisi Europea." In Cesaratto and Pivetti, 26–43.

Cesaratto, S., and M. Pivetti (eds.). 2012. *Oltre l'austerità*. Rome: Micromega.

Cesaratto, S., and A. Stirati. 2011. "Germany in the European and Global Crises." *International Journal of Political Economy*, 39, 56–87.

Chen, S., and M. Ravaillon. 2001. "How Did the World's Poor Fare in the 1990's?" *Review of Income and Wealth* 47, 283–300.

Chen, S., and M. Ravaillon. 2007. "Absolute Poverty Measures for the Developing World: 1981–2004." World Bank Policy Research Working Paper Series N. 4211.

Chen, S., and M. Ravaillon. 2008. "The Developing World Is Poorer than We Thought, but No Less Successful in the Fight against Poverty." World Bank Policy Research Working Paper N. 4703.

Chen, S., and M. Ravaillon. 2012. "An Update to the World Bank's Estimates of Consumption Poverty in the Developing World." World Bank, Briefing Note, http://siteresources.worldbank.org/INTPOVCALNET/Resources/Global_Poverty_Update_2012_02-29-12.pdf.

Chesnais, F. 1998–9. "Actualizar la noción de imperialismo para comprender la crisis en curso." *Herramienta. Revista de debate y crítica marxista*. Autumn, 13–37.

Chesnais, F. 2011. *Debiti illegittimi e diritto all'insolvenza*. Rome: Derive Approdi.

Chick, V. 2009. "The Current Bank Crisis: An Evolutionary View." Paper presented at the Workshop *The Complexity of Financial Crisis in a Long-Period Perspective: Facts, Theory and Models*, University of Siena.

Collier, P., and D. Dollar. 2002. *Globalization, Growth, and Poverty: Building an Inclusive World Economy.* World Bank Policy Research Report. Oxford: Oxford University Press.

Confindustria. 2013. *Progetto Confindustria per l'Italia: Crescere si può, si deve.* http://www.astrid-online.it/La-produtt/Documenti/CONFINDUSTRIA-Progetto-per-l-Italia_23_01_13.pdf.

Corn, D. 2008. "Foreclosure Phil." http://motherjones.com/politics/2008/05/foreclosure-phil.

Cornia, A. G. 2003. "The Impact of Liberalization and Globalization on Income Inequality in Developing and Transitional Economies." CESifo Working Paper N. 843.

Correia, I., E. Farhi, J. P.Nicolini, and P. Teles. 2011. "Unconventional Fiscal Policy at the Zero Bound." NBER Working Papers N. 16758.

Correia, I., J. P. Nicolini, and P. Teles. 2008. "Optimal Fiscal and Monetary Policy: Equivalence Results." *Journal of Political Economy*, 116, 141–70.

Costabile, L. 2009. "Current Global Imbalances and the Keynes Plan: A Keynesian Approach for Reforming the International Monetary System." *Structural Change and Economic Dynamics*, 20, 79–89.

Cowling, K., and R. Sugden. 1998. "The Essence of the Modern Corporation: Markets, Strategic Decision-Making and the Theory of the Firm." *The Manchester School*, 66, 59–86.

D'Angelillo, M., and L. Paggi. 2012. "Deutschland, Deutschland… Über Alles." In Cesaratto and Pivetti, 55–70.

De Cecco, M. 1999. *L'oro di Europa.* Rome: Donzelli.

De Angelis, M. 2004. "Separating the Doing and the Deed." *Historical Materialism*, 12, 57–87.

De Grauwe, P. 2006. *On Monetary and Political Union.* Catholic University of Leuven, Department of Economics, May.

De Grauwe, P., and J. Yuemei. 2012. "Self-Fulfilling Crises in the Eurozone: An Empirical Test." CESifo Working Papers N. 3821.

Devereaux, C., R. Z. Lawrence, and M. D. Watkins. 2006. *Case Studies in US Trade Negotiation*, vol. 1, *Making the Rules*, vol. 2, *Resolving Disputes.* Washington, DC: Institute for International Economics.

Dixit, A. 1984. "International Trade Policies for Oligopolistic Industries." *Economic Journal Supplement*, 94, 1–16.

Dollar, D., and A. Kraay. 2001a. "Growth Is Good for the Poor." World Bank Policy Research Working Paper N. 2587.

Dollar, D., and A. Kraay. 2001b. "Trade, Growth, and Poverty." World Bank Policy Research Working Paper N. 2615

Dooley M. P., D. Folkerts-Landau, and P. Garber. 2003. "An Essay on the Revived Bretton Woods System." NBER Working Paper Series N. 8871.

Drahos, P. 1995. "Global Property Rights in Information: The Story of TRIPS at the GATT." *Prometheus*, 13, 6–19.

Drahos, P., and R. Mayne. 2002. *Global Intellectual Property Rights: Knowledge, Access and Development*. Houndmills: Palgrave Macmillan.

Dreher, A., and N. Gaston. 2008. "Has Globalization Increased Inequality?" *Review of International Economics*, 16, 516–36.

Driskill, R. 2007. "Deconstructing the Argument for Free Trade," http://www.vanderbilt.edu/econ/faculty/Driskill/ DeconstructingfreetradeAug27a2007.pdf .

Dunning, J. H. 2000. "The Eclectic Paradigm as an Envelope for Economic and Business Theories of MNE Activity." *International Business Review*, 9, 163–90.

Eggertsson, G. B., and P. R. Krugman. 2011. "Debt, Deleveraging, and the Liquidity Trap: A Fisher-Minsky-Koo Approach," http://faculty.wcas. northwestern.edu/~gep575/seminars/spring2011/EK.pdf.

Eichengreen, B., and M. D. Bordo. 2002. "Crises Now and Then: What Lessons from the Last Era of Financial Globalization?" NBER Working Paper N. 8716.

Eichengreen, B., and R. Hausmann. 1999. "Exchange Rates and Financial Fragility." NBER Working Paper Series N. 7418, http://akson.sgh.waw. pl/~cwojcik/teaching/ee_fall/er%20and%20financial%20fragility%20 Eichengreen.pdf.

Eichengreen, B., and J. Sachs. 1985. "Exchange Rates and Economic Recovery in the 1930s." *Journal of Economic History*, 45, 925–46.

Elbers, C., J. O. Lanjouw, and P. Lanjouw 2003. "Micro-Level Estimation of Poverty and Inequality." *Econometrica*, 71, 355–364.

Ellis, L., and K. Smith. 2007. "The Global Upward Trend in the Profit Share." BIS Working Papers N. 231, Bank for International Settlements.

Ellwood, W. 2001. *The No-Nonsense Guide to Globalization*. London: Verso.

Emmanuel, A. 1972. *Unequal Exchange: A Study of the Imperialism of Trade*. New York: Monthly Review Press.

Epstein, G. 2011. "The Role and Control of Multinational Corporations in the World Economy." In J. Michie (ed.), *The Handbook of Globalization*, 2nd edition. Cheltenham: Elgar.

European Commission. 2012. *Annual Macro-Economic Database*. Bruxelles. http:// ec.europa.eu/economy_finance/ameco/user/serie/SelectSerie.cfm.

Eurostat. 2002. *European Social Statistics: Income, Poverty and Social Exclusion, Second Report*. Luxembourg: Office for Official Publications of the European Communities.

Eurostat. 2012. *Statistics by Theme*. http://appsso.eurostat.ec.europa.eu/nui/ show.do?dataset=ilc_li02&lang=en.

Evans, G. E. 1994. "Intellectual Property as a Trade Issue: The Making of the Agreement on Trade-Related Aspects of Intellectual Property Rights." *World Competition*, 18, 137–80.

Fabbrini, S. 2012. "I Quattro doveri della politica verso i cittadini." *Il Sole 24 ore*, September 19.

Farhi, E., G. Gopinath, and O. Itskhoki. 2011. "Fiscal Devaluations." NBER
    Working Paper Series N. 17662, http://www.nber.org/papers/w 17662.
Farhi, E., G. Gopinath, and O. Itskhoki. 2012. "A Devaluation Option for
    Southern Europe." *Project Syndicate*, March 4.
Feenstra, R., and G. Hanson 1999. "The Impact of Outsourcing and High-
    Technology Capital on Wages: Estimates for the United States,
    1979–1990." *Quarterly Journal of Economics*, 144, 907–40.
Felipe, J., and J. Lim. 2005. "Export or Domestic-Led Growth in Asia?" ERD
    Working Paper N. 69.
Ferreira, F. H. G., and M. Ravaillon. 2008. "Global Poverty and Inequality: A Review
    of the Evidence." World Bank Policy Research Working Paper N. 4623.
Ferrero, P. 2012. *Pigs! La crisi spiegata a tutti*. Rome: Derive Approdi.
Ferri, P., and A. M. Variato. 2009. "Financial Fragility in a Macro Model à la
    Minsky with Regime Switching." Paper presented at the Workshop *The
    Complexity of Financial Crisis in a Long-Period Perspective: Facts, Theory
    and Models*. University of Siena.
Financial Stability Board. 2012. *Global Shadow Banking Monitoring Report*,
    November. http://www.financialstabilityboard.org/publication-
    s/r_121118c.pdf.
Fiorentini, R. 2011. "The Increasing Inequality in Income Distribution: A Note."
    Working Paper Series N. 19, Department of Economics, University of
    Verona.
Fiorentini, R., and G. Montani. 2012. *The New Global Political Economy: From
    Crisis to Supranational Integration*. Cheltenham: Elgar.
Fisher, I. 1933. "The Debt Deflation Theory of Great Depressions." *Econometrica*,
    1, 337–57.
Fornasari, F. 2009. "I dati e gli insegnamenti della crisi finanziaria USA."
    Economia Italiana, 1, 53–110.
Foster, J. B. 2003. "The New Age of Imperialism." *Monthly Review*, 55, N. 3.
Franco, F. 2011. "Improving Competitiveness through Fiscal Devaluation: The
    Case of Portugal." Universidade Nova de Lisboa. http://competitivi-
    dade.com.sapo.pt/documentos/fiscaldev.pdf.
Fratianni, M. 2008. "Financial Crises, Safety Nets and Regulation." *Rivista Italiana
    degli Economisti*, 2, 169–208.
Fratianni, M., and F. Marchionne. 2009. "Il ruolo delle banche nella crisi finanzia-
    ria dei *subprime*." *Economia Italiana*, 1, 11–51.
Fuchs, C. 2010. "New Imperialism: Information and Media Imperialism?" *Global
    Media and Communication*, 6, 33–60.
Fujimoto, T., and Y. Shiozawa. 2011–2012. "Inter and Intra Company
    Competition in the Age of Global Competition: A Micro and Macro
    Interpretation of Ricardian Trade Theory." *Evolutionary and Institutional
    Economics Review*, 8(1), 1–37; 8(2), 193–231.
Gabriel, J. 2000. *The Dollar Hegemony: Dollar, Dollarization and Progress*.
    Bloomington IN: Writers Club Press.

Gallino, L. 2000. *Globalizzazione e disuguaglianze.* Rome: Laterza.

Gandolfo, G. 1998. *International Trade Theory and Policy.* Berlin: Springer.

Ghosh, A., et al. 2002. "IMF-Supported Programs in Capital Account Crises." Occasional Paper 210. Washington, D.C.: International Monetary Fund.

Ghoshal, S., and N. Nohria. 1997. *The Differentiated MNC: Organizing Multinational Corporations for Value Creation.* San Francisco, CA: Jossey-Bass.

Giacché, V. 2009. "Karl Marx e la crisi del XXI secolo." Introduction to K. Marx, *Il capitalismo e la crisi.* Rome: Derive Approdi.

Giacché, V. 2012a. *Titanic Europa: La crisi che non ci hanno raccontato.* Rome: Aliberti.

Giacché, V. 2012b. "Quattro errori sulla Cina." *Essere Comunisti,* 6, 28–39.

Gibson, B. 1980. "Unequal Exchange: Theoretical Issues and Empirical Findings." *Review of Radical Political Economics,* 12, 15–35.

Gilpin, R. 2000. *The Challenge of Global Capitalism: The World Economy in the 21st Century.* Princeton: Princeton University Press.

Godley, W. 1992. "Maastricht and All That." *London Review of Books,* October 8.

Goldberg, P. K., and N. Pavcnik. 2007. "Distributional Effects of Globalization in Developing Countries." *Journal of Economic Literature,* 45, 39–82.

Goldstein, A., and L. Piscitello. 2007. *Le multinazionali.* Bologna: Il Mulino.

Gollin, D. 2002. "Getting Income Shares Right." *Journal of Political Economy,* 110, 458–74.

Gowan, P. 1999. *The Global Gamble.* London: Verso.

Graham, E. M. 1998. "Market Structure and the Multinational Enterprise: A Game-Theoretic Approach." *Journal of International Business Studies,* 29, 67–83.

Gram, H. 2010. "Samuelson, Sraffa and Steedman on Comparative Advantage." In Vint, Metcalfe, Kurz, Salvadori, and Samuelson, (2010) 69–81.

Graves, R. 1960. *The Greek Myths,* revised edition, http://www.24grammata. com/wp-content/uploads/2011/12/Robert-Graves-The-Greek-Myths-24grammata.com_.pdf.

Guscina, A. 2006. "Effects of Globalization on Labor's Share in National Income." IMF Working Papers N. 06/294.

Haass, R. N. 2002. *The Reluctant Sheriff: The United States after the Cold War.* New York: Council on Foreign Relations Books.

Hahn, F. 1998. "Reconsidering Free Trade." In G. Cook (ed.), *The Economics and Politics of International Trade.* London: Routledge.

Hamilton, J. 1987. "Monetary Factors in the Great Depression." *Journal of Monetary Economics,* 19, 145–69.

Hamilton, J. 1988. "The Role of the International Gold Standard in Propagating the Great Depression." *Contemporary Policy Issues,* 6, 67–89.

Hardt, M., and A. Negri. 2000. *Empire.* Cambridge, MA: Harvard University Press, http://www.angelfire.com/cantina/negri/HAREMI_unprintable.pdf.

Harman, C. 2003. "Analysing Imperialism." *International Socialism*, 99, 3–81.

Harvey, D. 1996. "Il problema della globalizzazione." *Marxismo Oggi*, 9, 125–40.

Harvey, D. 2003. *The New Imperialism*. Oxford: Oxford University Press.

Hayes, C. 2009. "Bankers' Paradise: Capitolism." *The Nation*, June 8.

Helpman, E. 1984. "A Simple Theory of International Trade with Multinational Corporations." *Journal of Political Economy*, 92, 451–71.

Helpman, E. 2011. *Understanding Global Capital*. Cambridge, MA: Harvard University Press.

Helpman, E., and P. R. Krugman. 1985. *Market Structure and Foreign Trade: Increasing Returns, Imperfect Competition, and the International Economy*. Cambridge, MA: MIT Press.

Helpman, E., and P. R. Krugman, 1989. *Trade Policy and Market Structure*. Cambridge MA: MIT Press.

Heshmati, A. 2005. "The Relationship between Income Inequality, Poverty, and Globalization." Working Papers RP2005/37, World Institute for Development Economic Research.

Hess, C., and E. Ostrom. 2006. *Understanding Knowledge as a Commons: From Theory to Practice*. Cambridge MA: MIT Press.

Hilferding, R. 1910. *Das Finanzkapital: Eine Studie über die jüngste Entwick-lung des Kapitalismus*. Vienna: Wiener Volksbuchhandlung. *Finance Capital*. London: Routledge and Kegan Paul, 1981. (Trans.)

Himanshu, 2009. "New Global Poverty Estimates: What Do These Mean?" http://docs files.com/pdf_new_global_poverty_estimates_what_do_these_mean.html.

Hobson, J. A. 1902a. *Imperialism: A Study*. London: Nisbet.

Hobson, J. A. 1902b. "The Economic Taproot of Imperialism." *Contemporary Review*, August.

Hobson, J. A. 1902c. "The Scientific Basis of Imperialism." *Political Science Quarterly*, September.

Hoffman, A. 2009. "U.S. Global Hegemony: The Beginning … and the end." *GoldSeek. com*, April 19, http://news.goldseek.com/GoldSeek/1240158180.php.

Hogrefe J. and M. Kappler. 2013. "The Labor Share of Income: Heterogeneous Causes for Parallel Movements?", Journal of Economic Inequality, 11, 303-319.

Hubbard, R. G. (ed.). 1990. *Asymmetric Information, Corporate Finance, and Investment*. Chicago: University of Chicago Press.

Husson, M. 2008. "The Upward Trend in the Rate of Exploitation." *International Viewpoint*, February.

Husson, M., and D. Bensaïd (eds.). 2001. *Il nuovo disordine mondiale: L'imperialismo oggi e il movimento che lo contesta*. Milan: Nuove Edizioni Internazionali.

Hymer, S. H. 1976. *The International Operations of National Firms: A Study of Direct Foreign Investment*. Cambridge MA: MIT Press. (Posthumously Published PhD Dissertation [1960]).

Hymer, S. H. 1979. *The Multinational Corporation: A Radical Approach.* Cambridge: Cambridge University Press.

Ietto-Gillies, G. 2002. "Hymer, the Nation-State and the Determinants of Multinational Corporations' Activities." *Contributions to Political Economy*, 21, 43–54.

Ietto-Gillies, G. 2011. "Strategies of Transnational Companies in the Context of the Governance Systems of Nation-States." In M. Ugur and D. Sunderland (eds.), *Does Economic Governance Matter? Governance Institutions and Outcomes.* Cheltenham: Elgar.

Ietto-Gillies, G. 2012. *Transnational Corporations and International Production: Concepts, Theories and Effects.* Cheltenham: Elgar.

ILO. 2008. *World of Work Report 2008: Income Inequalities in the Age of Financial Globalization.* Geneva: International Institute for Labor Studies.

IMF. 2011a. *Enhancing International Monetary Stability: A Role for the SDR.* Washington: IMF.

IMF. 2011b. *Strengthening the International Monetary System: Taking Stock and Looking Ahead.* Washington: IMF.

IMF. 2011c. *Addressing Fiscal Challenges to Reduce Economic Risks.* World Economic and Financial Surveys, *Fiscal Monitor*, September, http://www.imf.org/external/pubs/ft/fm/2011/02/pdf/fm1102.pdf.

IMF. 2012a. *World Economic Outlook*, http://www.imf.org/external/pubs/ft/weo/2012/01/index.htm.

IMF. 2012b. *Currency Composition of Official Foreign Exchange Reserves (COFER).* http://www.imf.org/external/np/sta/cofer/eng/index.htm.

IMF. 2013. *Currency Composition of Official Foreign Exchange Reserves (COFER).* http://www.imf.org/external/np/sta/cofer/eng/index.htm.

IMF. 2014. *World Economic Outlook Update: Is the Tide Rising?* January, http://www.imf.org/external/pubs/ft/weo/2014/update/01/index.htm.

Jaffe, A. B., and J. Lerner. 2004. *Innovation and Its Discontents: How Our Broken Patent System Is Endangering Innovation and Progress, and What to Do about It.* Princeton: Princeton University Press.

Jaumotte F, and I. Tytell. 2007 "How Has the Globalization of Labor affected the Labor Income Share in Advanced Countries?", IMF Workig Paper N. 298.

Kaldor, N. 1966. *Causes of the Slow Rate of Economic Growth of the United Kingdom.* Cambridge: Cambridge University Press.

Kaplan, R. D. 2010. "A World with No One in Charge." *The Washington Post*, December 5.

Kautsky, K. 1892. *The Class Struggle (Erfurt Program).* London: Charles H. Kerr & Co, 1910, http://www.marxists.org/archive/kautsky/1892/erfurt/index.htm.

Kemp, T. 1967. *Theories of Imperialism.* London: Dobson.

Kiely, R. 2005. "Capitalist Expansion and the Imperialism-Globalization Debate." *Journal of International Relations and Development*, 8, 27–57.

Kiff, J., and V. Klyuev. 2009. "Foreclosure Mitigation Efforts in the US:

Approaches and Challenges." *International Monetary Fund Staff Position Note*, SPN/09/02, Feb. 18.

Kindleberger, C. P., 1978. *Manias, Panics and Crashes: A History of Financial Crises*. New York: Basic Books.

Kindleberger, C. P. 1984. "Banking and Industry between the Two Wars: An International Comparison." *Journal of European Economic History*, 13, 7–28.

Kindleberger, C. P., and R. Aliber. 2005. *Manias, Panics and Crashes: A History of Financial Crises*. Houndmills: Palgrave Macmillan.

Klein, N. 2007. *The Shock Doctrine: The Rise of Disaster Capitalism*. Toronto: Knopf Canada.

Knickerbocker, F. T. 1973. *Oligopolistic Reaction and Multinational Enterprise*. Boston: Graduate School of Business Administration, Harvard University.

Kose, M. A. 2002. "Explaining Business Cycles in Small Open Economies: How Much Do World Prices Matter?" *Journal of International Economics*, 56, 299–327.

Kose, M. A., E. Prasad, K. Rogoff, and S.-J. Wei. 2006. "Financial Globalization: A Reappraisal." IMF Working Papers N. 189.

Kregel, J. 2008. "Minsky's Cushions of Safety." Public Policy Brief N. 93, The Levy Economics Institute.

Krueger, A. 1999. "Measuring Labor's Share." *American Economic Review*, 89, 45–51.

Krugman, P. R. 1979. "Increasing Returns, Monopolistic Competition, and International Trade." *Journal of International Economics*, 9, 469–79.

Krugman, P. R. 1986. *Strategic Trade Policy and the New International Economics*. Cambridge, MA: MIT Press.

Krugman, P. R. 1991. "Increasing Returns and Economic Geography." *Journal of Political Economy*, 99, 483–99.

Krugman, P. R. 1998. "What's New about the New Economic Geography?" *Oxford Review of Economic Policy*, 14, 7–17.

Krugman, P. R. 2009. "Actually Existing Minsky," http://krugman.blogs.nytimes.com/2009/05/19/actually-existing-minsky/

Krugman, P. R., M. Obstfeld, and M. J. Melitz. 2012. *International Economics: Theory and Policy*, 9th edition. New York: Pearson.

Kurz, H. D., and N. Salvadori. 2010. "Trade Equilibrium among Growing Economies: Some Extensions." In Vint, Metcalfe, Kurz, Salvadori, and Samuelson (2010), 106–14.

Lane, P.R. 2006. "The Real Effects of European Monetary Union." *Journal of Economic Perspectives*, 20, 46–66.

Langot, F., L. Patureau, and T. Sopraseuth. 2012. "Optimal Fiscal Devaluation." IZA Discussion Paper Series N. 6624, http://ftp.iza.org/dp6624.pdf.

Lanoszka, A. 2003. "The Global Politics of Intellectual Property Rights and Pharmaceutical Drug Policies in Developing Countries." *International Political Science Review*, 24, 181–197.

Lapavitsas, C., et al. 2010. "Eurozone Crisis: Beggar Thyself and Thy Neighbour." *RMF Occasional Report*, March, http://researchonmoneyandfinance.org/media/reports/eurocrisis/fullreport.pdf.

Lardy, N. R. 2006. "China: Toward a Consumption-Driven Growth Path."
        Policy Briefs in International Economics. Washington, DC: Institute for
        International Economics.
Layne, C. D. 2009. "America's Middle East Grand Strategy after Iraq: The
        Moment for Offshore Balancing Has Arrived." *Review of International
        Studies,* 35, 5–25, http://journals.cambridge.org/action/
        displayAbstract?fromPage=online&aid=3291800.
Leaven, L., and F. Valencia. 2008. "Systemic Bank Crises: A New Database." IMF
        Working Paper WP/08/224.
Lemmi, A., and G. Betti. (eds.). 2006. *Fuzzy Set Approach to Multidimensional
        Poverty Measurement.* New York: Springer.
Lenin, V. I. 1915. Preface to N. Bukharin, *Imperialism and the World Economy.*
        Lenin Internet Archive, 2004, http://www.marxists.org/archive/
        lenin/works/1915/dec/00.htm.
Lenin, V. I. 1917. *Imperialism, the Highest Stage of Capitalism: A Popular Outline.*
        Lenin Internet Archive, 2005, http://www.marxists.org/archive/
        lenin/works/1916/imp-hsc/.
Leonardi, R., and R. Nanetti (eds.). 1990. *The Regions and European Integration:
        The Case of Emilia-Romagna.* London: Pinter.
Lim, M.-H. 2008. "Old Wine in a New Bottle: Subprime Mortgage Crisis–Causes and
        Consequences." Working Paper N. 532, The Levy Economics Institute.
Lindert, P. H., and P. J. Morton. 1989. "How Sovereign Debt Has Worked." In J.
        D. Sachs (ed.), *Developing Country Debt and Economic Performance,* vol.
        I. Chicago: University of Chicago Press.
Liu, H. C. K. 2002. "Dollar Hegemony Has Got to Go." *Asia Times Online,* April
        11, http://www.atimes.com/global-econ/DD11Dj01.html.
Longo, M. 2012. "Quei rialzi sincronizzati e il timore di un ribasso." *Il Sole 24 Ore,*
        February 23.
Lorentz, A. 2009. "Evolutionary Micro-Founded Technical Change and the
        Kaldor-Verdoorn Law: Estimates from an Artificial World." *Papers
        on Economics and Evolution,* Max Planck Institute of Economics,
        Evolutionary Economics Group, Jena.
Maddison, A. 2010. *Historical Statistics of the World Economy: 1–2008 AD,*
        Horizontal-file_02-2010.xls.
Maddison Project. 2013. *GDP per capita,* mpd_2013-01.xlsx.
Maffeo, V. 2012. "La crisi economica e il ruolo della BCE." In Cesaratto and
        Pivetti (2012), 111–21.
Malinconico, R. 2001. "Quando i minuti diventano ore: Tentativo di ragiona-
        mento sul neoimperialismo." In Husson and Bensaïd (2001).
Mandel, E. 1975. *Late Capitalism.* London: NBL.
Mandelbaum, M. 2005. *The Case for Goliath: How America Acts as the World's
        Government in the Twenty-first Century.* New York: Public Affairs.
Markusen, J. R. 2002. *Multinational Firms and the Theory of International Trade.*
        Cambridge MA: MIT Press.

Marx, K. 1848. *On the Question of Free Trade.* In *Panarchy,* http://www.panarchy. org/engels/freetrade.html

Marx, K. 1857–8. *Grundrisse,* translated by M. Nicolaus. Harmondsworth: Penguin, 1973.

Marx, K. 1863–6. *Results of the Immediate Process of Production,* translated by R. Livingstone. In Appendix to K. Marx, *Capital,* vol. I. Harmondsworth: Penguin, 1976.

Marx, K. 1867. *Capital,* vol. I, translated by B. Fowkes. Harmondsworth: Penguin, 1976.

Marx, K. 1894. *Capital,* vol. III, translated by D. Fernbach. Harmondsworth: Penguin, 1981.

Marx, K., and F. Engels. 1848. *Manifesto of the Communist Party,* in K. Marx, *The Revolution of 1848.* Harmondsworth: Penguin, 1973.

McCombie, J., M. Pugno, and B. Soro (eds.). 2003. *Productivity Growth and Economic Performance, Essays on Verdoorn's Law.* Houndmills: Palgrave Macmillan.

McCombie, J., and M. Roberts. 2007. "Returns to Scale and Regional Growth: The Static-Dynamic Verdoorn Law Paradox Revisited." *Journal of Regional Science,* 47, 179–208.

McMichael, P. 2000. *Development and Social Change: A Global Perspective.* Thousand Oaks, CA: Pine Forge.

Melitz, M. J. 2003. "The Impact of Trade on Intra-Industry Reallocations and Aggregate Industry Productivity." *Econometrica,* 71, 1695–1725.

Metcalfe, J. S., and I. Steedman. 1973a. "Heterogeneous Capital and the Heckscher-Ohlin-Samuelson Theory of Trade." In J. M. Parkin and A. R. Nobay (eds.), *Essays in Modern Economics.* London : Longman. (Also in Steedman, 1979a.)

Metcalfe, J. S., and I. Steedman. 1973b. "The Non-Substitution Theorem and International Trade Theory." *Australian Economic Papers,* 12, 267–9. (Also in Steedman, 1979a.)

Metcalfe, J. S., and I. Steedman. 1974. "A Note on the Gain from Trade." *Economic Record,* 50, 581–95. Also in Steedman, 1979a.

Milanovic, B. 2002. "Can We Discern the Effects of Globalization on Income Distribution? Evidence from Household Budget Surveys." World Bank Policy Research Working Paper Series N. 2876.

Milanovic, B. 2009. "Global Inequality and the Global Inequality Extraction Ratio: The Story of the Past Two Centuries." World Bank Policy Research Working Paper Series N. 5044.

Milanovic, B. 2012. "Global Inequality Recalculated and Updated: The Effect of New PPP Estimates on Global Inequality and 2005 Estimates." *Journal of Economic Inequality,* 10, 1–18.

Milios, J., and D. P. Sotiropoulos. 2009. *Rethinking Imperialism: A Study of Capitalist Rule.* Houndmills: Palgrave Macmillan.

Milner, H. V., and D. B. Yoffie. 1989. "Between Free Trade and Protectionism:

Strategic Trade Policy and a Theory of Corporate Trade Demand."
International Organization, 43, 239–72.

Minsky, H. P. 1982. *Can "It" Happen Again? Essays on Instability and Finance.* New York: Sharpe.

Minsky, H. P. 1986. *Stabilizing an Unstable Economy.* New York: McGraw-Hill.

Morin, F. 2006. *Le nouveau mur de l'argent.* Paris: Seuil.

Mundell, R. 2005. "The Case for a World Currency." *Journal of Policy Modelling*, 27, 465–75.

Nesvetailova, A. 2008. "The End of a Great Illusion: Credit Crunch and Liquidity Meltdown." DIIS Working Paper N. 2008/24. Copenhagen: Danish Institute for International Studies.

NPR. 2012. "Poverty in the U.S. by the Numbers," http://www.npr.org/2012/07/10/156387172/poverty-in-the-u-s-by-the-numbers

Oatley, T. 2007. *International Political Economy: Interests and Institutions in the Global Economy.* Harlow: Longman.

Obstfeld, M. 2009. "International Finance and Growth in Developing Countries: What Have We Learned?" *IMF Staff Papers*, 56, 63–111.

OECD. 2008. *Growing Unequal? Income Distribution and Poverty in OECD Countries.* Paris: OECD Publishing.

OECD. 2011. *Divided We Stand. Why Inequality Keeps Rising. An Overview of Growing Income Inequalities in OECD Countries: Main Findings.* Paris: OECD Publishing.

OECD. 2014. "Labour Productivity Growth in Total Economy," http://stats.oecd.org/Index.aspx?DataSetCode=PDYGTH.

Onado, M. 2012. *Finanza shock.* Milan: Il Sole 24 Ore.

O'Rourke, K. H. 2001. "Globalization and Inequality: Historical Trends." NBER Working Paper N. 8339.

Ottaviano, G. I. P. 2010. " 'New' New Economic Geography: Firm Heterogeneity and Agglomeration Economies." *Journal of Economic Geography*, 11, 231–40.

Palma, J. G. 2006. "Globalizing Inequality: 'Centrifugal' and 'Centripetal' Forces at Work." DESA Working Paper N. 35.

Palma, J. G. 2009. "The Revenge of the Market on the Rentiers: Why Neoliberal Reports of the End of the History Turned Out to Be Premature." *Cambridge Journal of Economics*, 33, 829–66.

Panić, M. 2011. *Globalization: A Threat to International Cooperation and Peace?* 2nd edition. Houndmills: Palgrave Macmillan.

Panitch, L. 2000. "The New Imperial State." *New Left Review*, 11, 5–20.

Panitch, L., and S. Gindin. 2004. "Global Capitalism and American Empire." In L. Panitch and C. Leys (eds.), *The New Imperial Challenge*, in *Socialist Register 2004*, London: Merlin, 1–42.

Panitch, L., and S. Gindin. 2005. "Finance and American Empire." In L. Panitch and C. Leys (eds.), *The Empire Reloaded*, in *Socialist Register 2005*, London: Merlin, 46–81.

Pape, R. A. 2009. "Empire Falls." *The National Interest*, January 22, http://

nationalinterest.org/article/empire-falls-2952.

Parrinello, S. 1970. "Introduzione a una teoria neo-ricardiana del commercio internazionale." *Economia Internazionale*, 25, 267–321.

Parrinello, S. 2010. "The Notion of National Competitiveness in a Global Economy." In Vint, Metcalfe, Kurz, Salvadori, and Samuelson (2010), 49–68.

Patel, P., and K. Pavitt. 1991. "Large Firms in the Production of the World's Technology: An Important Case of Non-Globalization." *Journal of International Business Studies*, 1, 1–21.

Patel, P., and K. Pavitt. 1994. "The Nature and Economic Importance of the National Innovation Systems." *STI Review (OECD)*, N. 14, 9–32.

Peoples, J., and R. Sugden. 2000. "Divide and Rule by Transnational Corporations." In C. N. Pitelis and R. Sugden (eds.), *The Nature of the Transnational Firm*. London: Routledge, 174–92.

Perelstein, J. S. 2009. "Macroeconomic Imbalances in the United States and Their Impact on the International Financial System." Working Paper N. 554, The Levy Economics Institute.

Petras, J., and H. Veltmeyer. 2001. *Globalization Unmasked: Imperialism in the XXIst Century*. London: Zed Books.

Petri, F. 2012. "Una prospettiva disincantata sulla crisi economica contemporanea e sulla teoria economica contemporanea." In P. Della Porta (ed.), *Crisi dell'economia e crisi della teoria economica?* Naples: Liguori.

Pietroburgo, A. 2009. "The End of American Hegemony." *Enzine Articles*, April 5, http://ezinearticles.com/?The-End-of-American-Hegemony&id=2207395.

Pizzuto, P. 2012. *Disuguaglianza e povertà nell'economia globale contemporanea*. Degree Dissertation, University of Siena.

Pogge, T. 2010. "How Many Poor People Should There Be? A Rejoinder to Ravallion." In S. Anand, P. Segal, and J. E. Stiglitz (eds.), *Debates on the Measurement of Global Poverty*. Oxford: Oxford University Press, 102–114.

Quaresima, G. 2011. *La globalizzazione e le nuove teorie dell'imperialismo*. Pistoia: Petite Plaisance.

Qureshi, M. S., and G. Wan. 2008. "Distributional Consequences of Globalization: Empirical Evidence from Panel Data." *Journal of Development Studies*, 44, 1424–49.

Rajan, R. G. 2010. *Fault Lines: How Hidden Fractures Still Threaten the World Economy*. Princeton: Princeton University Press.

Rajan, R. G., and I. Tokatlidis. 2005. "Dollar Shortages and Crises." *International Journal of Central Banking*, 1, 177–220.

Ravaillon, M. 2001. *Growth, Inequality, and Poverty: Looking beyond Averages*. World Bank Policy Research Working Paper Series N. 2558.

Ravaillon, M. 2004. "Pessimistic on Poverty?" *The Economist*, April 7, http://www.economist.com/node/2571960.

Reddy, S. G. 2008. "The World Bank's New Poverty Estimates – Digging Deeper into a Hole." Working Paper, Institute for Social Analysis, Columbia University, http://www.columbia.edu/~sr793/response.pdf.

Reddy, S. G., and C. Minoiu. 2007. "Has World Poverty *Really* Fallen?" *Review of Income and Wealth*, 53, 484–502.

Reddy, S. G., and T. W. Pogge. 2005. "How *Not* to Count the Poor." Working Paper, Institute for Social Analysis, Columbia University, http://www.columbia.edu/~sr793/count.pdf.

Reddy, S. G., and T. W. Pogge. 2009. "How Not to Count the Poor." Initiative for Policy Dialogue Working Paper Series, May.

Rees, J. 2006. *Imperialism and Resistance*. London: Routledge.

Reich, R. B. 2010. *Aftershock*. New York: Knopf.

Reinhart, C., and K. Rogoff. 2009. *This Time Is Different: Eight Centuries of Financial Folly*. Princeton: Princeton University Press.

Roach, S. S. 2011. "Ten Reasons why China Is Different." *Project Syndicate: A World of Ideas*, May 27, http://www.project-syndicate.org/commentary/ten-reasons-why-china-is-different.

Robinson, W. I. 2004. *A Theory of Global Capitalism*. Baltimore: Johns Hopkins University Press.

Robinson, W. I. 2005. "Gramsci and Globalization: From Nation-State to Transnational Hegemony." *Critical Review of International Social and Political Philosophy*, 8, 1–16.

Robinson, W. I. 2007a. "Beyond the Theory of Imperialism: Global Capitalism and the Transnational State." *Societies without Borders*, 2, 5–26.

Robinson, W. I. 2007b. "Theories of Globalization." In G. Ritzer (ed.), *The Blackwell Companion to Globalization*. Oxford: Blackwell.

Rodrik, D. 2000. "Comments on 'Trade, Growth and Poverty' by D. Dollar and A. Kraay." Research Paper, Harvard University, www.hks.harvard.edu/fs/drodrik/Research papers/Rodrik on Dollar-Kraay.pdf.

Rodrik, D. 2007. *One Economics, Many Recipes*. Princeton: Princeton University Press.

Rodrik, D. 2011. *The Globalization Paradox: Democracy and the Future of the World Economy*. London: Norton.

Rodrik, D., and A. Subramanian. 2005. "From 'Hindu Growth' to Productivity Surge: The Mystery of the Indian Growth Transition." *IMF Staff Papers*, 55, 193–228.

Rodrik, D., and A. Subramanian. 2009. "Why Did Financial Globalization Disappoint?" *IMF Staff Papers*, 56, 112–38.

Ross, R. J. S., and K. Trachte. 1990. *Global Capitalism: The New Leviathan*. Albany: State University of New York Press.

Rothman, A., and J. Zhu. 2012. *Misunderstanding China: Popular Western Illusions Debunked*. Hong Kong: CLSA, http://www.slideshare.net/jpitak/misunderstanding-china.

Sala-i-Martin, X. 2002. "The World Distribution of Income (Estimated from Individual Country Distributions)." NBER Working Paper N. 8933.

Sala-i-Martin, X. 2006. "The World Distribution of Income: Falling Poverty and
       . . . Convergence, Period." The Quarterly Journal of Economics, 121,
       351–397, http://qje.oxfordjournals.org/content/121/2/351.short.
Samuelson, P. A. 1962. "The Gains from International Trade Once Again." The
       Economic Journal, 72, 820–29. (Reprinted in The Collected Scientific
       Papers of Paul A. Samuelson, vol. 2, 1966, Cambridge, MA: MIT Press,
       792–801.)
Samuelson, P. A. 2001. "A Ricardo-Sraffa Paradigm Comparing Gains from Trade
       in Inputs and Finished Goods." Journal of Economic Literature, 39,
       1204–14.
Screpanti, E. 1989. "Monetary Dynamics, Speculation, and the Term Structure of
       Interest Rates." Economic Notes, 18, 167–91.
Screpanti, E. 1996. "A Pure Insider Theory of Hysteresis in Employment and
       Unemployment." Review of Radical Political Economics, 28, 1–18.
Screpanti, E. 1997a. "Banks, Increasing Risk, and the Endogenous Money
       Supply." Economic Notes, 26, 567–87.
Screpanti, E. 1997b. "La mitologia del postfordismo e la soggezione ideologica
       della sinistra: quali fondamenti per la politica dell'occupazione?"
       Marxismo Oggi, 10, 118–149.
Screpanti, E. 2000. "Wages, Employment, and Militancy: A Simple Model and
       Some Empirical Tests." Review of Radical Political Economics, 32,
       171–196.
Screpanti, E. 2001. The Fundamental Institutions of Capitalism. London: Routledge.
Screpanti, E. 2004. "L'imperialismo globale e le leggi 'naturali' dell'accumula-
       zione capitalistica." Proteo, part I, N. 1, 100–105; part II, N. 2, 116–122.
Screpanti, E. 2006. Il capitalismo: Forme e trasformazioni. Milan: Punto Rosso.
Screpanti, E. 2010. "La grande crisi e l'imperialismo globale." Quaderni del
       Dipartimento di Economia Politica N. 590, April, University of Siena.
Screpanti, E. 2011. "Globalization and the Great Crisis." In Brancaccio and
       Fontana (2011), 201–16.
Screpanti, E., and S. Zamagni. 2005. An Outline of the History of Economic Thought.
       Oxford: Oxford University Press.
Sen, A. K. 1983. "Poverty, Relatively Speaking." Oxford Economic Papers, 38,
       153–69.
Serfati, C. 2004. Impérialisme et militarisme. Lausanne: Éditions Page Deux.
Sklair, L. 2001. The Transnational Capitalist Class. Oxford: Blackwell.
Sklair, L. 2002. Globalization: Capitalism and Its Alternatives. Oxford: Oxford
       University Press.
Sklair, L., and P. T. Robbins. 2002. "Global Capitalism and Major Corporations
       from the Third World." Third World Quarterly, 23, 81–100.
Sklair, L., and D. Miller. 2010. "Capitalist Globalization, Corporate Social
       Responsibility and Social Policy." Critical Social Policy, 30, 472–95.
Slovik, P., and B. Cournède. 2011. "Macroeconomic Impact of Basel III." OECD
       Economics Department Working Papers N. 844.

Soros, G. 2012. "How to Save the Euro." *The New York Review of Books*, February 23.

Spencer, B., and J. Brander. 1983. "International R&D Rivalry and Industrial Strategy." *Review of Economic Studies*, 50, 707–22.

Srinivasan, T. N., and S. D. Tendulkar. 2003. *Reintegrating India with the World Economy*. Washington, D.C.: Institute for International Economics.

Steedman, I. 1979a. *Fundamental Issues in Trade Theory*. London: Macmillan.

Steedman, I. 1979b. *Trade amongst Growing Economies*. Cambridge: Cambridge University Press.

Stiglitz, J. E. 2001. *In un mondo imperfetto: Mercato e democrazia nell'era della globalizzazione*. Rome: Donzelli.

Stiglitz, J. E. 2002. *Globalization and Its Discontents*. New York: Norton.

Stiglitz, J. E. 2010. *Freefall: America, Free Markets, and the Sinking of the World Economy*. New York: Norton.

Stiratai. 2010. "La riduzione del prodotto che va al lavoro." *Economia e Politica*, November, http://www.economiaepolitica.it/index.php/distribuzione-e-poverta/la-riduzione-del-prodotto-che-va-al-lavoro/#.Uca_79jeBv8.

Summers, L. H. 2006. "Reflections on Global Account Imbalances and Emerging Markets Reserves Accumulation." L. K. Jha Memorial Lecture, Reserve Bank of India.

Sutcliffe, B. 2004. "World Inequality and Globalization." *Oxford Review of Economic Policy*, 20, 15–37.

SWIFT. 2013. "RMB Now 2nd Most Used Currency in Trade Finance, Overtaking the Euro," December 3, http://www.swift.com/about_swift/shownews?param_dcr=news.data/en/swift_com/2013/PR_RMB_nov.xml.

Taylor, J. 2007. "A Symbiotic Relationship between the United States and China." *Seeking Alpha*, June, 8. http://seekingalpha.com/article/37861-a-symbiotic-relationship-between-the-united-states-and-china

Taylor, J. B. 2009. *Getting Off Track: How Government Actions and Interventions Caused, Prolonged, and Worsened the Financial Crisis*. Stanford, CA: Hoover Institution Press.

Temin, P. 1989. *Lessons from the Great Depression*. Cambridge, MA: MIT Press.

Toporowski, J. 2009. "The Economics and Culture of Financial Inflation." *Competition and Change*, 13, 147–58.

Townsend, P. 1979. *Poverty in the United Kingdom*. London: Penguin.

Trading Economics. 2013. *GDP Growth Rates*, http://www.tradingeconomics.com

UNCTAD. 2011. *World Investment Report. Annex table 34: Number of Parent Corporations and Foreign Affiliates, by Region and Economy, Latest Available Year*, 28/07/11, Geneva: United Nations, http://archive.unctad.org/sections/dite_dir/docs/WIR11_webpercent20tabpercent2034.pdf

UNCTAD. 2012. *World Investment Report 2012: Toward a New Generation of Investment Policies*. Geneva: United Nations, http://www.unctad-docs.org/files/UNCTAD-WIR2012-Full-en.pdf

Ulubasoglu, M. A. 2004. "Globalization and Inequality." *The Australian Economic Review*, 37, 116–22.

Vercelli, A. 2009. "A Theory of Minsky Moment: A Restatement of the Financial Instability Hypothesis in the Light of the 'Subprime' Crisis." Paper presented at the Workshop *The Complexity of Financial Crisis in a Long-Period Perspective: Facts, Theory and Models*, University of Siena.

Verdoorn, J. P. 1949. "Fattori che regolano lo sviluppo della produttività del lavoro." *L'Industria*, 1, 45–53. (Trans. in L. Pasinetti (ed.), *Italian Economic Papers*, II, Oxford: Oxford University Press, 1993.)

Vernengo, M., and E. Pérez-Caldentey. 2012. "The Euro Imbalances and Financial Deregulation: A Post-Keynesian Interpretation of the European Debt Crisis." *Real-World Economics Review*, 59, 83–104.

Vint, J., J. S. Metcalfe, H. D. Kurz, N. Salvadori, and P. A. Samuelson (eds.). 2010. *Economic Theory and Economic Thought: Essays in Honour of Ian Steedman*. London: Routledge.

Volpi, A. 2013. *La globalizzazione dalla culla alla crisi: Una nuova biografia del mercato globale*. Milan: Altreconomia.

Wade, R. 2002. "Globalisation, Poverty and Income Distribution: Does the Liberal Argument Hold?" Paper presented at the Reserve Bank of Australia Conference, http://www.rba.gov.au/publications/confs/2002/wade.pdf.

Wade, R. 2004. "Is Globalization Reducing Poverty and Inequality?" *World Development*, 20, 567–89.

Wade, R. 2008. "The First-World Debt Crisis in Global Perspective." Paper presented at the Conference on Subprime Crisis, University of Warwick.

Wallerstein, I. 1974–89. *The Modern World-System*, 3 vols. London: Academic Press.

Wallerstein, I. 1999. "States? Sovereignty? The Dilemmas of Capitalists in an Age of Transition." In D. A. Smith, D. J. Solinger, and S. C. Topik (eds.), *States and Sovereignty in the Global Economy*. London: Routledge.

Wallerstein, I. 2003. "U.S. Weakness and the Struggle for Hegemony." *Monthly Review*, 55, August, http://monthlyreview.org/2003/07/01/u-s-weakness-and-the-struggle-for-hegemony.

Wallison, P. J. 2008. "Fair Value Accounting: A Critique." *Financial Services Outlook*, American Enterprise Institute for Public Policy Research, July.

Watal, J. 2001. *Intellectual Property Rights in the WTO and Developing Countries*. Alphen aan den Rijn: Kluwer Law International.

Went, R. 2002. *The Enigma of Globalization*. London: Routledge.

Wessel, D. 2009. *In Fed We Trust: Ben Bernanke's War on the Great Panic*. New York: Crown Business.

Whalen, C. J. 2007. "The U.S. Credit Crunch of 2007: A Minsky Moment." Public Policy Brief N. 92, The Levy Economics Institute.

Williamson, J. 1989. "What Washington Means by Policy Reform." In J. Williamson (ed.), *Latin American Readjustment: How Much Has Happened?* Washington, D. C.: Institute for International Economics.

Williamson, J. 2004. *Short History of the Washington Consensus*, Washington, D.C.:
      Peterson Institute for International Economics, http://www.iie.com/
      publications/papers/williamson0904-2.pdf.
Wolf, M. 2005. *Why Globalization Works.* London: Yale Nota Bene.
Wood, E. M. 2002. "Global Capital, National States." In M. Rupert and H. Smith
      (eds.), *Historical Materialism and Globalization.* London: Routledge,
      17–39.
Wood, E. M. 2003. *The Empire of Capital.* London: Verso.
World Bank. 1990. *World Development Report 1990: Poverty.* New York: Oxford
      University Press.
World Bank. 2013a. *Capital for the Future: Saving and Investment in an
      Interdependent World,* http://econ.worldbank.org/WBSITE/
      EXTERNAL/EXTDEC/.
World Bank. 2013b. *World Economic Outlook: Hopes, Realities, Risks*, April,
      http://www.imf.org/external/pubs/ft/weo/2013/01/pdf/text.pdf.
Wray, L. R. 2008. "Financial Markets Meltdown: What Can We Learn from
      Minsky?" Public Policy Brief N. 94A, The Levy Economics Institute.
Xiaokun, L. 2010. "Wen Upbeat on US Relations Despite Strains." *China Daily*,
      March 23, http://www.chinadaily.com.cn/cndy/2010-03/23/con-
      tent_9625705.htm
Yang, D. T., J. Zhang, and S. Zhou. 2011. "Why Are Saving Rates So High in
      China?" NBER Working Paper Series N. 16771.
Yongnian, Z. 2010. "America's Loss of Its Hegemony Causes China to Face
      Greater International Pressure." *Lianhe Zaobao*, November. (Trans.
      in *Watching America*, http://watchingamerica.com/News/79192/
      america%E2%80%99s-loss-of-its-hegemony-causes-china-to-face-grea-
      ter-international-pressure/.)
Zakaria, F. 2009. *The Post-American World.* New York: Norton.
Zezza, G. 2012. "La crisi dell'euro: Invertire la rotta o abbandonare la nave?" In
      Cesaratto and Pivetti (2012), 89–103.
Ziegler, J. 2002. *Les nouveaux maîtres du monde et ceux qui leur resistent.* Paris:
      Fayard.
Zhou, X. 2009. "Reform the International Monetary System." Beijing: People's
      Bank of China. Also in BIS, http://www.bis.org/review/r090402c.pdf.

Notes

1. In Screpanti (1997), I outlined some criticisms of the "good globalization" ideology. Here I adjust my argument, taking account of various recent contributions, including Beck (2000), Anonymous Authors (2002), Stiglitz (2002), Ziegler (2002), Ellwood (2003), Dal Bosco (2004), Driskill (2007), Rodrik, (2011), Volpi (2013).

2. The UN defines these as Least Developed Countries. They include all nations with: an annual per-capita income of less than $905; a high rate of Human Resource Weakness; and high economic vulnerability. There are currently forty-eight such countries (thirty-three of which are African), with 880 million inhabitants. They represent 12 percent of the global population and less than 2 percent of the GDP.

3. Williamson (1989) uses this expression to summarize the political philosophy that emerged at the end of the 1980s in the wake of exchanges between the main leaders of the global economy. The consensus was built around the following principles: reduction of the degree of tax progressiveness in order to boost investment; broadening of the tax base to include less well-off social classes so as compensate for the reduction in tax revenue; liberalization of financial markets to lower interest rates; guarantee of equal treatment between foreign direct investment and national investment; deregulation of markets and privatization of state enterprises to foster competition; strengthening the protection of private property; liberalization of foreign trade; encouragement of economic sectors oriented toward exports; limitation of public budget deficits; abolition of state subsidies to achieve market transparency; reorientation of public spending toward the provision of the *minimum* services necessary to provide for the poor and foster development (*primary* education, *primary* health services, infrastructures). For a reconstruction of the genesis of the *Washington Consensus* see Beaud (1999) and Williamson (2004).

4. Here are some of the most bizarre. Markets are intertemporally and conditionally complete, that is to say, there are markets for any future good in any possible event. For example, an umbrella to be delivered on a particular day of next year in case it rains that day; prices are fixed by an omniscient

auctioneer who operates in a logical time different from real time; information is complete and symmetric; technology is known and accessible
to everyone; returns to scale are constant; transport and transaction costs
are nil; production factors are fully employed; consumers have identical
and exogenous preferences; no externalities exist; equilibrium is stable
and unique. Particular problems arise when dealing with capital, which in
most models is treated as a homogenous factor available in a given quantity.
Only recently, prompted by the criticisms of various Sraffian economists
(such as those I refer to below), have models been designed (for example,
Samuelson, 2001) that take into account the use of produced capital goods
and confirm the main conclusions of the HOS model *under very special
hypotheses*. However, it has been demonstrated that under other hypotheses
the introduction of heterogeneous capital with a uniform rate of profit in a
constant growth model can lead to realistic results that are disconcerting for
HOS theory. Opening up to foreign trade can, for example, produce losses
instead of improvements in welfare, and a large country can produce all
goods while a small one specializes in the production of a single good. For
criticisms from the Sraffian school see Parrinello (1970; 2010), Steedman
and Metcalfe (1973a; 1973b; 1974), Mainwaring (1974; 1975), Steedman
(1979a, 1979b); Gram (2010), Kurz and Salvadori (2010).

5.   The modern ordinalist approach does not allow for interpersonal comparisons of utility. Thus, even if a change were to produce a net monetary
advantage in the aggregate (the greater profits of some exceeding the losses
of the others), it would not be possible to say that an improvement in collective welfare had occurred. It is necessary to use the Pareto criterion to assess
the aggregate effects of change: improvement occurs only when somebody
is better off and nobody is worse off. The adoption of a cardinal measure
of utility would complicate rather than solve the problem, as it would be
impossible to conclude anything about aggregate welfare changes without
knowing the utility functions of all the individuals. Nor could we resort to
a simplifying assumption typical of general equilibrium models, that is, that
all individuals have the same utility function. Suppose there is an increase
in aggregate output, with the rich people's income rising more than that of
the poor shrinks. Given the assumption of decreasing marginal utility, the
welfare improvement of the former might be lower than the welfare loss of
the latter.

6.   The four IMF researchers claim that this empirical evidence is slightly less
apparent when research focuses on microeconomic rather than macroeconomic effects. They live in hope, arguing that if things are not so good at the
moment, it doesn't mean that they can't improve in the future. To help foster
hope, they have developed a new growth model in which the positive effects
of financial globalization are felt through some *"potential* collateral benefits"
rather than through the traditional channels of savings and investments.
Once a certain threshold effect has been triggered, these benefits should

produce the desired positive results. As if to say that the causal link between financial globalization and growth has not been empirically demonstrated, at least for today, but there is a possible, *potential*, nexus and nothing to say that it couldn't become true in the future. The important thing is that governments act to favor the achievement of the threshold effects, for example, by encouraging the development of financial markets.

7. The last effect was brought to light by the *New Trade Theory* and *New Economic Geography*, begun by Paul Krugman and developed in various more recent reformulations. See Krugman (1979; 1991), Brewer (1985), Helpman and Krugman (1985), Gandolfo (1998), Melitz (2003), Ottaviano (2010), Fujimoto and Shiozawa (2011), and Helpman (2011). These theoretical models follow heterodox approaches: neo-Keynesian, post-Keynesian, or Sraffian. They adopt different combinations of the following hypotheses: increasing returns to scale, endogenous technical progress, underemployment of factors, centrality of multinational firms, imperfect or oligopolistic competition, fixed prices. They demonstrate that a country's endowment of factors, and especially of capital, is *path-dependent* and determined both by historical events and by industrial policies; most trade is intra-industry and involves countries with similar production structures and factor endowment; multinational firms play an essential role in increasing production on a global scale.

8. Most emerging and developing countries have followed the same time scale. From the 1950s through the 1970s, protectionism and import substitution policies propped up forced industrialization. Between the end of the 1970s and the early 1980s, internal liberalization policies were implemented. In 1980 development began to accelerate and, for the first time, exports of manufactured goods overtook exports of agricultural products; in the early 1980s exports exceeded imports, and average tariffs began to decrease. In China and India growth rates jumped at the beginning of the 1980s, and accelerated in the 1990s. See Srinivasan and Tendulkar (2003), Rodrik and Subramanian (2005), Rodrik (2007), Krugman, Obstfeld and Melitz (2012).

9. *Strategic trade policy* was theorized to account for certain neo-mercantilist policies adopted even by advanced countries. It differs from previous theories of protectionism in that it assumes industrial markets are oligopolistic and economies of scale and age play a crucial role in creating competitive advantages for the first firms to open up a market. Strategic trade policies are implemented by governments wishing to favor the birth and expansion of national firms in industries where, given the large market shares of already established companies, there would be no space for new firms. See Brander and Spencer (1981; 1985), Spencer and Brander (1983), Dixit (1984), Krugman (1986), Milner and Yoffie (1989), Oately (2007).

10. Some significant contributions are Gallino (2000), O'Rourke (2001), Acocella (2004), Heshmati (2005), Anand and Segal (2007), Ferreira and

Ravaillon (2008), ILO (2008), Atkinson and Brandolini (2009), Fiorentini (2011), Fiorentini and Montani (2012), Pizzuto (2012).

11. Among the most outstanding contributions extolling the successes of the global battle against poverty, see Bhalla (2002), Bourguignon and Morisson (2002), Chen and Ravaillon (2001; 2007; 2008; 2012), Collier and Dollar (2002), Dollar and Kraay (2001a; 2001b), Ravaillon (2001; 2004), Sala-i-Martin (2002; 2006).

12. An innovative multidimensional method of measurement has been developed by Betti, Cheli, Lemmi and Verma (2006), Lemmi and Betti (2006). Eurostat (2002) has used a multidimensional approach over the last decade or so, and even the World Bank has recently shown signs of wanting to move in this direction (Elbers, Lanjouw and Lanjouw, 2003; Betti, Dabalen, Ferré and Neri, 2013).

13. Some researchers claim that setting two thresholds—one for poverty ($2.50) and one for extreme poverty ($1.25)—helps contextualize measurements, as the first is suitable to measure the phenomenon in some countries (Latin America, Eastern Europe, and the Caribbean) with medium-to-low incomes, and the second to measure it in the poorest countries. If this were the case, though, the two thresholds should not be applied indiscriminately to all countries. The first should only be valid for medium-to-low income countries and the second only for the poorest nations.

14. For methodological criticisms, see in particular Wade (2002; 2004), Reddy and Pogge (2005; 2009), Reddy and Minoiu (2007), Reddy (2008), Himanshu (2009), Pogge (2010).

15. To deal with some methodological problems the World Bank has pledged to develop a PPP for the poor (PPPP). However, calculation of this index might involve a circular reasoning: to define a PPPP, the consumption of the poor needs to be measured. But in order to identify the poor, we first need to identify the poverty threshold, which in turn requires knowledge of the PPPP. The problem could be resolved by explicitly defining a basket of subsistence goods, using this as a basis to calculate minimum income with the indirect method, and then applying PPPP. But in this case different poverty thresholds should be accepted for every single country, as the baskets would vary according to the standard of living in each one. Another problem with PPP is that, if the same base year is always maintained, the data would be comparable in time, but their ability to account for the most recent situations would change, as consumption habits evolve with the passing of time. To avoid wearing out the base, the World Bank adopted new PPP conversion factors with new base years. This produced new datasets that are not comparable with the old ones and, above all, make the new criteria inadequate to evaluate the old levels of poverty. There are further methodological difficulties. With the passing of time, not only have the base years changed, but so have the formulas used to construct the PPP indices (from the Geary-Khamis formula to that of Eltetö-Köves-Szulc), as well as the sources used for their

calculation (from the Penn World Tables to the International Comparison Program). The sample of countries selected to define the poverty threshold has also changed (in 1990 the minimum income was established by observing that of the eight poorest countries in the world; in 1993 the median of the minimum income of ten countries was used; in 2005 the mean minimum income in fifteen countries). Moreover, the threshold values have also been altered (for extreme poverty they increased from $1 to $1.08 then $1.25, while for poverty they escalated from $2 to $2.15 and $2.50). Lastly, it must be recalled that the data used for the various countries are not entirely homogeneous: in some countries they were taken from family surveys, in others from national accounting indicators, and in some cases from both. In some countries income was observed, in others consumption; in some actual prices and quantities were used, in others estimations; in some detection was carried out only in certain cities, in others throughout the country.

16.   This kind of research would be very difficult, as it requires an evaluation of the extent to which policies are oriented toward free trade. An attempt in this direction was made by Dollar and Kraay (2001a, 2001b), who produced an econometric study of the correlation between poverty, growth, and globalization. They subdivided countries into globalizers and non-globalizers, and obtained an impressive result: the globalizers have succeeded in reducing poverty most, as their income has grown more than that of the non-globalizers. Even more impressive is that China is classified as a globalizer. Rodrik (2000), commenting on a previous version of the paper, pointed out that the result obtained by Dollar and Kraay is determined by an arbitrary grouping of countries and that their methods of classification are flawed.

17.   This is how European bureaucrats euphemistically define the conditions of the social strata with a disposable income below the threshold of relative poverty (set at 60 percent of the national median). It would seem that there are no poor people in Europe, only people *at risk* of becoming poor.

18.   Other interesting research has been performed by Cornia (2003), Ulubasoglu (2004), Palma (2006), Goldberg and Pavcnik (2007), Dreher and Gaston (2008), OECD (2008), Qureshi and Wan (2008), Berg and Nilsson (2010), Celik and Basdas (2010), Berg and Ostroy (2011). Problems with the use of PPP and the choice of base years also arise in measuring inequality. Milanovic, to be sure, supplemented the above-mentioned indices (calculated with a 2005 base year) with others calculated with a 1993 base year. The trend remains ascending, although the values are lower. See also Milanovic (2002; 2009).

19.   Sutcliffe (2004, 26), for example, showed a case in which the Gini coefficient decreased from 0.67 to 0.63 between 1980 and 2000, while the ratio of the income of the richest 1 percent of the population to that of the poorest 1 percent rose from 216.17 to 414.57.

20.   The exceptions are the eastern European countries, Russia, the Middle East, and North Africa, where the wage share has fluctuated around a flat trend.

21.   I originally presented an outline of the arguments developed in this and the following chapter in two seminars held in Florence in 1999 and 2000. I later published them in Screpanti (2004; 2006).

22.   Two articles on the same subject (Hobson, 1902b; 1902c) are also worthy of attention. Note that Kautsky (1892) had anticipated some of Hobson's ideas on the roots of imperialism.

23.   Wallerstein (1974–89), Amin (2002), Milios and Sotiropoulos (2009) are among the authors who have developed this notion with greatest clarity.

24.   Kemp (1967), noting that Lenin is rather evasive about Hobson's under-consumption hypothesis, identified a weakness in his theory in that he does not develop an alternative conjecture regarding the roots of imperialism, not even one based on the falling profit rate. To me this seems a strong point, as it frees his theory from ad hoc hypotheses. Hilferding also touched upon underconsumption without giving it much weight.

25.   Of course, qualifications could be made, but not to the extent that the substance would change. For example, with the financialization of global markets the relationship between financial and industrial capital became much more complex than Lenin and Hilferding, studying the German econ-omy in the early 1900s, could have imagined. Likewise, the prevalent market regime in modern global capitalism is that of oligopolistic competition, rather than monopoly in the strict sense. A corollary of this qualification is that technological progress, rather than being hampered by competition between large firms, is actually helped by it, and consequently capitalism tends not to "putrefy," as Lenin maintained, but, if anything, to metastasize.

26.   For this reason I am unconvinced by attempts to update Lenin's theory and repropose the notion of the essential nature of inter-imperial contradictions by shifting their application from the national scale to that of the continen-tal imperial poles (see, for example, Casadio, Petras and Vasapollo, 2004). Similar arguments were made by Callinicos (1991a; 1991b) who wisely adjusted his position in the light of subsequent events (Callinicos, 2005). According to this vision, of which Mandel (1975) was one of the first and most prestigious advocates, we would now be living in a system character-ized by conflict between three great continental imperial powers: the United States, Europe, and Japan. This argument may have had its attractions in the 1970s and 1980s, when Japan was storming the American market and Europe had already established its predominance in world trade, while planning a leap forward with the euro. Nowadays it is difficult to see these "super-contradictions," or at least to see anything essential in them.

27.   Milios and Sotiropoulos (2009, 70–71, 82–83), having noted that various (more or less neo-Leninist) contemporary theories of imperialism tend to postulate some form of autonomy of the political, observe that they have nothing to do with Marx's theory and attribute their origin to Weber.

28.   Hardt and Negri (2002) explicitly refute the thesis of U.S. super-impe-rialism. Nonetheless, they slip into it on several occasions, such as when

attributing special roles in the building of the empire to America's military power and Constitution. In other ways the thesis of the postmodern empire can be reduced to that of ultra-imperialism (Callinicos, 2007, 535).

29. For instance Boròn (2001; 2002), Petras and Veltmeyer (2001). For a critical review see Quaresima (2001).

30. See in particular Arrighi (1994; 2005), Gowan (1999), Harvey (2003), Harman (2003), Callinicos (2005; 2007; 2009), Serfati (2004), Bello (2005), Ashman and Callinicos (2006), Rees (2006).

31. Together with the works of Ross and Trachte (1990), McMichael (2000), Sklair and Robbins (2002), Went (2002), Sklair and Miller (2010), they contribute to developing an innovative approach that updates, and in many ways goes beyond, the twentieth-century theories of imperialism. For critical reviews of the new theories of imperialism, see Kiely (2005), Robinson (2007a; 2007b), Callinicos (2007), Milios and Sotiropoulos (2009), Quaresima (2011).

32. In this sense see also Arrighi (1994).

33. The Europeanization of America and Oceania predates nineteenth- to twentieth-century imperialism and is ascribable to sixteenth- to eighteenth-century mercantilism.

34. For Malinconico (2001) the capitalist relationship "totalizes," for Wood (2003) it "universalizes."

35. As already theorized by Emmanuel (1972). See Gibson (1980) for a thorough formalization.

36. Following a long period of stagnation, Africa underwent a relatively intense process of development between 2001 and 2007, with a mean annual GDP growth rate of between 4.9 and 6.7 percent. This jump was made possible by a rise in raw material prices and a drop in interest rates. But also very low wages gave their contribution: in 2007 85 percent of workers in Sub-Saharan countries earned less than 2 dollars a day. With the present crisis the growth rate fell to 1.7 percent in 2009. Obviously the situation varies from one country to another: some (for example, South Africa, Angola, Chad, Guinea, Ethiopia, Mauritania, Sudan, Uganda) have had very high growth rates in some years, while others (such as the Central African Republic, Eritrea, Liberia, Madagascar, Seychelles, Zimbabwe) had negative growth rates even in the global boom years. The fact remains that thirty-three of the forty-eight countries defined by the UN as Least Developed Countries are African. In any case, according to some forecasts, Sub-Saharan Africa should grow at high rates (about 5.5 percent) in 2014.

37. These include some countries "in transition" toward market capitalism.

38. The *imperium* was the set of decision-making and coercive powers attributed by the Roman people to the magistrates (consuls, praetors, quaestors, aediles, etc.). Under the republic a distinction was made between *imperium domi* and *imperium militiae*. The first was exercised within the boundaries of the *pomerium* (the inner city) and could be limited by the *provocatio ad populum*

(through which the people could withdraw magistrates' coercive powers). Thus the *imperium* did not infringe upon the sovereignty of the people, at least formally. The second was exercised outside the city, and was not limited by the *provocatio*. With Octavian an *imperium maius* was established. This was attributed by the Senate to the *Princeps*, making him *Imperator*, assigning him the power of command over proconsuls and provincial governors, as well as over the kings of *socii* states. As the *Imperator* was also endowed with *tribunicia potestas*, the prerogative to represent the people in the Senate (with the right of veto), the *provocatio ad populum* could not be used against him. His power was superior to that of any state, administrative entity, or democratic appeal. In this sense it could be said that *imperium superat regnum*, meaning that imperial power as an institution prevailed over any state or administrative power, as well as the will of the people.

39. Note that this concept is mentioned by Hardt and Negri (2000, 3) to stigmatize a theory they disagree with.

40. What makes Marx's formulation of this law illuminating is not so much the idea that the market pushes the prices of goods toward labor values, but his description of the competitive process through which labor is efficiently allocated and exploited.

41. In financial markets this means uniformity of rates of return for all assets of equivalent maturity and risk.

42. The problems caused by this type of specialization are explained well by Adda (1998, chap. 2).

43. The European Union's agricultural policy is calculated to cost the South of the world 20 billion dollars of damage per year in terms of lost exports (Bonaglia and Goldstein, 2008, 40).

44. Besides, international commodity prices are rather volatile and, as exports represent a high percentage of the GDP in many developing countries, their growth is subject to significant fluctuations (Adda 1998; Kose, 2002; Broda and Tille, 2003).

45. Countries at the forefront of scientific and technological research have seen a significant increase in the salaries of highly qualified staff. These are mostly engineers, scientists, managers, and executives: a rather limited circle of people who would not accept the label of "working class."

46. On the 1980s debt crises, see Lindert and Morton (1989), Ghosh et al. (2002), and Reinhart and Rogoff (2009).

47. Harvey retrieves this concept from the Marxist theory of primitive accumulation. De Angelis (2004) speaks even more explicitly of the extraction of surplus value by "enclosure," and stretches this concept to cover various forms of global capitalist exploitation, such as the cases of environmental dumping that allow multinationals to acquire surplus value by producing negative externalities. It is a fact that exploitation by expropriation or enclosure is a key characteristic of global imperialism. It serves, above all, to demolish pockets of precapitalist resistance to the penetration of multinational capital

in the Peripheral countries, and to create in them the economic and social conditions for the exploitation of wage labor in the capitalist factory. As Callinicos (2006, 129) observed, dispossession and enclosure are prerequisites for the expanded reproduction typical of the capitalist system, a system whose essential form of surplus value extraction remains the exploitation of wage labor.

48. Amin (2008) speaks of "oligopolistic financial capital." The financial sector is the most concentrated of all. In 2006, it accounted for the highest percentage (24.6) of mergers and acquisitions worldwide; in 2008, it covered the highest percentage (75.96) of world capital (Fuchs, 2010, 36, 40).

49. When the banks of the North have brought home profits and capital gains, the great countries occasionally come to the aid of those in difficulty, but they ask for real security. The United States, for example, helped Mexico out of its 1994 financial crisis by granting it new loans. In exchange, U.S. multinationals obtained control of Mexico's oil resources.

50. In the IMF and WB, decisions are made based on the rule "one dollar, one vote." As the advanced countries put the most money in, together they have the overwhelming majority, at over 60 percent. In any case, the rule of super-majority (85 percent) rather than absolute majority applies, which means that the United States, with more than 16 percent, has veto power. The EU countries together have more than 32 percent, so that they would also have the power of veto if they voted univocally. As for the WTO, in its constituent body (the Ministerial Conference) and its managing body (the General Council), the rule "one state, one vote" and the "consensus" method apply. The decision-making power of developing countries would therefore seem to be greater. Except for the fact that, due to the complex technical knowledge necessary to actively participate in negotiations, the difficulty of conducting talks involving hundreds of ministers and experts, and especially the great political strength of the advanced countries, the most important decisions are effectively made in informal *mini-ministerial meetings* held in the Green Room at the WTO headquarters. In these meetings only a handful of influential countries, the *rule makers*, mold negotiations, the results of which are then proposed to the *rule takers*.

51. For example, when the Italian government was considering whether to participate in the "liberation" of Afghanistan, all the press at the service of big industry unleashed a media campaign using the following argument, among others: if Italian forces did not participate in the war, Italian firms would subsequently be excluded from participation in the peace.

52. See Screpanti and Zamagni (2005, chapters 9–10) for a critical review of contemporary liberal theories.

53. Germany, the United States, and Japan, to mention three nations chosen at random, made heavy and prolonged use of protectionism to defend nascent national industry, becoming free trade advocates once their processes of industrialization had been completed. Great Britain, the harbinger of free

trade, underwent a long and painful political battle for the acceptance of free trade, which ultimately occurred when the Industrial Revolution had been accomplished, in 1846.

54.   In this context it should be pointed out that many governments and central bankers have proven more astute than some fundamentalist economists, refusing to grant central banks full autonomy. The countries of Euroland are an exception, having accepted German imperiousness without saying a word. The EU has adopted an extreme form of separation of central bank and government, as its treaties refuse to attribute responsibility to the ECB for achieving full employment and prohibit it from acting as a lender of last resort toward states.

55.   Whoever thinks that university professors and scientists are immune to ideological bias because they are interested in the pursuit of truth is often surprised when faced with the blatant bad faith of some great contemporary oracles. We would need to refer to the sociology of science to explain the mechanisms of ideological allegiance of many economists. Petri (2012) identified five psycho-social mechanisms. First, almost all university professors come from middle to upper social classes, so have a certain propensity to accept ideological positions that justify unequal distribution, as well as a material interest in maintaining their income, prestige, and power privileges. Second, those wishing to pursue an academic career will tend to avoid opposing the ideas of the professors who award professorships and select articles for publication in the most prestigious journals. Third, research centers and universities receive funding from capitalist firms and cultural associations supported by big capital, which understandably orient funds partly on the basis of the ideological contents of research and teaching. Fourth, academics who support critical and heterodox theories are distanced from the most influential universities and confined in peripheral ones, while their scientific contributions are declined by the most highly regarded journals, so the majority of students are unlikely to get to know their theories. Fifth, once an economist has begun a career based on a certain ideological allegiance, the interpretative schemes he uses become consolidated in his mind and he will find it difficult to abandon them simply because they do not effectively explain reality.

56.   In the early 1960s about half of the global stocks of foreign direct investments belonged to U.S. firms. The European multinationals grew by first investing in the countries of the European Common Market, only penetrating the U.S. market in the 1970s. Japanese firms also launched a massive attack with direct investments in the United States (and Europe) only in the 1970s (Goldstein and Piscitello, 2007, 22–37).

57.   Among the various theoretical works I have drawn on, I would like to mention in particular those of Knickerbocker (1973), Buckley and Casson (1976), Dunning (2000), Graham (1998), Helpman (1984), Cowling and Sugden (1998), Bartlett and Ghoshal (1991), Ghoshal and Nohria (1997),

Krugman (1998), Cantwell (1989; 1992), Markusen (2002), Peoples and Sugden (2000), Barba Navaretti and Venables (2004), Ietto-Gillies (2002; 2011; 2012).

58.   This is not to be confused with the notion of *ownership*. Whether it belongs to a single capitalist, many shareholders, or the state is irrelevant for the purposes of *control* over resources. What counts is that the decision maker with the entrepreneurial function has control over the production process by virtue of his power of command over labor (Screpanti, 2001).

59.   This can occur following serious economic crises and due to the "reforms" and "structural adjustment plans" imposed by the IMF and WB as a prerequisite for granting bailouts and funds to relaunch growth.

60.   The following kinds of provisions are sanctioned: measures to determine the administrative value of transactions (for example, subsidized bills), the number of employees (for example, to boost employment), the number and types of suppliers (for example, national companies), the type of legal entity that manages production (for example, nonprofit organizations or social cooperatives)—all policies that clash with the *market access* clause.

61.   The 2001 Doha Conference introduced a partial rectification to this scandalous situation, by providing for the practice of "compulsory licensing." In cases of public interest, patent abuse, and noncommercial government use, this allows for generic drugs to be produced locally, without the payment of patent royalties. The problem is that the countries most in need of low-cost drugs lack the technological and organizational capacity to produce them. An attempt was made to resolve this problem in an agreement, signed in Geneva on August 30, 2003, by virtue of which low-cost drugs can be imported if the countries that need them are not capable of producing them. They will be produced by emerging countries, such as India or Brazil. The pharmaceutical multinationals put up some resistance but finally gave in charitably, having received assurance that the low-cost drugs will never be exported to the North. After all, the markets of the poor countries are not very rich.

62.   The lobbies of the U.S. multinationals in this sector began forming in the 1970s to push the government into taking action against countries that permitted the counterfeiting of U.S. products. The chemical and pharmaceutical industries began, followed by cultural ones, and many others. The most important organizations founded to protect intellectual property rights are the International Federation of Pharmaceutical Manufacturers Association, the International Anti-Counterfeiting Coalition, the U.S. National Agricultural Chemicals Association, the Intellectual Property Committee, the International Intellectual Property Alliance (originally a coalition of five other associations: the Motion Picture Association of America, Recording Industry Association of America, National Music Publishers' Association, American Film Marketing Association, Association of American Publishers). With Section 301 of the 1974 Trade Act, the lobbies ensured that the

government could intervene (through international investigations, negotiations and reprisals) to defend the intellectual property rights of U.S. firms. Then, in 1986, they succeeded in including intellectual property issues in the Uruguay Round of the GATT. When negotiations began it immediately became clear that U.S. government representatives were acting on behalf of the lobbies. At last, after heated and drawn-out negotiations to counter the resistance of developing countries, and with the backing of European countries and Japan, they obtained the TRIPs agreement. The European representatives initially supported the developing countries, but were finally convinced by the American negotiators to back their proposals, in exchange for protection for the typical products of European agriculture. Instead, the Peripheral countries were bribed with the promise of opening the Northern markets to their agricultural, textile, and manufactured goods, and with that of expanding the multinationals' foreign direct investments and technology transfers. On this subject, see Evans (1994), Drahos (1995), Watal (2001), Devereaux, Lawrence and Watkins (2006), Caldarelli (2013).

63.   Such as the requirements of local content, local employment, manufacture, exports, trade balance, technology transfer, local shareholders, as well as restrictions on currency exchanges and exporting profits.

64.   See Anonymous Authors (2002, 41–46) for a reconstruction of the political initiatives undertaken to achieve the GATS by American Express, Citigroup, AIG, the Coalition of Service Industries, the Financial Leaders Group, the European Services Forum, and the High Level LOTIS Group, all lobbying organizations of the financial multinationals.

65.   Cases in which allocation through the market prevents the determination of the prices or quantities most conducive to public welfare.

66.   By way of example, theories of state failure sought to contrast theories of market failure. The doctrine of contestable markets tried to argue that even oligopolistic markets are allocatively efficient. The Coase theorem, by which efficiency rises when commons are privatized, suggested to resolve the "tragedy of the commons" through the dismantling of public policies aimed at disciplining negative externalities. The theory of central bank autonomy sought to contrast Keynesian arguments on the use of monetary policy to stabilize financial markets and support full employment policies.

67.   It is no coincidence that the most roaring emerging country, China, is also the one that contributes most to global environmental degradation, and is home to sixteen of the twenty most polluted cities in the world.

68.   Such as South Korean chaebols, to which part of the blame for the Asian crisis of 1997–98 is attributed (Gilpin, 2000, chap. 5).

69.   Two wide-ranging historical reconstructions of economic crises can be found in Kindleberger and Aliber (2005) and Reinhart and Rogoff (2009).

70.   Thus I do not define crises confined to a specific area as "great crises," even when they are very intense, such as the recent crises in Southeast Asia, Argentina, Mexico, and Russia.

71.   On the role played by the gold standard in the crisis of 1929 see Kindleberger (1984), Eichengreen and Sachs (1985), Temin (1989), Hamilton (1987; 1988), Bernanke and James (1991).

72.   I made a first attempt in Screpanti (2010; 2011).

73.   In 2008 military spending represented 17.1 percent of overall public spending. Education and health care accounted for 3.2 percent and 11.2 percent, respectively (Fuchs, 2010, 51).

74.   Gramm is considered one of the most prominent advocates of the bank lobbies, a "handmaiden to Big Finance." He was a Democratic congressman from 1979 to 1983, Republican from 1983 to 1985, and a Republican senator from 1985 to 2002. In 2002, he was engaged by the major Swiss bank UBS AG as vice chairman of the Investment Bank Division. He carried out lobbying activities in Congress, the Senate, the Federal Reserve Bank, and the Treasury Department. As chairman of the Senate Committee on Banking from 1995 to 2000, he championed financial deregulation. He played a crucial role in writing the law that abolished the Glass-Steagall Act, as well as in providing the key sections of the Commodity Future Modernization Act. For other information on Gramm, see Corn (2008).

75.   In 2007, the assets of non-bank financial institutions in the major advanced economies (twenty countries plus Euroland) amounted to 128 percent of their GDP. Following the explosion of the crisis, this percentage shrank to 111 percent in 2011 (Financial Stability Board, 2012, 9–10).

76.   In Italy this "divorce" was decided in 1981 by Minister Beniamino Andreatta, with the purpose of controlling inflation by cutting wages. The Bank of Italy was no longer obliged to buy the government securities the treasury was unable to sell in public auctions. It was thought that this would prevent fiscal policies from attempting to accommodate "excessive" wage rises. However, the actual consequence was that, since the government wanted to assuage class conflict and avoid severe recession, public debt began to rise sharply. The problem was aggravated by the upswing in interest rates of the 1980s and early 1990s (Maffeo, 2012).

77.   In 2005, the American shadow banking system accounted for 44 percent of the world total (actually twenty countries plus Euroland, which together represent almost the entirety of the world financial markets), while the European system (including the UK and Switzerland) accounted for 41 percent. In 2011 the first dropped to 35 percent and the second rose to 47 percent (Financial Stability Board, 2012, 10). Bear in mind that these changes also reflect modifications in exchange rates and accountancy systems. In any case, the weight of some intermediaries, such as hedge funds, is somewhat underestimated, as most of them are registered in offshore tax havens.

78.   In the boom preceding the crisis, banks appeared to appreciate this criterion, as the speculative bubble inflated the market value of their assets. After 2007, in contrast, they strongly opposed it. The U.S. Congress slackened it in May 2009 (Hayes, 2009).

79. On the role of banks in the endogenous creation of money, see Screpanti (1997a).

80. The riskiest assets, those based on irrecoverable loans, are defined *toxic*. *Subprime* are those based on loans to risky borrowers (people who have already been insolvent or who do not provide sufficient documentation on their income and wealth). *Alt-A* (alternative A-paper) assets are less risky than subprime but more risky than *prime*. The latter are based on loans to trustworthy borrowers. As for derivatives, there are many kinds: ABS (Asset-Backed Securities), MBS (Mortgage-Backed Securities), RMBS (Residential Mortgage-Backed Securities), CMBS (Commercial Mortgage-Backed Securities), CDO (Collateralized Debt Obligations, second-degree derivatives combining MBS and other kinds of assets), and CDS (Credit Default Swaps, insurance policies on asset exchanges).

81. In principle, industrial concerns are not devoted to speculation, as they aim to make profits by producing goods. In reality, most corporations are engaged in financial speculation. In contemporary capitalism the big multinationals are public companies. Their ownership is dispersed among many shareholders and their control is assigned to managers paid with salaries, bonuses, and stock options linked to the firm's value. They tend to behave as speculators, since they are more interested in the current value of their company shares than in long-run profitability (Toporowski, 2009). Besides that, big corporations have financial management divisions that tend to maneuver capital by continually shifting investments from production to portfolio trading, depending on which is most convenient at the time.

82. In reality, speculative transactions are a little more complex than this, as they are mostly based on futures or option contracts. In any case, the simplification based on spot contracts does not change the substance of the reasoning.

83. Stabilizing speculation is based on a comparison between the current market price of an asset and its trend price, which is assessed with long-sighted expectations. This assessment may be performed using a *fundamental analysis* to evaluate firms' real profitability. If the difference between the two prices is positive, most long-sighted investors expect the current price to diminish, and take a bearish flier. When such a behavior prevails, current prices tend to approach the fundamentals. Destabilizing speculation, instead, is moved by myopic expectations of the adaptive or extrapolative kind. Speculators try to assess the *variation* of an asset price on a very short-run horizon. They do so based upon knowledge of variations that occurred in the recent past. When this kind of expectation prevails, most speculators forecast that prices will go on increasing when they are increasing. Then, targeting immediate capital gains, they buy assets. Demand rises and so do prices. For a formal analysis of financial instability see Screpanti (1989).

84. A robust explanation was proposed by Fisher (1933). His theory was then developed in various models. Especially interesting are those of Kindleberger (1978) and Minsky (1982; 1986). For a review, see Berger and

Udell (2004). A consistent part of contemporary literature accounts for the subprime crisis as a consequence of the financial instability and fragility that grew with the speculative bubble. Minsky's theory of financial instability has become very popular, with the crisis being christened *a Minsky moment* even in the newspapers. Minskian explanations of the current crisis have been put forward by Whalen (2007), Wray (2008), Krugman (2009), Bellofiore (2009), Ferri and Variato (2009), Vercelli (2009), Eggertsson and Krugman (2011). However, Kregel (2008) recommended some caution, arguing that Minsky's theory does not enable us to grasp the full complexity of the present crisis. I would add that it does not even enable us to comprehend the fundamental causes, which I will deal with in chapter 6.

85. The Federal Fund Rate is the interest rate at which a bank lends overnight to another bank the funds maintained at the Federal Reserve. The LIBOR is an estimate of the average interest rate the leading banks in London pay for borrowing from each other. It is considered the yardstick for short-term interest rates around the world.

86. For an accurate reconstruction of the crisis timeline, see Fornasari (2009) and Kiff and Klyuev (2009).

87. For an account of U.S. monetary policy during the first period of the crisis, see Wessel (2009).

88. Soros (2012). In studying the effects of Basel III, Slovik and Cournède (2011) forecast an annual GDP drop of 0.5 percent as a consequence of Core Tier 1 being gradually raised to reach 8.5 percent in 2019.

89. Moody's immediately threatened downgrading if the recommendation was not complied with.

90. Germany and a few other countries resisted for a few months as the temporary euro depreciation caused by the crisis favored an increase in extra-European exports, and because the capital flight from Italian and Spanish securities toward the "more reliable" German markets produced an increase in liquidity and a drop in interest rates there. In the last quarter of 2011, Germany faced a slight GDP decrease, which became a slight rise in the first three quarters of 2012, followed by a severe slowdown in the last quarter.

91. For instance, Taylor (2009) blames the Federal Reserve for its excessively expansive monetary policy and for not following the "Taylor rule," according to which the regular interest rate must be determined taking into account the rate of inflation and the output gap. Stiglitz (2010) interprets the crisis as a case of market failure determined by wanton deregulation, which magnified information asymmetry problems, reduced transparency in risk assessment, and hence induced a high number of investors to take excessive risks.

92. In reality, this pact is not so "implicit." As I argued in chapter 4, the TRIPs and the GATS emerged from the Uruguay Round following lengthy negotiations between the developing countries and the lobbies sustained by the United States.

93. See Archibugi and Iamarino (2002), Drahos and Mayne (2002), Archibugi and Pietrobelli (2003), Lanoszka (2003), Jaffe and Lerner (2004), Hess and Ostrom (2006).

94. See Feenstra and Hanson (1999), Krueger (1999), Gollin (2002), Blanchard and Giavazzi (2003), Guscina (2006), Ellis and Smith (2007), Arpaia and Pichelmann (2008), ILO (2008, chap. 1), Husson (2008), Stirati (2010).

95. Adjusted wage shares at factor costs. The figures for Germany refer to West Germany up until 1990, and to unified Germany afterward. In 1991 the wage share was 65.48 percent in West Germany and 66.96 percent in unified Germany.

96. The importance of this factor was well corroborated by empirical research. See Jaumotte and Tytell (2007), Atkinson (2009), Hogrefe and Kappler (2013).

97. The Taylorist assembly line prevailed in the great factories producing mass consumption goods. The big concentrations of unionized workers provided for increasing bargaining power of the worker movement. Class conflict was domesticated by governments playing the role of national collective capitalist, favoring high profits and GDP growth rates, full employment, and increasing direct and indirect wages.

98. However, after a first impact of disorientation, immigrant workers learn to organize and fight, and today there are many cases of struggles conducted by organized migrant workers (Bacon, 2008; 2013). There is no doubt that, once they understand their exploitation and that they have a common enemy in capitalism, local and immigrant workers will sometimes fight united.

99. Verdoorn (1949), Kaldor (1966). See also McCombie and Roberts (2007), Britto (2008), Lorentz (2009), and the essays collected in McCombie, Pugno and Soro (2003). The "Verdoorn coefficient" is about 0.5. With a 4 percent output increase, productivity rises by 2 percent. This is a long-run process. There is also a short-run one. In recessionary phases labor hoarding takes place in firms that use skilled workers. In order not to lose human capital, firms' dismissals of workers are less than proportional to their reduction in output. Thus productivity slows down and sometimes even diminishes during crises.

100. In the period 1970–80, the yearly percentage rate of growth in labor productivity was 4 in France, 3.8 in Germany, 4.1 in Italy, 4.3 in Japan, 2.7 in the United Kingdom, and 1.5 in the United States. In the years 1995–2012 it was 1.2, 1.3, 0.3, 1.5, 1.6, and 2.0, respectively (OECD, 2014). In the last period the United States did better than the other advanced countries not only in productivity growth, but also in GDP growth (see Table 3). In the crisis years 2009–12, GDP growth diminished drastically in all advanced countries and labor productivity slowed down in the United Kingdom and the United States too: 0.3, 1.3.

101. Notwithstanding this vocation, the debt-to-GDP ratio is growing. Some projections forecast a 150 percent ratio in Italy, France, and the United States by

2020; 200 percent in the UK and 300 percent in Japan (Cecchetti, Mohanty and Zampolli 2010, 9). Notice that these projections were formulated in a recovery period. Today they should be considered somewhat optimistic.

102. In any case, they do not seem to be the result of a plan elaborated by a strategic mind. Instead, they emerged from the interaction of many political and economic forces (lobbies, administrations, banks, firms). The American ploy, as I argued in chapter 5, resulted from the convergence of pressure from bank lobbies (which aimed for financial deregulation and an expansive monetary policy) and the political demands of the Clinton and Bush administrations (which sought to nurture growth).

103. China enjoyed a permanent trade surplus from the early 1990s. In the period 1993–2003, net exports contributed about 10 percent to GDP growth, while investment expanded more than consumption (Felipe and Lim, 2005). Notice that the driving role of exports is not limited to this 10 percent, as they stimulate investments through the accelerator mechanism. Such a driving capacity shrank drastically with the crisis. The growth rate of China's exports, which had been 26 percent in 2007, plummeted to –16 percent in 2009. The subsequent slackening in demand induced a slowdown in investments, whose ratio to national income contracted from 35 percent to 27 percent. In any case, the trend of the investment ratio was increasing from 2001 to 2010, while those of consumption and public expenditure were decreasing (Rothman and Zhu, 2012).

104. According to the Kaldor-Verdoorn law, productivity can rise even if domestic technological research is not particularly advanced. In fact, most Chinese productivity growth resulted from technology transfers from advanced countries. True, in the last ten years or so Chinese R&D investments have increased rapidly, but apart from a narrow sector of sophisticated technologies (which is nonetheless growing) a large portion of domestic innovations results from the imitation and improvement of imported know-how. Nowadays, even if it is the second country in the world (after the United States) in R&D expenditure, China is still far from taking a leading role in scientific and technological research.

105. There was a slight surplus in 1991. Then a deficit emerged, which rose to 2 percent of GDP in 1997 and 6 percent in 2006 (Perelstein, 2009), when the U.S. current account deficit contributed 2 percentage points to the growth of world demand (Summers, 2006).

106. Several economists have pinpointed this factor as a crucial determinant of the bubble and the crisis. See in particular: Barba and Pivetti (2009; 2011), Palma (2009), Rajan (2010), Reich (2010), Screpanti (2010; 2011), Fiorentini and Montani (2012).

107. In the German case, as in the American, the economic policy model emerged from the interaction of various political and economic forces, rather than from a strategic plan. The euro expedient resulted from the need to adapt to a policy strongly coveted by France in order to harness the Bundesbank's

power. The German government initially refused the single currency proposal, but eventually complied (in exchange for France's approval of German unification, it would seem). However, when drawing up the treaties, Germany asserted its strength and imposed its own philosophy upon the European Union: an independent European Central Bank with a strong deflationary inclination and strict constraints on national fiscal policies. This philosophy helped to reconcile the interests of national big industry, bank bureaucracy, and the political class.

108. European economic policies in the Single Currency era have been variously interpreted. See Blanchard and Giavazzi (2002), Acocella (2005), Baldwin (2006), De Grauwe (2006), Lane (2006), Lapavitsas et al. (2010), Cesaratto and Stirati (2011), Alessandrini et al. (2012), Bagnai (2012), Cesaratto (2012), D'Angelillo and Paggi (2012), De Grauwe and Yuemei (2012), Zezza (2012), Vernengo and Pérez-Caldentey (2012).

109. The definitions come from the Bank of Italy, and are especially focused on public finance problems. Here I will use them by superimposing this classification on the most common grouping into "core" and "non-core" countries. A basic discrimination is based on current account balances, which exhibit surpluses in the former countries and deficits in the latter. The first group includes Austria, Belgium, Finland, Germany, Luxemburg, and The Netherlands; the second, Cyprus, Greece, Ireland, Italy, Malta, Portugal and Spain. France and The Netherland,s which were originally core countries, are sliding into the second group as a consequence of the crisis.

110. See Correia, Nicolini and Teles (2008), Correia, Farhi, Nicolini, and Teles (2011), Franco (2011), IMF (2011c), Farhi, Gopinath, and Itskhoki (2011), Langot, Patureau, and Sopraseuth (2012), Farhi, Gopinath, and Itskhoki (2012).

111. I thank Ugo Pagano for calling my attention to this phenomenon.

112. See Cesaratto (2011), Cesaratto and Stirati (2011), Chesnais (2011), and Amoroso and Jespersen (2012). Bellofiore (2012, 16–20) talks about "strong neo-mercantilism," rightly including Japanese and Chinese policies. Here, though, I am mainly interested in Germany, as its policy is at the origin of the present euro crisis.

113. Until the 1980s a system of *organisierter Kapitalismus* triumphed in Germany. This took the form of bank-oriented corporate capitalism (Screpanti, 2006) in which national banks, in concert with the government and the Bundesbank, performed functions of corporate governance and national planning. From the 1990s, a transformation toward the Anglo-Saxon model of corporate governance took place. By the beginning of the new millennium the main banks had withdrawn from the boards of directors of most industrial companies and transformed themselves into universal banks.

114. In the same period the percentage wage share passed from 66.39 to 65.69 in France, from 61.56 to 62.06 in Italy, and from 71.96 to 70.44 in the United Kingdom. Subsequently, in the years 2008–9, the wage share increased in

all four countries as a consequence of a GDP decline and a less pronounced decrease in industrial employment due to corporate practices of labor hoarding.

115. In 2011, the Italian debt/GDP ratio was 120.1 percent. In 2012, as a consequence of the "salva Italia" decree and other austerity maneuvers of Mario Monti's government, it jumped to 127 percent, then to 132.6 in the second quarter of 2013.

116. In Italy the households capable of saving were 35 percent in 2011 and 28 percent in 2012.

117. The euro/dollar exchange rate experienced a decreasing trend from April 29, 2011, when it was at $1.484. By July 25, 2012, it had fallen to $1.206. Afterward it recovered, reaching the value of $1.364 on February 2, 2013. This appreciation can be accounted for by the currency war that began in mid-2012, when the major advanced countries tried to relaunch growth through exports. I will come back to this problem in chapter 7.

118. In the fourth quarter of 2012 the percentage GDP growth rate was –0.1 in the United States, –0.3 in France and the UK, –0.4 in Japan, –0.7 in Germany, –0.9 in Italy (Trading Economics, 2013).

119. In the third quarter of 2013 the percentage GDP growth rate was 0.5 in Japan and 0.8 in the United Kingdom. In Euroland it was 0.1 , but in July industrial production fell by –1.5 . At any rate, the divergence between virtuous and non-virtuous countries remains: the percentage GDP growth rate in the third quarter of 2013 was 0.3 in Germany, –0.1 in France and Italy (Trading Economics, 2013). Moreover, the divergence in labor costs and competitiveness has widened, since the negative growth in non-virtuous countries blocked their productivity increases.

120. From 2010 to 2013, the yearly percentage rate of GDP growth passed from 10.4 to 7.7 in China, from 11.2 to 4.6 in India, from 7.5 to 2.3 in Brazil, from 3.1 to 1.8 in South Africa, from 4.5 to 1.5 in Russia. As to 2014, the most optimistic forecasts predict a percentage growth rate of 7.5 in China, 5.4 in India, 2.3 in Brazil, 2.8 in South Africa, 2 in Russia (IMF, 2014).

121. However, this situation is likely to change in the near future as a consequence of the discovery of vast shale gas reserves. Gas production is rapidly increasing, and the White House is already dreaming of achieving energy independence and using exports to bring down international hydrocarbon prices and enhance its geopolitical influence.

122. See Taylor (2007). Dooley, Folkerts-Landau and Garber (2003), as well as Fiorentini and Montani (2012), talk of an "implicit bargain."

123. $1.3 trillion in 2008, equivalent to 22 percent of all global foreign currency reserves (Lim, 2008).

124. Unemployment, especially as a consequence of the privatization of state companies, increased continually from 1985 to 2002, when the official rate stabilized at around 4 percent, which means tens of millions of unemployed people. But the official rate underestimates real unemployment. The Chinese

Academy of Social Sciences assessed a 9.4 percent rate in 2009. According to a declaration of former premier Wen Jiabao, there were 200 million jobless people in that year (Xiaokun, 2010).

125. This would seem to be fulfilling the hopes of Lardy (2006) and other economists that China will convert to a growth model driven by domestic consumption. Roach (2011), Rothman and Zhu (2012), and Giacché (2012b) argue that these hopes are in fact being fulfilled. However it seems that so far growth has been mainly led by investment expenditures sustained by an easy credit policy.

126. In the last eight years the yuan exhibited a revaluation trend against the dollar, in the last five years against the euro and the pound. It is in a trend of significant revaluation against the yen since November 2012.

127. The ideological dress of this stupidity takes the form of a theory of "expansive austerity," according to which fiscal austerity would reduce the risk of sovereign debt default, restore market confidence, reduce interest rates and therefore feed economic recovery.

128. The intention to implement a "shock therapy" was made explicit in an official Confindustria (2013) document, with which the Italian capitalist association "proposes [that] candidates for government" relaunch the "industrial logic," that is, accumulation, making "a clear break" from the policies of the past. I recall it here because, given Italy's crucial position in the current Euroland crisis, it can be seen as a policy strategy for all the big multinational capitals, even beyond Europe. The basic idea is to relaunch growth through exports as well as the "promotion of internationalization and the attraction of foreign investments." The main proposals for the achievement of these goals involve: reducing labor costs by 8 percent in three years, intensifying labor flexibility, increasing working hours by forty hours a year, transferring employment rules traditionally dictated by the law to private bargaining, privatizing public property, reducing public expenditure by 1 percent a year, reducing taxation on firms and financial profits, shifting part of tax revenues from direct to indirect taxes, and increasing incentives for firms that export and invest.

129. This year, "mini-jobs," meaning jobs for very low wages without payroll taxes, have become widespread in Germany. In 2003 there were 5.9 million, which climbed to 7.5 in 2012. In mid-2013, 30 percent of German workers earned less than 8.5 euros/hour, a wage that the OECD considers below the poverty line. Unsurprisingly, other European countries first complained about social dumping, then rushed to imitate Germany.

130. It goes without saying that his policies were warmly welcomed by the ultra-liberal German leaders, who sought to smooth their way by hampering the ECB's stabilizing policies. In fact, German Minister of Economy Philipp Rösler and Bundesbank president Jens Weidmann prefer monetary policy to remain restrictive. This attitude is partly motivated by the fact that German industry gains from the crisis in southern Euroland (where it can shop for

corporate control at fire-sale prices), while German banks profit from the flight of liquidity from non-virtuous toward virtuous nations. Above all, though, it is inspired by a political philosophy that is trying to take over the whole of Europe. In Rösler's words: "If you take away the interest rate pressure on states, you also take away the pressure for them to reform" (cited in Carrel and Heller, 2012).

131. Keynes put forward the idea of an International Currency Union in 1941. His proposal has recently been revived and updated by various economists, among whom I would mention Mundel (2005) and Fiorentini and Montani (2012, 164–76).

132. Amin (2002, 33) calls the first "principal" and the second "fundamental."

Index